Airy Nothing

a novel by

Clarissa Pattern

tRaum
Books

Airy Nothing by Clarissa Pattern
A tRaum Book

Cover art by Rysz Merey

For Mum and Dad,
who smiled as they read stories about dead plants coming back to life.

For Dearest J,
who told me I had something important to say.

For Kathryn,
who believes in hobgoblins with the power to stop the lost and lonely from descending into darkness.

For Patrizio,
who can conjure up the rainbow magic of the Globe
while sitting in a tiny café eating sponge cakes.

For Rysz,
who is my hobgoblin and makes magical visions come to life.

The poet's eye, in fine frenzy rolling,
Doth glance from heaven to Earth, from Earth to heaven.
And as imagination bodies forth
The forms of things unknown, the poet's pen
Turns them to shapes and gives to airy nothing
A local habitation and a name.
Such tricks hath strong imagination,
That if it would but apprehend some joy,
It comprehends some bringer of that joy.
Or in the night, imagining some fear,
How easy is a bush supposed a bear!

From 'A Midsummer Night's Dream'
By William Shakespeare

To unpathed waters, undreamed shores

John ran, his feet thumping on the uneven ground. His lungs heaved against the tightness of his bodice, and his skirts clawed at his calves, clinging to the flesh of his thighs. When he stumbled, the hobgoblin bobbed around him, pulling at his clothes so they didn't trip him and steadying his shoulder with its small, powerful hands, but there was only so much a house sprite could do. And an almost infinite list of things it couldn't.

It couldn't stop his muscles from feeling like they were worn to threads.

It couldn't ease the pain that ripped through him every time his concentration slipped and images of his family flickered.

And it couldn't prevent the pounding of horse hooves which came closer every second.

His breath too gone to speak, John begged the faerie folk in his mind. Please. You've always been kind, please take pity now. Please protect me. But the air around him remained empty and cold.

He kept running, his legs cramping, the earth beneath him vibrating with the thump of his pursuers. Suddenly, he twisted around a sharp bend in the path and fell. He didn't see what had tripped him, only knew that one moment he had hope; the next he was on the ground, his head barely missing a stone that would have been the end of him. His hands pushed against the dirt and he clenched his teeth, summoning everything that remained of his strength and his willpower to scramble to his feet.

Then he saw it: a twinkling within the thick hedgerow. As he stumbled towards it, the foliage opened and revealed a hollow space where the hobgoblin was waiting, dancing a spinning jig. John crawled in, and the branches closed around him. He breathed in the woody aroma of leaves and earth.

The hobgoblin leapt up and floated in the air, touching him on the lips soft as a spider's web, and his body fell still, caught in the space between two heartbeats.

A horse, two horses, stopped by the hedge: beasts of fire, with spiked hooves and curled horns on their heads. Their riders were skeletons with black hearts visible through yellowing ribs. They bellowed out all the pain in the world.

John blinked, and then all that was visible from his hiding place were normal horse legs of a dunny brown colour. The voices that spoke belonged to ordinary men.

'Zounds! Where has that little nymph gone?' Delight rather than disappointment rang in the man's tone, as if John's whereabouts were a fun mystery, soon to be solved.

'Aye, she's disappeared, but where? There's nowhere to go.'

Neither man was Da, John realised with a jolt. Or anyone from the village. The people chasing him weren't here to drag him back home. The first man spoke again.

'Come now, my pretty maiden, show yourself. Don't be shy. We will use you well.' He dropped from his horse and paced backwards and forwards. John could hear his breathing.

'Harry!' The second man protested. 'We've wasted enough time. If a person vanishes into thin air, it's best to leave well alone.'

'You're not scared are you, old friend?' The man called Harry laughed. 'Did you see how long and golden her hair was? How could it ever be a waste of time to pursue beauty like that? And you call yourself a man!' Harry paused. If he but reached through the branches, his fingertips would brush John.

'Do you think she could be hiding in the hedgerow?'

'Only if she's transformed into a mouse. No one could fit through there without being scratched to death. Let's go. You've had your fun.'

'That's the problem though, I haven't.' Harry's voice was honeyed, as if reminiscing about a long-lost sweetheart. 'She was small though, wasn't she? You don't see many as finely made as she was. And how fast she ran—like a sweet, startled deer.'

'Enough of this nonsense! I'm not spending the day chasing wisps with you. If my horse can manage it, I plan to make London before they close the gates tonight. You may do as you wish.'

'My good friend, you fright too easily. But as that fair girl has escaped, you're the only companion I have, and I suppose it's my lot to protect you from highwaymen, witches, wisps and maidens too pretty for belief.' Harry chuckled as he climbed back into the saddle. They trotted away in the direction they'd come from.

Soon, the only sounds were birds and the rustling of the wind. John's heart began to beat again. He held his hands in front of his eyes, his fingers shaking.

He opened his mouth to take a calming breath, but instead his lips started to move through a recitation.

A whispered copy of their booming certainty.

'Come now, my pretty maiden, show yourself. Don't be shy. We will use you well.'

'Come now, my pretty maiden, show yourself. Don't be shy. We will use you well.'

'My pretty maiden.'

'My pretty maiden.'

'We will use you well.'

His hands formed tight fists and he squeezed his eyes shut.

London.

It was a place the elders spoke of in hushed voices.

Forbidden, to be avoided, not for the likes of the villagers. But he knew how to listen and he'd heard the important words: gold, and riches, and Queene.

Whenever Da had dragged him to the corner of the room and kicked him into silence, John didn't see the dank straw matting his face was ground down into, or smell the animal stink of his father, or even taste the blood in his own mouth.

He was faraway in London.

Trees towered above his head, their tops kissing the clouds. They were dressed in glittering bark and their branches bowed under the weight of spring blossoms magically mixed with the plenty of autumn fruit. In the shade of the trees, foxes and rabbits munched together on green grass and greeted him with sparkling eyes. There were more faeries than he could count and his own hobgoblin played with them through the day, then came back to him, grinning in the night. John's fingers were permanently stained purple from the baskets and baskets of berries he'd gathered to keep all the faeries fed.

Those men might ride as hard as they liked for the beautiful city, but the gates wouldn't open for them.

The Faerie Queene wouldn't allow it.

They were men, ordinary men, and there'd be no space for men who tried to... for men like that, in the most magical place in the whole kingdom.

In London, everything would be perfect.

Nothing could be wrong.

Not even John.

He opened his eyes and smiled at the small faerie dancing carefree around the clearing in the hedgerow.

'The Faerie Queene will keep us safe, and no one'll ever hurt us... me again.' His mouth became a straight line.

The hobgoblin met John's gaze, its eyes flowing through all the colours of nature before finally settling on the fresh green of spring grass. It climbed into John's lap and curled up into a tight ball, as if to sleep.

But the hobgoblin never needed sleep, not like humans.

It was a sign for John.

'Is it safe to stop here?' he asked.

He was tired. Escaping the horsemen had used the last of his strength. And if they hadn't seen him when they'd been so close, that had to mean that no one else would spot him either. His head drooped and he closed his eyes. 'Just a few more days... a few more days,' he murmured.

In his dreams, he danced through a forest of silver and gold trees.

A woman appeared, her body made of spring's earliest buds. Her face was of snowflakes and her eyes of morning dew. Her hair flowed down to her ankles and crackled with the orange and yellow of autumn leaves.

She looked at him for less than a heartbeat, then swirled

away. He skipped after her, knowing he would never catch her, but it didn't matter. He had to follow her.

His slumbering body twitched and he cried out.

The hobgoblin's eyes turned grey, and it stroked John's hair until he was peaceful again.

Life's but a walking shadow,
A poor player that struts and frets his hour upon the stage, and then is heard no more

There was a peace to waiting. John waited and listened to the songs of the birds above him and breathed in the earthy scent of the ground below, while the hobgoblin jigged in front of him with enough energy to tear the whole hedgerow apart. John put a finger to his lips, although in truth, the sounds the faerie made were just the ordinary rustling of nature.

'There might be more,' he whispered.

More what he couldn't say. Not out loud.

The horsemen must be long gone. Had he slept through the chill of night and into the warmth of a new day? Yet his heart still thumped and terror prickled his skin. He bit his lip. How was it possible to be more scared now that he was alone, than when they had been chasing him?

'I'm safe,' he said.

But what if they caught you?

The question trilled through his mind; an angry changeling trapped inside him. Back there, at least you knew Da. At least you knew the village. Now you know nothing.

'I still know Da.'

He stared down at his body as if he could see the old scars and bruises through the fabric of Jetta's dress.

The hobgoblin stopped dancing and gazed at him with wide green eyes.

John looked down at the worn material.

'You're right. Now that Da's not here to tell me what to wear, I should be in breeches by now. Like every other boy my age. And I will be.' He smoothed the dress over his knees. 'Soon. Maybe.'

The hobgoblin's eyes glimmered into a red.

'I know. You don't really care about what clothes I wear. I try to forget about the things frightening me, by fretting on the things that make me hurt.' He held his hands out for the hobgoblin to jump onto. 'Are all humans as foolish as me?'

The hobgoblin danced onto John's palms, then leapt away and swung to a branch above his head, making the whole hedgerow shake.

John looked around the magical hollow.

'I understand. We have to go. We could be in London by now and not hiding in bushes.'

He moved forward to crawl out, hoping that whatever faerie magic had parted the brambles before would work in his favour again, else he'd be scratched to pieces. But then he heard voices. The world became midwinter cold. The mist of his breath transformed to ice on his tongue. Even the hobgoblin was still.

The delicate sounds of nature became nothing under the roar of the approaching humans. John could not tell how many there were, as their voices boomed together and the words he could distinguish made little sense. Patrons, nobles, licenses, fees.

The sentences cleared as the feet trampled closer:

'It is time to return to the city and try our fortune joining one of the companies,' a sharp voice said.

'Stop with that folly. There is nowhere that would accept all of us. We'd be separated,' an even louder voice replied.

'Aye, stop your moaning. I for one prefer the adventure of the road,' said a third man.

John wondered how many there were, but even the slightest peek through the branches seemed impossible.

'These villagers are more appreciative of our playing than any of the city rabble have ever been.' Another male voice. Loud again, but with a soothing quality.

'But these villagers pay us in days old potage and stale bread!'

There was a harmony to the group's conversation, as if

they'd had it many times and everyone knew when to speak and what to say.

'We'll do A Midsummer Night's Dream at the next place we stop. I stole more sheets of that than of any other. It'll be a sure success if we don't have to rely so much on making up the lines ourselves.'

'I am being the Faerie Queene this time! I've had enough of being Bottom. Let Bladwell sweat under that fly-bitten ass's head for once!'

John's eyes widened and his gaze snapped up towards the hobgoblin. How could anyone declare with so little fuss that they were going to be the Faerie Queene? What did it mean?

The hobgoblin tilted his head, then pointed at the group traipsing past. With a thumping heart, John followed its direction and managed to look outwards. Everyone had already passed, apart from one youth trailing at the back. He was not much taller than John, but still laden down with packs covering his back and filling his arms.

Despite his burden, he walked with a skipping stride and spoke in a sweet voice that carried far beyond the dusty road. Like one with a merry purpose beyond all this:

'Over hill, over dale,
Thorough bush, thorough brier,
Over park, over pale,
Thorough flood, thorough fire.
I do wander everywhere
Swifter than the moon's sphere.
And I serve the fairy queen
To dew her orbs upon the green.
The cowslips tall her pensioners be.
In their gold coats spots you see.
Those be rubies, fairy favors.
In those freckles live their savors.
I must go seek some dewdrops here
And hang a pearl in every cowslip's ear.
Farewell, thou lob of spirits. I'll be gone.
Our queen and all our elves come here anon.'

'In sooth, shut thy dark cavernous toothhole and use that energy to keep up with us, rather than showing off how well thou remembers thine lines!'

Such a gruff voice didn't seem possible next to the magic of the poetry, but the boy only laughed and trotted off towards it.

John gazed at the now empty track beyond the tangled hedgerow. He moved his lips in a silent repetition of the words the boy had so easily said. His skin shivered and goose-pimpled as if he was reciting a sacred vow. He kept staring forward, his heart thumping, expecting a queen and her elves to appear in response to the beautiful words.

The hobgoblin poked him in the ribs.

John startled from his reverie and turned towards the small faerie.

'Will the Faerie Queene... '

The hobgoblin shook its head, then made a sharp, whistling sound. Creaking like a rarely opened door, the branches separated. John didn't wait for them to fully part, but crawled through as quick as he could manage without tearing Jetta's dress.

When he stood out on the path though, the men were already nothing more than dots on the horizon.

'It hasn't been long... how have they got so far... I could still catch them.' John said to the empty air.

He turned to look directly at the hobgoblin floating next to him.

'Could I still catch them?'

The hobgoblin stared at him with sun-white eyes.

Sometimes, he felt how different he and the faerie were. And then there were times like now, when the hobgoblin seemed to know him better than he knew himself.

'Yes, I know. You're right. Even if I caught up with them, what would I say to them? What would they say to someone like me, trying to follow them?'

John looked downwards, his eyes fixing on a large stone protruding from the dirt; much like the thing he'd almost cracked his head on when he'd tripped while being chased. It was only a flash, but he saw the stone coated in sticky blood and his body lying pale and lifeless and naked.

He swallowed.

His mouth was dry, and his stomach felt heavy, as if lined with rock.

The hobgoblin wrapped its hand around one of John's fingers and pulled him forward.

'Yes,' he said. 'Towards London. I'm better with faeries and magic than with people.'

He took a final look at the distant group and then followed his faerie friend. As he walked, there was a fluttering to his heart that was different to the fear he'd felt before, although he did not know how to explain what it meant. He'd never felt the sparkle of magic in anything beyond his hobgoblin before, but something had changed since hearing the stranger's words. He noticed far more cowslips, their yellow heads dancing out of the dark foliage of the hedgerow like drops of sunshine, and all of them were decorated with lustrous, perfectly round, white gems.

For ne'er was dream so like a waking

He'd never spoken to a stranger before.

John looked up and down the empty road, at his feet, his hands, at anywhere except the wrinkled old woman. He was perfectly aware though of her toothless grin, musty scent, and the worn heaps of linen piled on her ramshackle cart. Da's voice thundered through his head: Never trust a female without a man by her side. They're all hags, witches, or worse.

John licked his lips, his tongue thick. A reedy squeak came from his throat and the old woman squinted at him.

'You're one of those that can't speak, my luvvie? Have no fear of me, I've travelled with your sort before. I bet you're good for plenty of coin a-begging—especially a pretty young lass like you.' She cackled. 'Point to what you want, and we'll work out the price together.'

John didn't correct her, only reached out and touched a pair of breeches with a trembling hand.

'You got a nice boy, a sweetheart you're buying things for? No? A brother, perhaps?' She peered at him shrewdly. 'Is he close by? Sent you on ahead, did he? Or... are you all on your own?'

She didn't seem to expect an answer, so he concentrated on gathering a selection of clothing, trying to stop the shake spreading throughout his whole body.

'Why are you so nervous, little one? Have you done something wrong? Someone after you? Thinking of disguising yourself?'

The garments slipped from his quaking hands into the dust. John stooped down to pick them up and saw the hobgoblin standing rigid by the old woman, its skin the colour of fresh blood.

When he looked up, the woman was looming over him, a scaly demoness with eyes of fire. Instead of hands, she had long claws, reaching out to sink into his flesh.

His breath faltering, John dodged away from her and ran, the hobgoblin darting through the air in front of him. The words thank you, thank you, thrummed in his mind like a lute.

They finally stopped by a large oak tree and John leaned against it panting, fear still pumping through his heart. His head twisted side to side, checking for pursuers that didn't appear. A breeze rustled the leaves above him, but there were no other sounds. The air smelt of early-morning undisturbed nature. Apart from him and the hobgoblin, there might have been no-one else alive. He was still clasping the bundle of clothes to his chest.

John sank to the ground and gazed at the faerie dancing in the grass, changing the colour of its skin and hair to match its meadow-green surroundings.

'Am I a thief? I didn't mean to steal... not this time. I got scared. She was going to hurt me... wasn't she?' He whispered, and the hobgoblin skipped and twirled as if it hadn't heard a word.

'Sorry. I don't doubt you. I doubt me. Whether what I see... what I think I see... is what you want to show me.' He tilted his head back and stared up at the blue sky. Perhaps he ought to find his way back to the woman and ask her what he owed? But even as he thought it, he knew he wouldn't—he couldn't.

John followed the hobgoblin through faerie paths with a much lighter step than when he walked amongst human tracks. It was a weakness in him that required curing. There would be other people in the Faerie Queene's city and he needed to be able to speak to them. Faeries were beautiful and awe inspiring, but it could be very lonely without any of his own kind to talk to.

John knew that faeries didn't follow any human rules of politeness and socialising. You could be talking and looking at one and it'd vanish with no sign of when it'd return. There were times while they were travelling when the hobgoblin would disappear, and John didn't know when he'd see it again. At these times, he kept walking forward, hoping it was the right direction and that his faerie would come back soon to guide him. Left alone, his mind would wander, dreaming about what it'd be like to be a different person. The kind who could have run after the group of men he'd seen, and ask what they knew about the Faerie Queene, and ask the boy to explain all of his magical words.

John sighed. He feared his mind was wandering right now, to avoid what he should be really doing. He looked around several times to make sure that him and the hobgoblin were truly alone. Then he gazed at the clothes he was holding and slowly began to get undressed.

He slipped off the bodice and skirt, leaving on the smock that he'd embroidered himself with the delicate leaf patterns he'd seen in his dreams. Cool tendrils of air slashed across his smock, despite the warm morning. He knew he should get dressed quickly, but he paused, running a finger over the ribbon that hung around his neck. It held three pouches. One of silk, holding the charm his mother had given him. A rougher pouch, with dried flowers. He pressed it to his nose. Did they still smell sweet?

The last one, made of old leather, he ignored.

'Me and you then for my breeching celebration?' John looked at the hobgoblin, forcing himself to smile. 'Do you want to make a speech about how I'm a man now, ready to work in the fields and make my father proud?'

The hobgoblin only sang in response. On occasion, John was sure he could understand the words of the faerie songs, but today all he heard was a melancholy tune that made him homesick. Despite everything.

'Nothing cheerier? It is supposed to be a happy occasion, to show I am accepted and... grown up.'

It was a mournful sound, but John hummed along as he struggled to put on his new clothes. The faerie hopped over to help him, but even working together, it took time to lace the breeches to the doublet. Normally, John had quick, deft hands, but today, his fingers were stiff and clumsy. His father wouldn't have worn clothes like this any more than he'd have worn a skirt, but these were definitely male garments. John's skin prickled with the spirits of the boys who had worn them before him. He could almost hear their loud cries, see their fierce games. Their energy, so different from his own, itched deep in his soul.

John rolled his sister's old clothes up. He would not need them again, but he put them to his face and breathed deeply. He was sure he could still smell the scent of Jetta's living body, though she'd outgrown these a year ago and he was the only one who'd worn them since. He tucked them under his arm. He could not leave them behind, discarded in this lonely world.

It had not rained for days, but the hobgoblin somehow managed to find a clear puddle at the edge of a cornfield. John walked over to inspect his reflection. First, his mother gazed up at him, with the tired blue eyes that were so like his own. Then he trilled the water with his little finger and his sister appeared. Born mere minutes before him, Jetta possessed none of John's softness; her youth was almost completely disguised by their father's heavy features. John reached out to touch her hair. He always combed and dressed it for her, and right now, it appeared a tangled mess.

The image rippled away and Eda appeared.

'Look, it's pretending it's a boy! It thinks putting boy's clothes on changes what it is: a feeble, useless, cursed thing!'

John widened his eyes; the hobgoblin splashed his toe in the surface and when the puddle stilled, all that was left was John's own reflection.

He stared at himself for a long time, moving occasionally to see other angles. He removed the new cap to try and shove his hair underneath, thinking he would cut it off as soon as he could. It was too bright and distinctive. He wished he'd thought to bring a knife.

'I'm a boy,' he said to his reflection.

The eyes of his reflection mocked him: But don't you know? When boys run away, they take daggers with them. Not pouches of flower petals to make their clothes smell nicer.

'I am a man,' John attempted in a deeper voice.

The reflection looked at him with pity.

'Maybe not now, but I will be soon.' He turned away from his image. 'We must be close to London. Everything will be different when we get there. Won't it?'

The hobgoblin leapt up and ran forward in the empty air,

tossing a careless glance at him over its shoulder. John wanted to shout for it to stop and wait for him to change back into his old skirt and bodice. Instead, he tightened his grip on Jetta's clothes and followed the creature into the midst of a field. The waist high grass itched at his legs far more now, without his normal skirts. He brushed the grass out of the way, avoided looking down at his exposed calves. Instead, he looked up and the sight of the hobgoblin brought warmth to his cheeks.

'London will be different,' John said. 'I know that it will.'

Before, his days had been governed by when Da left for the fields in the morning and when he returned in the evenings. John had measured his life out in the chores he could successfully complete before Da's hulking figure came back to fill up the single room of their home.

Now he felt time pass only through the base needs of his body—when he got hungry, when he got tired, when he needed to relieve himself. Within those boundaries he had moments of real terror—when his body tensed with fear, and he was certain that he was only minutes away from being captured and dragged back to the village. And then there were other moments, when it felt like he was a completely different, faraway John from a completely different, faraway lifetime from the one who had once belonged to Da.

Sometimes, he tried to work out how many nights had passed since he'd had a definite place to rest, but he never could. A tiny child inside begged him to turn around and go back home, but by the time he spotted the walls of what surely must be the great city, the tiny child had given up pleading.

John paused by a river, watching a skinny woman drag a dead dog across the street and kick it down into the water. She glanced up, catching his eye, and shot him a glare before stalking away.

'Sorry,' he mumbled, unsure why he was apologising.

It was the first word he'd said to a stranger and she hadn't even listened. His tongue flicked over his lips, but it made no difference: his lips were as dry as his tongue. Tongue as dry as his lips. The sound of running water had drawn him, but looking down into the river, he saw nothing refreshing—A great, red band flowed past him, boiling with blood and disease. A creature with a foot-long beak, bulbous eyes and a swollen belly broke through the surface then dived back down.

John looked around for the hobgoblin. He knew that it left sometimes, for days even, but it would always come back. So why did his heart ache now as if he'd been left forever? He turned back to the river, closed his eyes for as long as he dared, then opened them again. The crimson veins had finally stopped, but the water still festered. Butchered remains of unrecognisable animals tangled in the debris at the sides of the river, murky brown with human stink.

John swallowed the bile that rose in his throat. Boys didn't feel sick when they saw dead things. Neither did girls, come to think—just him. But not any more. He wiped his hand across the back of his mouth.

'You doing some fishing?'

He jumped at the voice by his elbow. At first, he thought it was the woman with the dog, but this was a newcomer. Younger, with a wide smile that revealed one lone tooth peeking out of red gums. Though he understood all of her words, they still sounded different to anything he'd heard before.

A child with matted hair peered from behind the bucket that hung by the girl's side.

'The only person who catches anything in the Fleet is the undertaker,' the child said in a strange pretend-adult voice and the pair threw their heads back and laughed.

John stood still, breathing quickly, feeling himself weaken as he transformed into a newly born fawn. His limbs shook beneath his body. The colours of the world around him changed, some fading into greys, others deepening into intense blues. He opened his mouth and bleated.

How was he supposed to make himself understood in a fawn's body?

The girl and child looked at him, then at each other. The girl tapped a finger against her single tooth. Their brows creased, as if undecided on whether John should be kept as a curious pet, or skinned and eaten.

Then he was a boy again, and the girl and child were talking to him with easy grins as if there was nothing odd about John. Nothing odd at all.

Emptying out her bucket into the river with a wide swing of her arm, the girl looked down at her muck-spattered clothes, shrugged, and turned back to John.

'It's not as bad here as further on at the ditch, but if you're new to these parts, take a bit of advice: cover your mouth and try not to breathe much. If you're not used to it, you can catch the plague, just by walking too close to the river.'

The child covered his mouth as he giggled.

'They don't even have to hang people here!'

And she nodded.

'That's right! That's a complete truth! You'd think criminals would be tougher, wouldn't you? But the ones at Fleet Prison die quick as you like when they have to drink the same water and breathe the same air as us.'

The child pulled a haggard face, as though he was dying right now.

'At least it's quick. I'd rather die that way than some others.'

The girl cuffed him amicably.

'You're such a pest, we all know you're going to die from a good thumping.' She beckoned to John. 'You look far too nice to be wandering around on your own. Come back with us, and we'll scratch up something for you to eat.'

John's eyes darted around, searching for the hobgoblin. Instead, he saw ramshackle dwellings clustered around a towering stone wall. As he watched, there was a flash of light, and a huge beast with a thousand mouths rose up from behind the city walls and spewed out fire with a thunderous roar. People scrambled away from it, screaming and shouting. As they ran, they transformed into bony rats, dressed in rags, scuttling away over piles of waste.

John backed away from the girl and the child and stumbled wordlessly towards the wall. As always, once the vision vanished, it was as if it had never existed, but the people he glimpsed from the corners of his eyes still seemed to have rat whiskers and twitching rodent noses. He shivered. Maybe the rat-people had once been like him, running to London to seek the protection of the Faerie Queene. But they'd grown older and sicker as they waited and waited, until there was nothing left but clinging to the sides and hoping that one day, the wall would crumble and admit them to the wonders of the city.

The one-toothed girl and the child hadn't been rats, though. He looked back, but they had gone. He thought through the conversation, wondering why he'd been so frightened. They'd been kind, hadn't they? How stupid he must have seemed, standing there witless. He needed to be better than this.

The child's words about plague hummed through his mind. John pulled the pouches out from under his clothes and breathed in the scent of dried petals. For the briefest moment, he was a flower, wide and open, warmed by the sun's rays, with nothing to think about, nothing to do, his only purpose just to be.

But the flower state passed quickly.

He put the pouch away.

Ignoring the river, John focused on the huge stone wall. There was no doubt that it hid the miracle of the Faerie Queene's city, which would be completely different from the foul dwellings sprawled around the outside. And John was sure of it—once he got into its protection, he too would be changed, no more this meek thing, crawling through life.

He pushed his shoulders back and lifted his chin, gripped Jetta's clothes against his chest with both arms. Boys walked with long strides, but not too long. It had to look natural. He focused his mind on his feet, but resisted looking at them, trying not to feel the leather digging into his toes with every step. The wall stretched onwards, across the whole of Time and England. It seemed hopeless—no matter how far or fast he went, he'd never find a way in.

John jumped at the sound of Da's voice, so clear right then that he almost whipped around to see if the big man was standing behind him. Whatever you are, you'll never be a man. He bit his lip. He'd been told many times that he was barely a boy, let alone a man, but none of those people who had jeered at him were here now. He looked up at the untouchable clouds.

He could be whatever he wanted to be.

When he lowered his eyes again he saw the city gate, as if it had always been there waiting for him. A whole village worth of people jostled in front of it, roaring together, an angry monster forcing itself forward, as if it would tear down the old stone walls with its rage.

As John got closer, he saw that there was no bellowing beast, only a vast, wounded animal broken up into men, women, and children, dirty and reeking, with shabby clothes. All of them stank, the younger ones like wet straw, the adults sour and sickly.

Some of them carried baskets on their backs, overflowing with wood, linen, fruit and herbs, which John could see were squashed beyond usefulness. Nevertheless, he sidled closer to a woman burdened with leaves, hoping that their aroma might mask some of the human stench. The mints were bruised and torn, all their refreshing properties lost to the wind. But there was marjoram too—a symbol of love and happiness ahead. He just had to get into the city.

No one looked at him or spoke to him, not even the people near enough to touch. It felt lonely, but it also meant there was nothing about him to make people stare. He was just one more limb of the injured creature limping through the city gates.

What country friends is this?

Drowning in the belly of a dragon, floundering in yellow bile, black bile, dark, thick blood. He clawed with his hands, trying to grab something, anything, to help him keep his head above the spew. John clutched at his throat, found the ribbon around his neck and followed it down to the pouch Ma had given him. In the second before his body was sucked under, he clasped the pouch in his fist.

He was out of the beast. His body was back to normal—or at least, the same as it had ever been which, he knew, was very far from normal. He was not drowning; he was not dying. He was standing on an ordinary street. London, at last!

But so many people. You'd think every single person in the whole world had gathered here. He turned his head in every direction. All these humans, but not a single faerie. No Faerie Queene. Not even a sign of his little hobgoblin.

John tucked Ma's pouch back under his clothes, brushing the other two pouches as he did so. Touching the old leather one sent a chill through his body that scratched into the marrow of his bones.

Shouldn't it be impossible to feel cold in this enormous city, with the heat of so many bodies around him?

He blinked and breathed, trying to rub the heat back into himself and his fingers paused on his legs, on the rough fabric of his stockings. The material separating his bare skin from the world seemed so much thinner than when he'd been alone in the country. Any stranger who glanced at him would see the exact shape of his legs! He shook away the traitorous wish for a skirt, adjusted his grip on the bundle of Jetta's clothes with a grunt and pushed on.

Through the sprawling mass of houses, he kept going even when the blood started to ooze between his toes. His body hurt more than after one of Da's worst punishments and the clamour split his head. Still, he tried to move forward in that way men had. That way Da had, of walking as if he couldn't see anyone else, but everyone saw him and would leap out of his way. Like he belonged here.

The upper storeys of the buildings hung over the edges of the street. Once he started looking at them, he couldn't stop, convinced they would crash down and crush him. He kept his head lowered, not out of nervousness, no, definitely not that, but to keep himself from stumbling on the churned-up ground. The road must have been chewed up by all the carts—two massive ones blocked his way, big enough to transport his entire village. With every step he took, this new world grew and his old village seemed to shrink away, until soon, it would be no more than a tiny speck. And then —Would it vanish altogether? Could it?

He didn't know how to comprehend that thought.

He didn't need to. Not right now.

He just had to focus on finding his way to the Faerie Queene.

Why were there so many people though? So much noise? So much stink?

John scurried back the way he'd come. He must've taken the wrong road, somehow. He needed to start again from the beginning and choose a different path. But he realised he had no idea how to get back to the city gate. Now he'd wandered into a street with vast hunks of red meat impaled on spits in the shop windows. All of the meat he'd eaten in his whole life wouldn't add up to what was in a single window.

Who ate this much? Who could be this hungry?

A thick-set man drove cows through the throng. The beasts strolled obediently onwards, as indifferent to the people they shoved aside as they were to their dead kin being bought and sold. The cows were silent, but something somewhere was howling. John surged with a deep, mad urge to throw his head back and howl too.

His breathing steadied, when a scream behind him made him jump. The noise had seemed human, but it must have come from an animal, the way everyone traipsed on. And the only thing John could see that he hadn't noticed before was a butcher inside one of the nearby shops, cleaving through cuts of meats.

The man's eyes remained focused down on his task. There was nothing unusual about him, but just as John was about to look away, a shadow with the blackness of a starless night started to spread out from the man. It grew and grew, swallowing up the street; a butcher holding a cleaver which chopped down with grim inevitably. John's stomach tensed as if a rat was clawing at his insides. He put a hand over it and swallowed down the vomit filling his mouth.

No time for madness. He had to find the Faerie Queene. Without his hobgoblin, he had no way of knowing if he was going the right way, and if he wasn't careful, night would come and he'd be alone, with nowhere to sleep, and nothing to eat or drink. He turned and was immediately lost again.

One voice cut above the ruckus and made his heart pound.

'Stranger, we don't want thy sort here! Get thou back where thou belongst!'

Boys surrounded him on both sides, their faces creased with hate, making them look far older and meaner. More of them took up the cry of 'Stranger,' and others shouted 'Spaniard,' which by the roughness of their voices must have been something even worse. John looked around, thinking perhaps he could get lost amongst the mass of people before they caught him, but then the boys started throwing clods of earth and stones, and John realised he was not their target. It was a man a few paces in front of him, who had the darkest skin he'd ever seen. The rest of the crowd had parted with one instinct: to give the boys a clear path to him.

John took a breath. Back in the village, whenever Wilkin pinned him down, or when Eda and her friends surrounded him, jabbing and sneering, he always hoped that someone would come to his aid. And now here he was, but what could he do? Could he try and cause a distraction? But the thought of that made sweat prickle at his brow. Had he really escaped the village to purposely put himself in the path of danger?

He was about to dart forward, still unsure, when a cry of 'Constable' went up and the boys scattered. The man vanished too, and only John remained standing there, his chest heaving and his mouth agape as if he had actually been in a fight.

Had he been brave?

No.

Almost.

But, no.

The flow of bodies bore him onwards.

Now he was in a different street, joined against his will in a queue of people, waiting for Death. Chains ensnared their arms and legs, but the chains were attached to nothing and hung in mid-air. And they weren't people, no; they were gaunt creatures with the flesh peeling away from their faces, all screaming and screaming.

John shut his eyes for a long time.

When he opened them again, the nearly-dead were only traders, bellowing out their wares. A blotchy-faced man with white patches of skin flaking away from his forehead stood just in front of him. John put his hand up to his own head, probing it with shaking fingers.

When people from the village talked about visiting the outside world for trading, he'd always imagined something similar to home. Like when Ma bartered with Tenney over how much weaving she could swap for him to re-sole a pair of worn boots. But here it was nothing like what he knew: All shouting and fighting, with more goods on display than surely even all these people could ever need.

Stalls and barrows, people with boxes on their backs, others with trays hoisted around their necks on fraying leather straps. A vast row of stalls layered with carefully folded linen. An old woman with a basket of fish that stared out with long-dead eyes.

His tongue felt rotten; the whole place was heavy with the stench of decay. There seemed no difference between the filth thrown on the ground for the rats to fight over, and the stuff people were expected to buy. John edged to the side, watching constantly and yet, he still managed to bump into a man.

He waited for an angry shout, but the man only stuck out his palm and spoke in a low whine.

'Alms for a poor wounded soldier, fresh returned from the wars in Ireland, young sir?'

He leaned on a long stick and John tried not to stare at the limb missing under his right knee.

'I... I don't have any... alms... I don't think. Is there any... other way I can help you, gentle sir?'

The man's face crinkled into a smile, but before he could reply, John felt a fluttering touch on his elbow. At last, the hobgoblin! He swung around, and saw instead a finely-dressed woman with wide skirts and a smart hat of a design John had never seen before. It took a moment to register that she was the one touching him.

Her cheeks coloured.

'No harm done. Just brushing a little dirt off.' She patted him again, looking past John at the soldier with narrowed eyes. 'Don't say a thing.'

The soldier laughed.

'I baited perfect for ye, but still the great Bess Porch ain't able to pick a simple country gull.'

The woman put her hands on her hips.

'Bring a waste!'

They were no longer paying him any attention and their voices had hardened. With a backward glance, John walked away. What on earth had just happened?

He skirted his way around a barrow filled with foods he didn't recognise, though his eyes saw well enough the rotting vegetables the fresh produce on top could not hide. Then he paused beside a tall man holding a tray of ribbons. Jetta would be wide-eyed with wonder to see such a rainbow of colours. It was like nothing he'd seen before, but obviously so commonplace in this world that no one else was stopping to marvel. He bit on his little finger, wishing Jetta could be here to share it with him.

For a moment, John felt peace in his heart. He imagined how she would tug on his sleeve, telling him to be brave and have a look with her. Even if they couldn't afford to buy, at least they could see treasures to visit in their dreams. The tall man noticed John's attention and beckoned him over.

'Come here, my pretty one, you deserve beautiful things to dress that golden hair.'

John's cheeks burned, his hand darting to his head, where his hair had tumbled free of the cap. He had to find somewhere quiet where he could stop and collect himself.

The houses were packed together, as if all these people wanted to be as near to one another as humanly possible. It still seemed certain that at any moment, one of the huge buildings would topple forward and pull the whole city down with it. Finally spying a gap between two houses, John crept into the shadows and leaned back against the wall. It felt damp and slimy; the air hung with the stench of stale urine. He imagined gangs of boy-dogs racing around every crevice of the city morning and night, marking everything as their own.

Sighing, he wished he could calm his mind.

So many people.

So many colours.

So many noises.

And no harmony—everything in constant battle.

A carnivorous monster so hungry it was trying to devour itself. Surely this couldn't be where the Faerie Queene dwelled?

Nowhere looked suitable to put Jetta's clothes down, so he struggled to balance, crooking them in his arm as he worked his hair back under the cap. He moved slowly—Concentrating on this meant he didn't have to think about anything else. But he had to decide what to do. He needed to work on the way he spoke and moved; he needed to pass as a normal boy without having to be conscious of it all the time. That would free up his mind to work out all the other truly important things.

'Good morrow,' he said in a voice quieter than his normal one.

'Good morrow,' he repeated.

The 'good' had sounded fine, but the 'morrow' disappeared into uncertainty.

He said the words again and again.

His eyelids got heavy and drooping. A pleasant thought drifted into his mind, that if he let his body fall into oblivion he would wake up at home, with Jetta and Ma praising him for how well he'd mended their clothes.

Then the daydream ripped apart—a noise startled him awake.

Clattering and panting, a person had come running into the alleyway and was pelting towards him. Whoever it was wore a dark, flowing cape. Inside its hood was a deep, black nothing that would swallow John whole. And no time to run.

The caped attacker was upon him.

I can express no kinder sign of love than this kind kiss

Good morrow,’ John squeaked.

The person tore off the cape, expertly folded it into a small square and threw it to the ground. That’s when he saw: They were a boy, just like John. Not like John—taller and broader, and even in the shadows of the alley, John could make out freckles on pale skin, hair as red as the sunrise on a clear day, and green eyes that sparkled like the hobgoblin’s.

‘Do you... do you mean to do me harm?’ The words were living things, scared to leave his mouth.

No. This wouldn’t do. He had to be stronger. He forced himself to stand up as tall as he could. He held Jetta’s clothes in one arm and turned the other hand into a tight, trembling fist.

The flame-haired boy’s eyebrows shot up, but instead of answering John, he responded with his own question, his face full of laughter and mischief.

‘Help me?’

John tried to keep his voice hard.

‘Why?’

‘By my troth, I’ll make it worth your while.’

The boy winked.

Some sort of starry light hung around him, an aura of... what? Maybe this was a test, sent by the Faerie Queene?

John blinked.

The stranger didn't transform into a monster or an animal, but remained a boy with dancing green eyes.

'What do you need me to do?' John asked.

The answer came in the form of hands gripping his waist, a body leaning into him, and full, warm lips pressed against his own.

John splayed his empty hand against the wall, unsure where to put it, unsure where to put anything. He held his bundle wedged between them, the familiar fabric against his palm, and the unknown material of the boy's clothes pushed into his knuckles.

John's mouth fell open, or the other boy's tongue pushed his lips apart. The moistness, the heat and the boldness of the kiss seemed to trap the very air in John's lungs.

The city faded. All that noise and stench, subdued by the taste of hot apples.

A sweltering sensation rushed through him. He knew pain, he was used to pain, but this was something completely new. Then he wanted to cry out. Not because it hurt. Though it did hurt, though not in a normal way. In a fierce, demanding way, in flames that wrapped around him and this stranger and burnt the rest of the world into ashes.

Realizing he'd closed his eyes, John opened them. The other boy was looking sideways at the entrance to the alleyway.

Unaware or uncaring of the effect he'd had on John's body?

Perhaps this was completely normal and unremarkable in this place... boys, kissing other boys?

A whimper escaped from John and disappeared into the other boy's mouth, and the other stepped back with a laugh. Thumped the wall with the side of his fist.

'Od's bod!'

John jumped, dropping the bundle of Jetta's clothes. He leaned down to retrieve them, but the boy did too, and John's head bumped his shoulder. As he grappled with his cap to stop his hair escaping, the boy picked up the clothes and tucked them under his arm.

The smell of the city was returning. John stared at the boy casually holding Jetta's clothes, unaware of his fingers tracing the lines of his own lips.

'Was it too much?' The other boy picked up the cloak he'd just abandoned and tucked it into John's bundle, talking all the while. 'Did I go too far? I thought it needed to look convincing. Marry, I will pay you well, though. That was closer than I like. And you saved me, you sweet thing.' He spun on one heel in a kind of half jig. 'Did you see them? The fools. They passed right by. To think such a simple trick saved me from riding the horse foaled by an acorn. And instead of hanging from the gallows, I'll be keeping company with the fairest maiden I've ever seen.'

John was following the boy's every movement. He opened and closed his mouth, but nothing came out. He should have denied being a maiden, but somehow the words wouldn't come.

The redhead tilted his chin, his brow creased.

'What an odd thing, though, I was certain when I first laid eyes on you that you were wearing a skirt. I can even picture it now, a plain, cheap country thing, but covered in the loveliest embroidery. Indeed, it was just like this.'

He held up Jetta's skirt.

John put his hands out for the clothes, but the tall boy stowed them back under one arm, and linked the other arm with his. John's feeble attempt at protest was smothered by the other boy chatting on.

'I'll be dragged to Bedlam, next thing I know!' He chuckled and shook his head. 'But don't you mind me, you're right to be wearing boy's garb. Few can pull off that trick, but it works for you; makes your face look even prettier. It's the contrast that does it, isn't it? I've got an eye for these things. ...When did you get here? You must be fresh. You'd never be on your own in an alley otherwise. Come now, we mustn't tarry.'

He strode forward, but John pulled back against his arm:

'You kissed me?'

The boy grinned down at him.

'The magic of your pretty red lips saved me from hanging. I am ever in your debt. You can tell me how to repay you over some ale—being so close to death makes a body thirsty.'

'I don't know your name,' John protested, then added in a rushed voice, 'And my lips are just—ordinary lips, like any b...'

A round-bellied man bumped into the other. The two of them cursed at each other, the red-haired boy refusing to back down, despite the man's size. The argument descended into a good-natured scuffle, until eventually the man stepped back, barked out a laugh, glanced at John and said in a low voice, 'You've found a rare precious mort there, Black Jack.' Then he boomed out, 'Stow you, wrench,' and barrelled away.

The boy winked at John.

'That was good distraction! You're bringing me even more good fortune, seeing Starving Robert like that by chance. He'll pay me well for that favour. Several finely-dressed gentlefolk paused to look at you.'

It was a dream where nothing made sense. John hadn't seen anyone stopping, finely-dressed or otherwise. But it wasn't a dream, was it? The sharp smell, slicing through his nostrils. The shouting, the hungry cries, the turbulence that seemed part of the city itself. And the living warmth of this boy next to him. It was no vision, not this time.

A group of children scampered around them, singing, 'Hark, hark, the dogs do bark, the beggars are coming to town!'

The boy next to him grinned.

'Fair Maiden, look, the Roaring Boys have gathered to greet you. Wherever you were before, I bet the day's lifts that you've never seen a sight like this.'

A ragged barrier of people formed across the street. None of them were boys though, and the roaring was coming from everyone else trying to get out of their way. They were dressed in ill-matched odds and ends, and their faces were scarred and pitted. Ears were missing, noses squashed in, and two of them only had one eye. Their stench was something real and solid: dirty feet, sour alcohol, emptied guts, weeping sores. They seemed a line of scarecrows, straggling between life and death, leaking filth from the pores of their skin. And his companion marched merrily towards them, taking John with him.

John wanted to run, but the boy's touch on his arm was all that kept him steady now. If he let go, he would fall.

And the smell would ooze over him and claim him and he'd be lost forever.

Once they got close, the men parted like a row of barley and let the two of them through. The smell was a wall of green meat, crawling with maggots. The red-haired boy stopped right in the midst of it, jesting and talking, leaning in to the closest man and whispering in his ear. The waxy gunk stuck to the wiry sproutings of hair on his head did not seem to concern him. The man wheezed and whistled, a death rattle that made John shiver, but he was also grinning, and the redheaded boy threw his head back in easy, open-mouthed laughter.

John's own mouth was clamped shut.

He swallowed and swallowed, desperate not to vomit and appear so weak in front of someone who was so—not-weak.

Eventually the row of men moved on, relinking their arms where they'd parted and stomping forward. They didn't take all their stink with them, but at least it lessened. The redheaded boy watched their unruly progress with a half-smile.

John fingered the scented pouch under his clothes, scared that if he brought it out into this miasma, it'd be forever destroyed. He gazed up at the taller boy, his eyes watering. Could he ask for another kiss? Would that beat the stench like it had in the alleyway? Could he say help me, like the other had said to him?

And the boy would put his hands on John's waist again—well, only one hand this time, as he was holding Jetta's clothes—he would put one hand on John's waist, and—

He realised the other was staring at him.

'What now? Does everyone smell like rose petals in your country?' He wiped a thumb across John's cheeks and his smile widened. 'Ah, forgive me, I've seen fellows bigger than Starving Robert faint dead away when the Roaring Boys pass by.' He watched the men move further down the street. 'Have you ever felt like that? Standing up and screaming and making all those people with their neat little lives take notice?'

'No,' John's voice was a croak.

'Never?'

'Never.'

'Why not? One as pretty as you would brighten the world of all who saw you.'

John only shook his head and looked at the ground.

It was a while before he could breathe again. They were in another street, crowded and overflowing with rubbish, but with stones underfoot rather than rough earth.

The boy spoke constantly without seeming to need any reply. John let the words flow around him, fluffy little clouds that tickled his ears and sheltered him from the fury of the city. He gathered that they were heading towards a tavern where there'd be food and drink—

A girl with dark, wild hair like Jetta danced by. John opened his mouth, ready to call, 'Jetta, it's me! I'm wearing breeches! I've been kissed! Do I look different?' But it couldn't be her—and he would never have said those things.

Instead, he asked the boy beside him:

'Are you ever going to give my clothes back?'

The other stopped mid-sentence, and turned to John.

'That's a serious question now, and I'll answer you likewise.' He blew air upwards. 'I aim to. There's no denying, I am a natural thief, but I've no wish to steal from you who saved me.'

'Should I believe you?'

The boy uncrooked his arm from John's, and for a moment, his limb stayed linked in the air to an invisible person before he let it drop to his side.

Then the boy slipped his hand around John's waist and pulled him close.

'Fair One, if you're going to survive even a day in this city, never trust anyone.' He leant in, his mouth next to John's ear, and John heard the words, but was barely aware of them. Right then, the hobgoblin appeared, perched on the other boy's shoulder and grinning its biggest grin. Its hair and eyes were the exact shade of the stranger's.

John made a sound at the back of his throat, a mewl more than anything:

'But I can trust you?' His cheeks reddened—he hadn't meant to speak the doubt out loud.

For the first time since they'd met, there was no hint of a smile on the other boy's face. His mouth set in a straight line. Finally, he nodded. Then he turned and walked on, chattering away as if there'd been no interruption.

Thy friendship makes us fresh.

The boy was telling a story about the tavern they'd stopped beside, but John had long lost track of it. Clearly, it was meant to be funny, as the other kept laughing—in contrast, the hobgoblin, skin grey, hair white and wiry, was staring through one of the tavern windows and hissing at something within.

He was still watching it when a hand gripped John's chin gently and lifted it up, until he was looking into a freckled face with merry green eyes and a slanted grin.

John bit his lip.

'I was just... '

'Not listening to a word I said.'

'Sorry. You're being so kind. I don't know why... but can we leave? Please? I don't think this is a good place.'

His words were somehow both hesitant and rushed, like he really did have a gift for sounding both like a blathering fool and a dithering one, all at the same time. But the other boy hadn't noticed, hadn't even heard.

'This is a bene place to have a drink and get to know each other. Likely many of my friends will be here and will be interested to meet you. But stay close to me until... '

The door swung open, releasing a waft of staleness and a clamour of voices. A man staggered out and slammed it closed behind him, pausing at a drooping angle. His body still deciding to stay upright or not. John couldn't tell if the man's clothes were falling off him, or if he was falling out of his clothes. As he watched, the man's head jerked upwards. It seemed impossible that he could focus on anything with his dazed, bloodshot eyes, but he raised a hand all the same and called out:

'What ho, Black Jack!'

As the other boy returned the greeting and chatted on in cant John couldn't follow, the man leaned against the tavern wall to relieve himself. His water trickled down to join a pool already darkening the ground outside the inn. He belched twice, then looked at John, his head falling sideways as if too heavy for his neck.

'You be boy or girl? Can't rightly tell,' he shrugged. 'No matter. I'm drunk enough, your face is pretty enough to—'

The hobgoblin spun away from the windows and kicked the man in the head with one crabbed little foot, and he fell face down with a grunt and lay there unmoving.

Sniggering, the redhead linked his arm through John's again.

'I think you're right, Fair One, you deserve somewhere finer for your first night in London. There'll be plenty of time for you to get acquainted with the likes of him.'

'Shouldn't we check he isn't hurt?'

'No need, he most certainly is hurt. Do not fret though, you tender-hearted thing. If he's so drunk that he cannot see clear you're a girl in boy's clothes, then he's too drunk to feel pain.'

The hobgoblin was now a pale green, dancing through the air away from the tavern. John's insides churned with an odd mix of disgust and pride: his new companion still hadn't realised—

But the redhead was in full flow again.

He seemed to be comparing the different quality of drinks you got in different places at different times of the year. The Dutch beer was apparently the best—if you could get friendly with the right people, which his companion was, of course. John imagined regaling him back with tales of the one alewife in the village with her single ale which always tasted the same. The thought made him smile, but he mustn't be distracted by idle thoughts: the other boy walked faster when he was talking about something he enjoyed, and John needed all his concentration and energy just to keep up. John had to take three quick steps to match one of the boy's long strides. He tugged on his arm.

'Black Jack?'

'Ay?' the boy slowed.

'Can I call you that? Is that your name?'

'Did I not introduce myself to you properly, Fair One? In all the excitement, I've lost my manners. Though some will tell you otherwise, I'm always polite—whatever else I'm doing.' He winked. 'Forgive me now, and let me correct my rudeness. Black Jack is what many know me as in these parts.'

John took a deep breath. He couldn't wait for a pause in Black Jack's talk before speaking; he might lose his courage by the time it came, but still, the other kept going,

'...Though going far back, I was originally a... '

'Well, my name is... '

'John,' they said together.

Black Jack threw his head back and gave a deep laugh.

'How did you guess? Right easy, with Jack being the friendly version of John!'

John tried to explain, but his voice was fading already.

How did you make yourself heard in this great, clanging city?

Surely it should have been simple to tell this merry near-stranger: I'm not a Fair Maiden, but a badly made boy called John with no friends in the world apart from a faerie only I can see. But they'd no doubt part ways soon, so what did it matter, really? John made a sound between a sigh and a whimper.

The boy didn't notice; there was not a breath's break in the whir of his voice. But the hobgoblin froze mid-somersault and gazed at John with round, brown eyes. It tugged at John's ear and pointed at Black Jack before continuing its flips. John looked up at the taller boy and listened more carefully to what he was saying.

'There was blood splattered everywhere. You would not believe it, nay, you could not believe it! How could something so small have that much blood in it? The mess I was in, it truly looked like I'd slain a giant. If my friends had not been there to bear witness, and be sure they told everyone I'd lost a fight with an old rat, then I'm certain I'd have been arrested for murder.' As he spoke, he constantly moved one arm, and his mouth looked always on the verge of bursting into laughter. 'And that's why I was known as Red Jack, though newcomers just assumed it was due to the shade of my hair, which is fine too, but as you and I are such fast friends, you should know all.'

But was John getting so confused that he couldn't keep track of someone's name? Was his companion Red Jack or Black Jack?

'Here's a confession just for you, Fair One: that story is also the reason why, no matter how empty my belly gets, I never try my luck with the rats. I play it that I am too good to be chasing about after the beady-eyed things.' He laughed. 'And that works well enough, even though my friends are roasting meat and I'm sneaking off to scavenge for rotten vegetables, or sucking old fish bones.'

John seized the gap in Jack's chatter.

'If you're hungry now... on the way here, before I reached London, I mean, I found a good supply of leaves and berries. I only ate a few, so there's plenty left... I could maybe find my way back, and... and... ' John sucked his lips. Sometimes, it was too easy to hear exactly why the sound of his voice had sent Da into such rages. A stinging like nettles prickled his entire body.

The taller boy gazed down at him for a moment, with his eyebrows turned up in the middle and a crooked smile dancing over his lips.

'Leaves and berries do sound like a fine feast, but today let me treat you to city dining. ...What were we talking of? How I became Black Jack? Ay, that is a tale.' Jack laughed. 'The like of which you've no doubt heard many times before, and will hear many times again, because it all revolves around a tavern brawl.'

John kept his head down, only glancing up occasionally at Black Jack or the hobgoblin, which was floating in front of the redhead's face, nodding along with his words.

'So there I was, away from my usual haunts, over at The Devil's Tavern doing a bit of this and that, outside my usual trade, when who should walk in?' He paused and gazed at John with wide surprised eyes. 'Black Jack! And what should he be clinging onto, as if it were passed down from heaven, but his blackjack, the drinking jug that he took everywhere with him and insisted all his ale was served in. And he immediately says... ' Black Jack unlinked his arm and mimed clutching a tankard against his chest, bunched his other hand into a fist, and screwed his face up into a livid scowl. He continued in a growl, 'Red Jack, you've no right to be here. You're out of place. And more than that, you have no right to your name, you're going to be Black Jack now, I have a mind to be Red Jack.'

The boy returned to his normal voice.

'Yes, you might well look confused, Fair One, because it was just like that, out of nowhere. Well, what's a body to do when someone tries to steal their name?' Keeping a hold of Jetta's clothes, Jack spread his arms out to their full span, and then leapt to the other side of John. In an exaggerated version of his own accent, he said, 'I have a right to be wherever I want to be, Black Jack, and to be called whatever I please. It is of no concern of yours.'

He jumped back, creasing up his face again and growling out his words. He shook a fist at John:

'If you'll be a fool and not do what I tell you, then there's only one solution.'

John's mouth hung open as he gazed at Jack, now walking backwards with an easy swagger. Even when Jack was pretending to be the man with the creased up face, there was somehow a joy to his movements, as if there was nothing merrier than beating each other up.

'In truth, there was more talk back and forth. But I won't bore you with all that; you know well how these things play out.'

Did John know it? He knew being punched in the gut so hard, that for a moment, you felt death. He knew lying on the floor with your eyes shut tight, picturing the delicate colours of faerie wings to distract from the spitting children all around...

'A whole roast chicken splattered into her face!'

'Have you ever seen a barrel thrown so hard that it splinters into nothing! It was a sight for sure!'

'Not just one spoon, but five in each hand, and she did not stop hitting him, even when he was on the floor!'

Jack spent longer acting out the attacking parts and gave them much more energy than the cowering defences. But of course—there wasn't anything entertaining about being curled up in pain, or pleading for mercy.

The taller boy fell into step again beside John and swung an arm around his shoulder.

'Oh, I wish you could've been there, you would have laughed and laughed. We all did. Me and Black Jack looked at each other, and all the lower half of his face was bloodied where I'd got good hits on his nose and split his lip open, and my face was all covered in bruises too. But there it was, the fight had shown us that it was a bene idea to swap names after all. And I've been Black Jack since that day.'

John licked his lips.

Now, he told himself—tell him now.

But Black Jack had more to say:

'Though the original Black Jack disappeared soon after.' He stared up at some birds, wheeling against the darkening sky. 'There was a rumour for a while that he got caught and hung for something that they wanted a Red Jack for. But I don't think that can be true.' He flashed John a wide smile. 'I suppose I could go back to Red Jack again, but I'm accustomed to the sound of Black Jack now. What thinks you, Fair One? Do you have a preference?'

If any answer was expected, it was beyond John's wit to give it.

As he spoke the last sentence, Black Jack spun them round, through a doorway and into a tavern.

It was the biggest room John'd ever seen. Tables and benches were everywhere, with no order to their arrangement, some placed so close together that even he wouldn't be able to squeeze through the gap. And still not enough furniture for everyone huddled in squashed groups. One man was trapped in a corner juggling three tankards, although people only seemed to notice him when he dropped one. Every mouth John could see was open—shouting, or stuffing in food or drink.

Unconsciously, he edged closer to Black Jack and searched for the hobgoblin, hoping to catch a glimpse of it dancing up in the beams. On the other side of the room, two musicians were winding their way through the tables, one strumming and the other singing. John hadn't noticed them before, but that's where he found his companion: Hovering close to the singer's mouth, as if trying to see where the sound was coming from. John watched, wondering if the hobgoblin would bless them all with the sweetness of faerie music, like it always did him. But the faerie only looked and did not touch the man.

Black Jack gave the musicians a nod of greeting and spoke quietly to John. 'You're taken with those two? You've got good instincts. They're people you can trust to make adequate distraction, and they never demand more than their share. But tonight I'm thanking you for saving my neck, not working.' He led John on, slipping easily through the crush of bodies.

The air was thick with voices calling. 'Good Even,' 'How Now!' 'What do you?' and just plain, 'Black Jack!'

Black Jack bent close to John's ear.

'It was a fine idea of yours to find a better place to eat. We've hit a lucky time: with so few people here, there'll be plenty of food left for us to bargain over. We'll get better fare at a cheaper price.'

John stared around, his breath quickening. So few people?

The other frowned into his eyes.

'Have you had a tiring day, my country girl?' He straightened up and put an arm around John. 'I know what to do. We'll celebrate being alive by spending the coin on a room, and we can eat there. It's not my custom to rent a bed, but this is a special day. We've found each other, and how often do you meet a new friend?'

'Never,' John murmured against his shoulder. 'Never.'

'What do I owe you for the food and lodgings?'

Later, John looked around the room that was too big for the two of them, larger even than the one his whole family had shared with their animals. A huge bed dominated, hung about with heavy curtains, and with a proper mattress and pillows instead of bug-ridden straw and logs. The hobgoblin would have loved twirling amongst all this finery, but the last time John had seen it, it'd been splashing about in burly men's drinks, leaving them to blame other burly men for spilling their ale.

For just the two of them, John and Black Jack had a tankard of ale, a bottle of wine, a crusty pie, a plate of oysters, and a handful of strawberries. They sat on the floor, backs against the wall, their legs stretched out and the food between them. There was still some daylight seeping through the window, but Black Jack had lit a candle which cast long shadows.

John's stomach growled, but he waited for the other boy to give him things rather than grabbing them. He glanced down at his knuckles, still feeling the raps he'd got when he took food before Da had finished. He asked again:

'What do I owe you for the food and lodgings?'

Instead of responding, Black Jack produced a knife and cracked an oyster shell open, deftly cutting the meat free and holding it up to the other's mouth. Without thinking, John tipped his head back and swallowed the ugly grey thing. To his surprise, he enjoyed the way it slipped over his tongue and the salty-sweet tang...

Then Jack passed him wine. John tried to take just a sip, but with a grin, Black Jack tilted the bottle and the liquid flooded his mouth. It had been sweetened, and John gulped it down as if it were fresh water.

'That's right, don't be shy, Fair One. I've paid, drink up.'

John frowned.

'I have money. You don't have to pay for everything. Tell me what I owe you.'

His mind blurred, as if the wine was washing thousands of separate images together. He had to concentrate to remember where he was and what he was doing here.

He was in London.

To become a man. And to be made new and clean in the sanctuary of the Faerie Queene.

Who was nowhere to be found, and yet he wasn't frightened. It must have been the sweet wine, or the tiredness, or the noise and stink of this city suffocating his capacity to feel things properly.

But wasn't he feeling something?

Not hollow disappointment, after running from home, and finding that his dream of London had all along been chasing a nightmare. He wasn't feeling the things he should have been, not since the alleyway, not since the kiss—

Black Jack had asked him a question.

For a moment, John gazed at the boy's freckles, dizzily thinking that they were like the stars in the skies—appearing random, but making beautiful patterns and stories if you looked at them in the right way.

He looked into Jack's eyes. The other was staring back at him with naked curiosity.

John felt his cheeks flush. He hiccupped, a little, high pitched squeak which made Jack laugh and look away. John tried to remember his purpose. Pulling the pouches out from under his clothes, he blurted again,

'I have money.'

'That is a fortunate thing, Fair One. It's always good to have coin in your possession.' Black Jack chuckled, but his eyes seemed different as he watched John's fingers play over the pouches.

The only one he needed was the worn leather pouch. Da's pouch. To become a man...

It was warm with the heat of John's skin, but John saw the stale odour of his father's body creeping out of it, a yellow fog, wrapping itself around his own fingers. He gulped, the saliva in his mouth tasting not of wine or oysters, but of hot apples. He gave his companion a quick glance and pulled the pouch open, tipping the contents out, then dropped the pouch as though it burned him and snatched his hands back into his lap.

Black Jack's eyes danced again. Without seeming to glance at the few coins, he said, 'You are fortunate. I want nothing. It is me that is in your debt. And if this, and the old clothes, are truly all you have, you really would've been in trouble—without my friendship, that is.'

'This isn't enough for the room?' John put a finger on one of the five coins.

'Not even for half of the meal, Fair One.'

'But it's all the money my Da had. It's all his money.' And John had stolen it, too. He didn't tell him that.

'Things must be different where you come from. This isn't even a real coin, it's just a shard of iron.'

Black Jack picked up one of the coins between his thumb and forefinger, stared at it for a moment, then dropped it back in the pouch, followed by the rest. They rattled dully as he handed it back to John.

'The iron is the most important thing of all,' John said, his voice sounding distant. 'It keeps the bad faeries away. Da didn't believe in faeries. He'd never believed ... But the iron'd protect him whether he believed or not... and I took it.'

Jack's brow creased, but his eyes still smiled.

'What about you? Do you believe in faeries?'

With a sickening lurch, John heard his mother's voice, clearer even than Black Jack's, like a crystal note that silenced the noise of the tavern below them. My dear child, promise me you'll never speak to anyone about these things you think you see. Not even Jetta. You may think she knows because she's your twin, but you must never say anything aloud. Don't mention it to me ever again. Not a thought of it in front of Da. And never, never speak of it in front of strangers.

Her voice vanished, and John was alone with Jack again. He gritted his teeth and made his hands into tight fists.

'No. They don't exist.' He was glad the hobgoblin was not around to hear his treacherous words.

Black Jack smiled.

'Who is to say what does and doesn't exist in this big beautiful world? What did you know of London before you came here? If someone had described it to you before you arrived, would you have believed them? In truth, I've oft wondered about these magical things myself.'

Normally an ever flowing river from Jack's mouth to John's ears, these words felt like sharp little hooks, aimed at his chest. John desperately hoped it were true, that Jack's willingness to believe in the faeries was real. He gazed down at the place where his stomach got snagged by Jack's words.

'You're not like anyone I've ever met,' he found himself saying. 'You have eyes like a faerie. I mean, what a faerie might look like, if they were real.'

Black Jack stood, stretching his arms above his head, and for the briefest moment, he was a content ginger tomcat with a mouse's tail hanging out of its mouth. But it was so quick that John couldn't be sure of what he'd seen.

'You're not like anyone I've ever met before either,' Black Jack declared. 'Though I cannot comment on whether your eyes are like a faerie's or not, never having seen one myself. But I can say they are blue like a summer sky, and they are certainly prettier than any I've ever seen before.'

Dazed, his cheeks afire, John stared down at his lap.

The room spun. Where had he left Da's pouch?

As he tried to gather his rambling thoughts, the hobgoblin appeared, leaving little beery footprints on the floor. It tapped on the oyster shells, lifting them up and staring into them. John smiled at it, though his mind fretted over Jack's words.

Black Jack laughed as he followed John's gaze.

'Sweet thing, are you starving away beside me while I talk on and on? Too shy to tell me how hungry you are, or to grab the food yourself?'

Jack's hand swooped down to take an oyster, so fast that the hobgoblin had to jump backwards to avoid being knocked across the room. John gasped. He was used to other people not seeing the faerie folk, but he'd never seen anyone move quick enough to surprise a hobgoblin. As Jack fed him another oyster, John watched his hands, so lively and bold. Surely if anyone could guide him to where he needed to be in this raucous city, it was this wild, brave boy. But would he still be friendly once he knew the truth? John needed to find out.

He dug his fingernails into his palms, and said:

'You've not asked my name.'

Jack grinned.

'I've been waiting for you to tell me.'

He forced himself to meet the quick green eyes.

'My name's... John, too. Like you. But just John, none of the extra bits you've got. It's what I've always been, nothing else.' There was no reason to add that Ma and Jetta were the only ones who'd used his real name.

Black Jack pushed himself upright.

'John? Did I hear correct? John? Not Jane?'

'John. Not Jane.'

'You'd have me believe you're a boy?' Jack's eyes went wide, and then creased up in merry laughter. 'You speak like a girl, you look like a girl, you smell like a girl, you taste like a girl, but you want me to call you John?'

John's stomach flipped at the words you taste like a girl, the heat rising to his face. Black Jack laughed again.

'And you blush more oft and prettier than any girl I've ever kept company with.'

John took some quick breaths.

'If you use your eyes you can see I'm wearing boy's clothes.'

'I am using my eyes and I can see you're a very fair maiden.' Jack's smile softened and he caressed John's cheek with the back of his hand. 'Do not fret, you don't have to pretend with me.'

'I'm not... ' John stared up at the beamed ceiling. 'Not... not in the way you say I am. I'm wearing boy's clothes because I am a boy, and since I've been wearing them no one 'til you thought I was a girl... apart from the ribbon seller, and that was only due to my hair falling out... '

With a deft movement Black Jack whipped the cap off John's head. For the beat of a butterfly's wings, as his hair tumbled down his back, John was wearing a gown of rose petals, standing with a boy dressed in leaves. They were on a wooded island, surrounded by the morning mist. All was silent. They looked into each other's eyes and knew who they were.

Then he was back. From below came the sound of revelry. The hobgoblin floated up in front of John's face, its eyes white starlight. Right now, John could no more look into them than he could look at Black Jack.

Finally, it was Jack who broke the silence. He balanced the cap back on John's head at an angle.

'Forgive me, coz. But you must understand my confusion. Surely you're used to people commenting on your prettiness?'

John shrugged.

'Yes. People have oft said things like that to me.' It wasn't a total lie. People had said things about his appearance all his life. Things he hoped Jack would never learn about.

'Starving Robert mistook you for my mort, my woman.' Black Jack put his hands behind his neck and leaned back, tipping John a wink. 'And I was heartily flattered. Now I know you are just a poor country boy, but I'm still heartily flattered. Even if you do see faeries.'

'I told you, I didn't, I don't... ' John protested.

'Right you did. My mistake.' Jack passed him a handful of strawberries that John hadn't even seen him pick up. 'Normally I savour them one by one, but they're best all together.'

'I know how to eat.'

'Well but you didn't know what oysters are.'

'You probably don't know ...something I know lots about is.'

Black Jack chuckled.

'Aye, I don't, and I heartily look forward to you teaching me.'

'Black Jack?'

'John?' The boy lounged back on his elbows again.

'You're not disappointed... I mean, you do believe I am a boy?'

Black Jack's face moved through several smiles: first a slight slant on the right side, then a definite slant on the left, a small glimpse of his front teeth, then his mouth open wide enough to reveal a crooked tooth on his lower jaw. How could anyone be so happy that they needed to possess more than one smile?

'If you tell me you want me to believe something, I'll believe it.'

John leaned forward, his hands clasped.

'Perhaps... Starving Robert mistook me for a woman because I was with you? You're... very much a boy, and perhaps that makes me look more like... what I'm not.'

'If you want to be something, be it, do not fret over what others are thinking.' Jack was breaking the pie into pieces; he did not seem able to stay still for a moment.

'But how can you be... something... if other people don't recognise you're... something? Don't you just end up being nothing?' John stared down at his hands, playing over each other. He didn't even understand his own question.

Black Jack handed John the largest part of the pie.

'I don't think that can be true, Fair John. If we were made by what others thought, I'd be a very different person from the one sitting beside you right now.'

The hobgoblin was grinning widely, rubbing its belly and pointing to the pie. John broke off a piece of crust and put it down on the floor. He listened to Black Jack's lilting words and tried to work out what it all meant.

'I think we truly exist in the places other people can't see, such as in the best memories stored in our heads, or the dreams in our hearts.' He flashed his brightest smile. 'Why, listen to me! Normally all my talk is about coin and hardship, who's in gaol, who's set for the pigeon-holes, who's hanging from the chats.'

He moved the dishes about and angled his body so that his arm was a feather away from John's.

'I don't think I can explain my dreams. But I am liking being here safe with you better than many of my memories.'

Black Jack finished his ale.

'We are in harmony, are we not? Though my dream is easy enough to explain, unlike yours. But I keep it close to my heart and tell none, because the telling would ruin it.'

John yearned to hear Jack's dream. But the other boy looked almost sad, suddenly. When John touched his hand, he gave a bright smile. 'All my talk has tired you. Let's get ourselves more comfortable.' He began to pull his shoes off, so John did the same, grimacing at the dark blood stains on his stockings.

Jack frowned.

'Let me look at your feet; see if I need to find the extra coin to cover a barber-surgeon.'

With flushed cheeks, John pulled off his stockings. Black Jack knelt and took his feet in his hands, twisting them gently.

'A body has to take good care of their feet: you won't last long if you can't run. A year gone, a girl I was friendly with, Lil Jennet, got so cold one night walking the streets that her feet froze in her shoes, but she refused to take them off because of the pain. It took days, nay, weeks, before she was finally in so much agony that she decided the shoes needed to go. And the skin had stuck to the leather, so when they were pulled off, it pulled her feet off too, and she was left with nothing but stubs. Needless to say, she didn't survive much past that.' Jack continued to study John's feet as he chatted away. 'You can carry on without a hand, or even a whole arm, but feet are a necessity.'

John's eyes were drooping. He murmured:

'I saw a man with only half a leg today.'

Black Jack cocked an eyebrow at him.

'What did he look like?'

'He had a beard and brown hair. His clothes... needed mending. But there was a woman, too, in a fine dress. She touched my elbow, and I thought it was my... I mean, I turned around, and the man said... ' John closed his eyes, and was back in the street with the two people. 'He said, I baited perfect for ye, but still the great Bess Porch ain't able to pick a simple country gull, and she...'

Black Jack roared with laughter.

'The moment I saw you, I knew you were a special one! All your innocence, but you must be quick as a crow to catch Bess with her hands on you.' He brushed his thumbs over the bones of John's ankles. 'Your poor feet. They're as dainty as everything else about you. But I believe they're tougher than they look, and in my expert opinion will do you well enough.'

John looked at the bed. Would Jack think him rude to fall asleep so soon?

Black Jack followed his gaze.

'This truly is a fortunate day—to get a room like this, just the two of us. Let's to bed early tonight, and enjoy it to ourselves before other guests turn up and we have to share.'

'Yester night, or it may have been the day before, or maybe the day before that, I slept in a hedge,' John mumbled. He stood, gazing down at his bare legs, which were somehow both stiff and boneless, unable to support his weight. He leant against the wall.

He was so tired that he barely gave a thought to sharing his bed with a near stranger for the first time in his life. Too much had happened today.

Too much had been said. He couldn't piece his thoughts together.

He drew the back of his hand across his eyes and walked with faltering steps towards the bed, then he fell forwards and let the darkness take him.

Fate, show thy force

Black Jack undressed down to his smock without taking his eyes off his find from the alleyway. The girl who was a boy looking finer than any girl he'd ever seen. She, no, he, appeared to have fallen asleep as soon as they climbed into bed. The pretty thing was scrunched up, eyes shut, breathing steadily.

Jack twirled his knife between his fingers. The Fair One's chest rose and fell, but there was no other movement. After a few minutes, Jack allowed himself to look out of the window. Nothing out of the ordinary. No one lurking in the shadows. Nobody whose business Jack didn't know.

He climbed under the covers without snuffing out the candle or drawing the bed curtains. He flipped his blade over in his hand a couple more times before stowing it under his pillow with a sigh and settling down.

If this little creature was working her own scheme with unseen others, they'd trained her... him so well, and covered their tracks so expertly, it'd be no shame to be taken down by them.

If his gut was right, and it almost always was, then John was alone and lost. And Jack would turn that treasure into gold. But now, he could rest. He closed his eyes, and in the darkness of his own mind, he first ran through the mistakes of the day that had led to him nearly being caught. Then, he moved on to his plans for the next few days. He rotated his shoulders and fidgeted his legs. It'd been some time since he'd slept in a proper bed or had this much sleeping space. Strange, how it was easier to adjust to cold floors than soft comfort.

Tossing from his side to his back, he thought about things he needed to do, things others wanted him to do, and things he himself desired. Before bribing the jailers on behalf of Old Osmund, convincing Sweet Maria to leave a window open after the family had gone to bed, seeking out Kind Kate and charming her into lowering her prices, he must deal with this curious find. With a little luck, he could find at least four people who would pay good coin for the beauty sleeping next to him.

Jack opened his eyes to gaze at the fine lines of the slumbering face. Then he grunted and shut his eyes again.

Would she struggle? She'd followed Jack along easily enough. Would she... he have any idea what was happening?

The price was a problem. He didn't know what good coin was for such a thing. The time and effort could all be wasted. It was better to dispose of his find to one who regularly worked such a trade. But who would cheat him the least? Was it better to get rid of the gull as quickly as possible, or cross the river to seek out Moll? He chewed on his lip and turned over again, stretching out his limbs. He had to see Moll anyway on other business, so—

A long, unearthly wail.

The blade was in Jack's hand.

'Ma, Jetta. Don't leave me. Don't.'

Jack's attention was fixed so tight on the door, it took him a moment to realise the voice was coming from inside the room.

'I'm sorry... Da... no... Da... please don't, please, I'm sorry.'

He glanced down at John. Small hands tangled through long hair; the brow glistened with sweat.

The boy's eyes were screwed shut, his whole face twitching.

Jack sighed. Just a nightmare. He tucked his blade away and reached out to shake the boy's shoulder. His fingers brushed a jutting collar bone, and the pretty thing flinched from his touch with a muted cry.

Jack looked in fascination at the way John's eyes flickered behind his shut eyelids, then lay back, crossing his arms and shaking his head. There was a story oft told, and one he encouraged for various reasons, that he'd slept right through a night when two of his friends had fought until one stabbed the other. He wished it was true. How was he supposed to rest with this constant whimpering, and the whole mattress shaking with the curious thing's trembling?

He turned to face the stranger, leaning his head on his elbow.

'Come now, you are far too beautiful to be haunted by the muck of this world.' Jack took a strand of stuck hair and smoothed it back.

Blue eyes flickered open. A whisper.

'I'm John. I'm a boy. A normal boy.'

'I know, shush now.'

Eyes closed again, the other's face stilled, the lips slightly parted. But the body continued to tremble, the breathing rapid and jerky.

Jack sighed, put his arms around John and pulled him against his chest. The boy curled up, became even smaller, but did not resist. Jack started to talk, about everything and nothing, tales of wonders he'd never seen and many that he had. Gradually John's breathing steadied, his body relaxed.

As Jack spoke, he gazed at the boy in the flickering candlelight and decided, even if he was being robbed of his sleep, and had made an unaccountable error in a simple pick, it had been a heartily fortunate day. Something so pretty, so innocent—whether female or male—would surely be worth enough coin to take him safely through spring, summer, autumn, and the coldest of winters.

I can raise no money by vile means

The London streets were still churned up, filled with constantly shouting people hemmed in by the too-big buildings and the stinking piles of human waste. But though it was only his second day in the city, John already felt like he was adjusting. Although it could have been the distraction of his constantly chatting new companion that was helping him cope.

Black Jack had a story about everything they saw. A trader selling lumps of fat with leaves sticking out of it launched Jack into a tale about the time he'd thieved a bar of soap and couldn't get anyone to buy it off him as it smelt so awful, he couldn't convince anyone that it was supposed to be for cleaning yourself.

During that long story, John opened his mouth several times to try and tell Black Jack that he knew how to mix young birch leaves and warm water to make something that would clean your skin of the stickiest dried-on blood. But he could never make the words interesting enough to leave his mouth.

Black Jack also had stories about things they couldn't see; fantasy food found in distant, newly discovered lands; people being round up off the streets and forced to fight and die in wars in other, older lands; ships that fell off the end of the world even though the world wasn't flat anymore but was now a circle; ships that attacked other ships and pirated enough gold to fill the heavens; stars that flashed through the sky and gave endless fortune to any who were quick enough to wish on them—

His new friend described so many marvels, that John felt even stories of the faeries he saw would sound plain in comparison.

He glanced at the hobgoblin somersaulting in the empty air and although it didn't look at him, John felt an accusation in the pit of his stomach. He'd left his village, stolen from Da, and travelled all this way to be safe with the Faerie Queene, not meander around crowded streets with a boy he didn't know.

John's heart slowed at the idea of leaving this person who'd been so kind to him. But maybe they didn't need to separate just yet. Black Jack did know this world, so perhaps John should stay with him for a little longer, and let Jack take him to where he needed to be.

He just needed to think of the right way of asking.

'Black Jack, earlier you said you were taking me somewhere to get the coin that I need to survive in the city? But we seem to be just walking around and going nowhere?' John wasn't used to talking, let alone interrupting.

The hobgoblin halted by his feet, hands on its hips, grinning wide enough to display both rows of pointed teeth, but the redheaded boy only sauntered on, chatting as if John was still right beside him.

John's eyes darted between Jack and the hobgoblin. He itched to trot after Jack, but the hobgoblin wanted him to stay here... Although, it had seemed to like Jack well enough yesterday. How was John supposed to make sense of anything in this stinking hole, when even his dear familiar faerie was behaving so oddly?

He stamped his foot; a gesture so unlike who he wanted to become that he immediately blushed.

Black Jack couldn't have heard anything, but he turned and laughed. Called out:

'What are you doing all the way back there, Fair One? Was I walking too fast? Come on now, I'll wait for you.' He tapped his fingers on his thigh as if calling to an obedient dog.

John glanced down again.

The hobgoblin's eyes shone, and it patted its hands on its

legs and made a sound like the whistling of the wind through the thatch at home.

Jack drew his attention back and John frowned: the boy was laughing so hard, John was worried he'd drop the bundle of Jetta's clothing he'd grabbed when they'd left the room this morning. He looked around, but could see nothing to amuse anyone. Near the hobgoblin, a woman with a skeletal face had dropped her basket and was scraping rotten fruit off of the floor. A young boy hung his head as a grizzled man cuffed and cursed him for being a milk-livered fool. A rat and a bird, both the same shimmering black, tugged on either end of a grey rope of intestine.

John tore his eyes away and looked back at Black Jack, but he was gone. The stench of the city rushed in, coating his teeth and tongue with yellow-brown fur. John stared, motionless, at the space where he'd last seen Jack.

Then from behind his shoulder, a merry voice chimed:

'Fair One, we must keep a tight hold of each other. Trust me, it's easy to get lost if you don't know where you're going.' Jack tucked a firm arm through his. 'You need me.'

John exhaled with relief, but his legs tensed for action, like they always did when he was scared.

His heart beat fast.

They'd only met yesterday, but this boy was already the closest thing to a real friend he'd ever had.

So why did his normally too soft voice sound so angry?

'I need to find a new home and a job.'

But Black Jack didn't seem to notice, or to mind.

'Pay attention, Fair One, I told you we have to wait until the right hours before we can conduct our business. Listen to me. I know these things. It doesn't do to... '

I do listen to you, John thought, but how do I get you to listen to me?

'I need to get a trade. It was you who said my coin wasn't enough, so I need to earn money.' John's heart felt like it would explode through his chest, interrupting this ever-talking boy for a second time.

'But I am helping you. I'm taking you to St Paul's. If we can't find something for you there, we'll find nothing for you nowhere. And if that happens to be the case, which I am sure it won't, but if by some chance of fortune it is like that, I can discuss other options with you.'

John looked back over his shoulder, though he allowed Jack to lead him on. The hobgoblin bobbed up and down in the same place for a moment, stamping its foot just as John had, before shaking its head, back flipping through the air, and landing weightless on top of John's cap.

John murmured a very soft thank you, not sure whether he was thanking the hobgoblin or Jack, or even what he was thanking them for. Then he squared his shoulders and tried to walk with the confidence of his companion; tried to look like someone capable and employable. He would have been fine on his own. Probably. But it couldn't be a bad thing to have someone who knew London so well by his side. Hopefully.

He tried to copy Jack's easy saunter when they walked into St Paul's, but it was no good. He wanted to run and run until he found a meadow with long whispery grass, and cow parsley and cuckoo flowers, where he could curl up and be safe.

The church was so big that he couldn't even comprehend it.

Why had he been so scared of the other tiny buildings in London? They were nothing compared to this one. He tried to imagine what would happen if these walls crumbled and fell. It would obliterate everything. His head spun.

The hobgoblin leaned over the peak of his cap and looked at him, upside down. It frowned, then grinned and blew sparkling air between John's eyes. His body begin to drift.

John felt his little finger gripped in its bony hand and they floated upwards, higher and higher, until they were flying among the great gabled arcs of the church roof. The faerie's skin and hair were the blue of the sky; little clouds drifted lazily over its belly.

Together, they circled the huge pillars and gazed down at the crowd far below. The whole building echoed with the bustle of humans. Men shouting about debts to be paid, women crying their wares, children scuffling over a ball, three boys pushing and pulling a mule along the thoroughfare between the north and south doors. If John listened hard, beneath all the voices he could hear the buzz of wood being sawn and hammered in the workshops around the edges of the building.

All the blare made his ears bleed, yet staring down from this height was somehow calming. How small everyone was! Then he saw the smallest person of all, shoulders hunched, head lowered, standing as close as possible to a tall, red-haired boy reading the bills covering one of the pillars. John snapped back into his body, stumbled and swayed.

Black Jack put a hand out to steady him without a glance.

'I am used to only feeding myself. If the bread of earlier was not enough, you must say. Do not be scared to say if your stomach is empty or your throat dry. ...Sorry this is taking so long, Fair One. There are many people asking for help, but I don't know yet if any of them will fit. We need someone special to be your master. You can tell a lot about a body by how they form their words, but you have to look hard.'

A master, John thought. But who would want such a cowed, fearful thing?

He straightened his back, and took a step away from Jack, then almost immediately found himself shuffling back towards him. He frowned at his rebellious feet, but did not seem able to stop them from moving in their chosen direction. But at least his head stayed up and his voice bold.

'Can you understand all that's written?' he asked.

'If it be plain English.' Jack tapped one of the papers, then shook his head and turned to another. 'I can make out some in other languages, enough that it's been useful on occasion. There is a certain magical Latin passage I'll have to teach you—the most important thing to memorise if you're not born rich. If you recite it perfect, it stops you from being hung. Not that you'll be needing it, mind, but it'll not hurt to know.'

John gazed at the hobgoblin, still soaring around the ceiling. All the happy hours he'd spent with faeries, learning to sing and dance and sew, and how to heal with herbs, but somehow he'd missed this 'most important thing.'

He looked back at Jack.

'Can you understand all the books in the stalls that we passed outside?'

Jack gave a low laugh.

'Knowing the words does not mean you understand them, Fair One. But to impress you, I'll lie and say yes, I understand all, and you can carry on staring at me as if I am the most marvellous person in all of London.'

John felt himself blush—again—. He turned from the other boy and stared at the bits of paper himself. The symbols that he knew were letters jumped from one place to another, finding new friends and dancing together in joyful circles.

'Is it difficult, learning to read? How do you go about doing it?'

John squinted until his eyes were nearly shut, but it made no difference: the letters refused to remain still.

'All things are difficult until you know the trick of them.' Black Jack tilted his head as he read one of the notices. 'Tell me, what you are good at, Fair One?'

John stared down at his boots. He waited for a moment to see if the other boy would ramble off onto another subject like he oft did. But it seemed Jack only became distracted when John had questions of his own. Finally, he mumbled:

'I worked in the field with me da and the other men.'

Jack took John's hand, rubbing his thumb over John's palm and each of his fingers in turn.

'You've very soft hands for a fieldworker. The only thing you've got near to callouses are more akin to what needle workers get.' He circled the pad of John's thumb, giving him a quick, sharp look.

'I worked with sheep too. I like animals—they're nicer than people.' John yanked his hand away, aware his bottom lip was sticking out like it did when Da yelled at him for being a sulking milksop.

Jack was smirking openly now.

'You may find this a mighty shock, but people who are good with sheep and mud are not in great demand in London. People who can sew as finely as this, though.' He tugged the hemline of Jetta's skirt free from the bundle. 'They can make enough coin with their soft hands to see them through until the faeries guide them home.'

John gritted his teeth. He had not come all this way just to continue with woman's work.

'I don't know how to sew. My hands are soft because of the wool.'

Black Jack laughed, his eyes creased at the corners.

'So I've learnt that you truly cannot lie, which means there's not one suitable job here for you. Forsooth, I know of no way to make coin which doesn't involve some brag and bluster.'

'I wasn't lying. Hammon said how good I was with sheep when I helped him on... many a time... all the time. He said that me da was wrong to... '

Something crashed into his shin, and he jumped back with a yelp. A battered ball lay at his feet, pieces of straw sticking through the pig bladder. The boys who had been playing with it were staring down now, horned beasts pawing the ground. John's heart pounded. Such a simple thing, just to kick it.

As John dithered, Black Jack's foot darted out and scooped up the ball, and he ran across the church as if it was attached to him. He weaved between the other boys, then slowed to allow a few to get close, before elbowing them out of his way.

John watched with an unconscious smile, then realised he was alone. A shiver snaked through him, and he ran to catch up with his friend.

Jack kicked the ball in the air, caught it with his free hand and threw it back over his shoulder to the players. He grinned down at John, wide enough to reveal his crooked canine.

John smiled too, but there was something in the other boy's eyes which made John want to prove himself.

'You should've left me to kick it, instead of stealing it away. I played it all the time... with all my friends at home... and me da, he loved playing football... with me.'

A shadow passed over Black Jack's face, but he spoke in a merry voice that didn't match his eyes.

'I would like to hear the tale of that. I've heard that the games between villages make our London version look dainty. I can't see you in a battle like that, mind. Bones broken, limbs twisted off... '

'I am fast for my size. That helped me escape the worst of it.'

Black Jack brushed his fingers down the back of John's neck.

'They still caught you. Didn't they, Fair One?'

John twisted his chin away.

'No. No, they didn't. I ran and ran and left them all behind and they all said that...'

His voice trailed into a whisper—

'They all said what? A body must finish a tale once they've started it.' Black Jack thumped him companionably on the back.

He didn't notice. A glint of rainbow colour sparkled in the corner of his vision. A dazzling, sky-blue faerie with translucent wings fluttered around a man who wore no hat over his shoulder-length brown hair. Beside the magnificent faerie, the man looked entirely plain. The only thing of notice was that he carried a bundle of parchment under one arm.

John'd never seen a faerie follow another so closely—his feet started to dreamily carry him in their direction, when a hand grabbed his upper arm and jerked him backwards. His new friend was talking, demanding his attention, but John's head whipped around desperately. The faerie and the man had vanished.

'Did you see where they went?'

'I try and see all, but you'll need be more specific than that,' Black Jack's voice was friendly, but his eyes were slightly narrowed as he gazed down at John.

'The magical man... the one with the blue... holding the parchment.'

'Ay. I thought that was the one that you were gazing after, leaving you all breathless. I can't see what's so special about him, he's just one of the theatre folk.'

'Theatre folk?'

'The ones that earn coin for pretending to be other people.'

'What are you meaning?'

'You've not seen a play before?'

John shook his head. His ears listened to all Black Jack said, anxious for explanation, but his eyes kept searching through the crowds for another glimpse of the faerie and its man.

'Now that I think upon it, perchance there is something special about the theatre folk after all. They're able to pull tricks that would get ordinary folks like you and I flogged in the street, most likely hanged. Men dressing up in all that finery, imagining that they are kings and queens... '

'Queens?'

'Of course. They've got some bene lads at the Rose playing

the women, you forget about what they've got under their skirts, they're that convincing. I was heartily sad when one of them got killed off in the last play I was at; he was providing fine distraction, allowing me to ply my own trade in peace.'

'Do boys wear dresses and truly become Queens? When I was travelling, I overheard a group of men, and they spoke about the Faerie Queene, and the words, they were so beautiful...'

Black Jack leant back on his heels and surveyed John up and down.

'Any company would think they could see faeries if you walked in the door.' He clicked his tongue against his teeth. 'Mayhaps I am not explaining it well. It's not the beauty you're dreaming of. Once they're off the stage, the actors dredge through the same old muck as the rest of us. On occasion, my trade has bumped me into a few of them and there's nothing magical about them, believe me. Don't look so dejected now, I'll take you to the theatre. I am just awarning you not to be in awe of it. You're worth more than any of them.' He patted John on the head, then looked away.

'There's Starving Robert. I'll see what he'll give us for the distraction of yesterday. Sit in the pew behind me... nay, two pews. If any bodies you don't like approach, shout out. And I mean shout, not your normal little mouse squeak.'

John obeyed, and sat quietly as Black Jack talked with the man he'd been cursing at yesterday. He stared down at his hands. There was a tremor in his fingers, and his excitement at seeing the blue faerie with that man, the thrill of hearing talk of the theatre, so quickly dissipated.

Not your normal little mouse squeak.

People had said much worse to him. There'd been no malice in Jack's voice. But still. He needed to stand taller, speak louder, kick poxy footballs when they landed at his feet.

A tap on his shoulder pulled him out of his reverie.

'When we met yester, why didn't you introduce yourself as a friend of Black Jack's?'

It took another long moment to recognise the woman who sat silently beside him. She wore simpler clothes than yesterday; and underneath a modest cap, black hair flowed down her back, though he was sure it'd been chestnut before. Her skin was sunbrown and blotchy.

'Are you... Bess Porch? You tried to... '

'Aye, aye, you did not tell Black Jack so, did you?'

John nodded.

'I tell him all.'

It was a strange thing to say, but already he felt as if it was a heart truth.

Bess cursed under her breath.

'Was he in a rage?'

'Why would he be? He laughed about me being quicker than you.'

She rolled her eyes, but smiled.

'Aye, that amused Nick mightily, too. I should've known right then that you'd be a connection of Black Jack's, but this look you have about you.' She waved her hand in a gesture that encompassed John's whole person. 'Though, now I look again, I can see that the whole wide-eyed country boy act is just too perfect. The stockings, the cap, that face... How have you done your painting so well? Even this close, I cannot see it.' She squinted at him, then said with a nudge, 'Take nothing I say amiss, it's all truly a compliment. ...I spied Black Jack looking at the notices. Is he going to get you into a grand house? It's a good play. Fine ladies, and some gents, would be glad to have you as a pet.'

'Yes,' John squeaked, cursing his treacherous voice.

'If you can keep this act up, they'll never suspect you.' Bess sighed. 'The truth is, the whoreson knave ministering physique to Nick is charging more bit than we can lay hands on. If you and Black Jack have a scheme that needs extra bodies, forget the mischance of yester and think kindly on me.'

'I told you to call out for me if anyone came near you.' Jack grinned in the pew in front of him, as if he'd always been there.

Starving Robert had vanished. The way people appeared and disappeared here—surely it must involve faerie magic?

'Did you forget what I told you?'

'What you said was... ' John puffed his chest out and mimicked Black Jack's voice. Why could he not make his own tones sound so gruff and bold? 'If any bodies you don't like approach, shout out for me and... '

Bess giggled.

'Ah, I see, you do like the company of my clever gossip, Mistress Porch.' Black Jack turned his head so he was looking only at Bess. His voice somehow slid away from the one John had copied, into an entirely different accent.

'Hast thou been busy making a new friend of my new friend, coz?'

'He's been telling me of your plans,' she replied with a cat's smile.

'That's bene.' Black Jack's voice dropped, confidentially. 'I'll trust thou not to be telling any my secret. I'd not like it known that my heart has softened and I'll be leaking coin trying to discover somewhere for sweet John to stay safe while he remains in London.'

Bess threw her head back. Her face and body mimed laughter, but no sound came out. She stood with a grunt. 'If you are of a mind to be serious, I'll be working the theatre later, the Rose.' Then she flounced away, as if she was wearing the wide skirts and big hat that John had met her in yesterday.

Black Jack pulled John to his feet.

'Fair One, sometimes it's worth telling the truth. It confuses people.'

By the south door, the group of boys still wrestled with their mule. They'd given up pushing and had decided to try beating it with sticks instead. John paused to watch, itching to intervene. Perhaps this was his chance to show Jack what he could do? He darted to the mule's head before his courage left him.

'You shouldn't hit it. You just need to ask nicely.'

'What are you talking about?' the largest boy growled.

Black Jack came over too, slipped seamlessly into a new role.

'My friend here is apprentice to a cunningman,' he said, legs spread and arms folded. 'He has a special way with stubborn mules and was kindly thinking of helping you.' Jack eyed the boys. 'I told him not to bother, when you're doing such a good job yourselves.'

John felt his skin flush, beads of sweat prickling his forehead.

Animals were much like magical creatures: you told them what you wanted, and sometimes they'd help, but more often, they wouldn't.

He stroked the mule's nose and looked into its brown eyes. His own head filled with images that he didn't entirely understand. The mule, walking to the door. Black Jack, laughing.

His own heart in a carved box.

Without thinking, John began humming a tune the hobgoblin liked to dance to. It swooped down from where it'd been hovering above his head and bounced onto the mule's back. The faerie jigged across the mule, and the animal skittered forward as if it were dancing too. The boys laughed and murmured among themselves. John was aware of Black Jack waving them back so that John could work in peace. As more people gathered to watch, Black Jack began to talk, weaving a web of words that snared the onlookers. John focused on humming his tune, coaxing the mule steadily forwards. When they'd finally passed through the great stone door, the hobgoblin leapt into the sky and disappeared high above the spire of St Paul's. John hummed for a few more seconds, but the mule squared its legs on the ground and refused to take another step.

Black Jack strode around the crowd, cheering loudly, and the people gradually joined in. Everything about him—his easy grin, his jaunty walk—looked relaxed and casual. But somehow, without ever seeming to try, Jack was always in front of anyone that tried to approach John. Coins jingled in Jack's hands, and he smiled and jested and accepted the money with overflowing gratitude. But as John watched, a third ethereal hand appeared, slipping like smoke into people's purses as they passed. John blinked a few times, and the extra hand vanished. He swallowed, and looked into the mule's ageless eyes until Jack came to his side.

Jack linked his arm through John's and led him away with a whistle and a hop in his step. When they were out of the shadow of the church, he laughed long and loud.

'If only Bess or Starving Robert had still been there, we could've got paid twice, nay three, four times over! But hark at me griping. Fortune blessed us once again, Fair One. You're such a natural performer; I'm sure we just earnt more coin than any practiced musician will in the taverns tonight. Could we make a regular thing of it, turn you into a known animal charmer, and... '

'Do mules oft get stuck in the middle of churches?' John asked.

Jack laughed even louder, slapping John on the back. He stumbled, and Jack steadied him with quick hands. The noise of the city rumbled on, but the air crackled between them with quiet. John looked down at Jack's hand. After a long moment, he said:

'You do believe me now, about working in the fields... with Da... and the sheep?'

Black Jack made a sound that was half a laugh, half a groan, and tugged John down one of the small streets by church.

'If you mention sheep again, I'll throw you over the city walls and dunk you in a tub of wool! Unless you think of a way we can make coin out of it, and then you are free to dunk me. Speaking of dunking, I have a surprise for you. We're going Bankside way: that's where most of my friends are, and they'll know what to do with you. And that means crossing the river.' Black Jack slipped his fingers through John's, walking backwards as he led him forwards. 'You'll be speechless, Fair One!"

Black Jack laughed and John giggled again.

Two laughs in as many seconds.

As Black Jack chatted on, John tried out different smiles. He remembered wondering how it was possible for one person to have—or need—so many. But was it possible that he, too, could feel enough happiness that it warranted different smiles, different laughs?

He looked at his new friend thinking, that maybe it was.

Too much of water hast thou

And that is how he ended up adrift on a river of death. They were balanced on sticks, teetering over an abyss. Nothing bound the sticks together, except the boys' hope. River Robin rowed with all his strength, sweat pouring down his face, his clothes dampening around his armpits and chest as his body strained. The river was still and stagnant; they were the only ones foolish enough to cross it. None of them knew why they'd started this journey or where they were going. In the water, bony fingers grasped. John felt the silver blue mist like a fist, pressing down on him from above. Where was the hobgoblin now, when he needed to fly away more than ever?

'You row this river every day and you still know nothing about the fog! It'll clear within the hour, I tell you.'

'You're a street rat! You'll never understand London fog like I do.'

John stared around.

He was back in the boat, which rocked with every movement. Black Jack waved his arms, leaning forward, jesting and talking as if he was entirely unaware of the vessel tilting beneath him. The red-faced boy Jack had introduced as River Robin rowed effortlessly, arguing amicably with Black Jack and flinging curses at people in other boats.

The river was like a street, crowded with people, noise and stink. They couldn't fill every inch like they did on land, but they tried. Boats of all sizes, some towering above him, some even smaller than theirs, bustled and jostled as if their business was more important than anyone else's.

John could have told them both that the mist had nothing to do with weather and everything to do with lives lost; despairing final breaths. But they wouldn't understand; they would think him mad. So he sat silent, resting his hands in his lap, fighting the urge to cling to the sides of the boat.

River Robin was in the middle of a particularly creative insult when he caught John looking at him. 'I mean nothing against your choice of company, coz, but... ' He raised an eyebrow at John. 'Do you not like the water, friend?'

'Yes... I like it very well ...thank you, Master Robin.' John tried to imagine himself anywhere but here. At the brook with Jetta. In winter, she always broke the ice. And all through the seasons, she carried the bucket until they were in sight of the village, where she'd pass it to him. In summer, he watched the water nymphs dance and wished that Jetta could know their beauty.

'Have you ever seen the sea?'

'No, I haven't... thank you, Master Robin.' His voice was clear, in spite of the tendrils of mist that wrapped themselves around his throat and tried to steal his breath away.

'I can take you one day.' Robin smiled at John. 'I can shoot the bridge—there's not many can do that. I'll show you now, if you like. The tides are right... '

'Thou canst not shoot the bridge,' Black Jack scoffed. 'Don't listen to him, John, he'll crash us into another boat before we get anywhere near.'

John was not listening. He was sitting perfectly still, holding his balance on the uneven sticks, as thin, white arms crept all around, reaching silkily from the water. Their voices were a chorus of flat misery.

'You belong with us.'

'Deep down below.'

'You belong with us.'

'Tangled in the weeds.'

'You belong with us.'

'Where none will see you.'

A hand of dripping ice pushed through his clothes, pierced his skin and found his heart. John had to bite his lip to stop himself from shrieking aloud.

Then Black Jack had his arms around him, pulling him close.

'Why, you're shivering! Not used to the fog yet? It's my blame. Next time, I'll make sure to choose a real waterman, one who'll give us a truly quick and smooth journey across, not this guts-griping lump.'

'There is none faster than me, thou knowst that, Black Jack.'

John blinked, unsure if he was alive or dead. The heat of the body holding him close was the only thing keeping him tied to the world of the living. Names formed in his mind: John... Jack... Red Jack... Black Jack... all the same person.

Black Jack urged the other boy on.

'Do your best, River Robin. We will make it in time. None be faster than you.'

'What got him? He's fading. We can't lose him, not the Fair One.'

'We won't lose him, he's Fortune blessed. You keep rowing and I'll keep him alive. How long will it take? Can we make it within the turning of a year?'

'We can. On my honour, we can.'

The sun set and the moon rose. The moon set and the sun rose. Again and again and again, too many times to be numbered. They passed the souls of men, heavy with rusting armour. Women, with stones sewn into their clothes. All of them sinking, drowning, then floating again, bloated, with fish nibbling on their eyeballs and fingers. One woman with long chestnut hair and dark, sunken eyes looked familiar. She cried out when she saw him looking. 'I've changed my mind. Please. I've changed my mind. I don't want to die. Please. Free me. Please.'

But whenever John tried to reach her, Black Jack tightened his grip.

'What's your favourite fish, John?'

John gasped. He wasn't curled up in Black Jack's arms. He was sitting normally, having a conversation with River Robin.

'I'm not sure. I don't know, Master Robin. Mostly at home

we ate potage. Me da... my father was not... is not skilled at catching fish. He's too busy working the land.'

'I can catch whatever you like. I just put my hand out and grab them, straight like that.' River Robin chuckled. 'Mostly I use cheese and tallow and nets though, like everyone else. I can get you tench and flounders and... '

'John likes oysters, which I can get him whenever he wants. Fresh off a stall.'

'Dace and eels and pike and... '

'He likes strawberries and wine, too, which you won't find swimming about in your dirty river.'

'Salmon and sturgeon and white bait and... '

'If you are so skilled at catching fish, I fear you be in the wrong trade, River Robin. Why break your back ferrying people back and forth when you could be... '

'Babies. Would you like a baby? I have one I found earlier.'

River Robin dropped his oars, letting them float off, and held a tiny, blue-tinged corpse up for John to inspect.

John jerked his head back with a moan.

He was still in this world, the real world with all the other boats and the people shouting at each other. But River Robin was a naked woman, holding the blue baby to her breast, her thighs splattered in crimson blood.

'I did no harm. He was already dead when I drowned him. I couldn't drown him, I tell you, he was already dead. What life would he have had if he'd continued to breathe? Only the long agony of awaiting death. I saved him from that.'

John closed his eyes.

When he opened them, there was still a woman with a small, fragile, blue baby held to one breast. But at the other there was now a large, dark-haired child suckling contentedly. The woman had long golden hair and her desperate eyes stared directly at Jack. John knew her, opened his mouth to cry out, but he had no voice for her to hear. He closed his lips and realised he didn't know her after all.

All she saw was Black Jack.

'Let him live,' she begged. 'Use your magic. He will be yours more than he'll ever be mine. I cannot bear another loss.'

Her voice merged into the mist, and then she was gone.

River Robin was in full flow. 'Thou willst pay all you owe me, thee clotpole, or I shall not allow thee off the boat!'

John's stomach twisted. He leaned over the side, but not quite fast enough. Vomit splattered onto his stockings and pooled at the bottom of the vessel.

River Robin murmured words of concern as Black Jack scooped him up and stepped lightly down from the boat.

'Fare thee well, Robin,' he called out as he strode away with John in his arms.

'God be wi' you both,' River Robin shouted back.

Gradually, time and space settled around John again. A minute, an hour, a day later he patted Black Jack on the chest.

'I can walk.'

Jack set him down, but laid a hand on his brow.

'I think we can ignore any employment that involves boats,' he said with a grin. Then added, not unkindly, 'It was just you not being accustomed to the motion of the water, was it not? The city has not made you so soon ill? You're not ailing, are you, my Fair One?'

John's legs shook. Black Jack kept an arm around his waist as though it was what he most longed to do. Even now, he was sparing John's feelings.

'It was not the rocking. It was... ' John bit his lip. How could he possibly explain? Especially now that the world was so solid and certain again. If he had spent a year in another world, being cared for by the boy beside him, he was the only one who had any memory of it. And even that memory was fading. 'It was you and him, arguing the whole time that made my head ache so. It was not kindly done.'

Black Jack laughed.

'I was being kind! I did not think on it before, but saw quick that you reminded River Robin of a little sister he doted on. You know how it is—if you live long enough, you see everyone die. So I distracted him with witty talk. I could've had him rowing us all the way to the sea and back without paying a thing. But I didn't.'

Like Robin's sister? John tried to swallow the ache in his throat and kept his voice light.

'You called him a gut-griping lump! And you mocked him

about the fish because, because you were jealous and... ' John's voice faltered as he remembered the blue-tinged skin of the baby.

'Jealous? Me? Didn't you notice how much he stinks? I do believe he catches all those fish he claims to, by the stench coming from him.'

'I didn't notice any smell, and even if there were, it wouldn't matter. He's nice, brave, true.'

'Nice? Brave? True?' Jack raised his eyebrows, then gave a crooked smile. 'Perchance I am a little jealous.'

'And you did get a free ride,' John said. 'You used me being sick to get away.'

'You miss nothing, do you? Your timing was so perfect though, it'd be wrong to waste it. I'll pay him all I owe, someday.'

'Will you?' John asked.

Black Jack shrugged.

'I have many things I aim to do, Fair One.'

'Like the dream you have?' John looked at him hopefully.

'Like my dream. Yes.'

There was a pause, and John realised that was all he was going to get out of Jack for the moment.

'We'll go over the bridge next time,' the other was saying. 'Foremost in the things I'm aiming to do is not give you another surprise that makes you ill.'

'No... I mean... I will be better next time... I'll know what to expect.' John's mouth went dry at the thought of another such trip, but if Jack saw, he did not show it.

'Next time we'll travel before we eat then. I'll not see such good bread go to waste more than once.'

John managed a smile.

'Before bread or travelling, I need to find where I belong, my trade. Otherwise how will I ever repay all your kindnesses... and surprises?'

'Aye. You'll be good for plenty of coin, I'm certain.' Black Jack looked to the side and clicked his teeth. Then he winked at John. 'Come then, even covered in your own vomit, you're fairer than any other. Let's go find your fortune.'

Unsex me here

There was an earthier, almost boggy feel to the air this side of the river. After the boat ride, John avoided looking at anything for too long, in case it turned into something else.

Black Jack stopped outside a house that looked like all the others. He rapped out a pattern on the door, then pushed it open.

'I will need some time to talk private. Now, where should you wait?'

This room was not as large as those at the tavern: it was closer to the size of John's own home, back in the village. But his family's house had just been the one room, whereas here there was another door opposite him, leading who knows where. John hoped it was somewhere more pleasant.

It was colder in here than it had been outside. The hearth was a mass of grey ash, so it must have been lit at some point, but it couldn't have been in the last few days. The dusty floor was covered in boot prints and clods of mud, tracks that crisscrossed each other as though a spiderlike creature had been scuttling in infinite circles. He saw the creature now, loping around the room, its breath loud and reeking... He blinked. Enough of monsters and death. When would he see the Faerie Queene?

'Stay right here by the hearth. Don't move,' Jack was saying.

As if the words were a secret signal, a person sauntered

into the room through the internal door, wearing long breeches and a cape wrapped around their top half. At their waist hung a thick and blunt and rather dangerous looking sword. The person searched their clothes with muttered grunts, finally producing a large pipe. When they caught sight of the dead fire, they tossed the pipe aside with a curse, and turned their attention to the boys as if they'd only just arrived.

'What are you doing, bringing a stranger here?' The voice was gruff.

'Moll Cutpurse, this is John. He's my friend.' Black Jack nodded towards him.

Moll scowled at John, her hand on her sword. He lowered himself in something that wasn't quite a bow or a curtsey. 'Pleased to meet you, Good Mistress Cutpurse.'

Jack raised his eyebrows. 'If that doesn't satisfy you, then we'll both be leaving, with no further trouble to you.'

'We'll see about that.' She jerked her chin at Jack, and he followed her out, leaving John alone by the hearth.

He stared down at the dirty floor. Being invisible usually made him feel free and light, but now, his toe dragged heavy semi-circles through the dust. Then he heard his twin's voice, echoing down through the years from a day long gone. 'John, why did you try and join in the dancing? All were merry and none were paying you any heed. It'd have been fine if you'd stayed out of sight.'

His Ma spoke next. 'Keep still and silent, John, and none will notice you. Your smallness can be your gift.'

Their voices were so loud and real that he spun around, hoping to catch a glimpse of them. But when he turned back, his father stood there, arms folded across his big barrel chest.

'You cannot hide from me, scobberlotcher. I will find you.'

The muscles in John's legs vanished, and he collapsed to the floor.

A small hand tapped his shoulder, and deceptively strong arms lifted him to his feet. John gave the hobgoblin a grateful smile. 'I'm glad it's you,' he whispered. 'I miss you when you go.' His hands instinctively went to brush down his clothes, but he stopped with a grimace as he saw the blotches of vomit still stuck to them. He gave the hobgoblin a sad smile. 'London is not what I expected, dear friend. I thought it'd be faerie light, not more darkness and nightmares.'

The hobgoblin hissed.

'But Black Jack is trying to arrange things for me right now, so I can meet more people who know beautiful words like the ones we saw on the road. We're going to a place called a theatre. Things are going to get better.'

The hobgoblin's eyes swam through shades of green. It cartwheeled through the air, over to the closed door and slammed it with both hands. The wood shattered into twigs and vines, leaving a ragged circle in the middle, and the hobgoblin beckoned him over.

'I don't know...' John looked around. 'Jack told me not to move.' But the hobgoblin was quivering with energy, baring its teeth at him, so he darted forward to peer into the other room.

Like the hold of a pirate ship, it brimmed with treasure. Fine clothes made of beautiful, shimmery materials, and a spread of rich-coloured linens. In a murky corner, silver plates and bowls glinted next to a pile of swords.

Moll and Black Jack stood in the midst of all these marvels, apparently oblivious to them. Moll had found another pipe, and a light for it; the smoke curled up around their faces and turned them into shadowy demons. Their heads were close together, and they spoke in muffled growls.

The hobgoblin stirred the air with its hands.

After that, John could hear them clearly.

'...One of Oliver's sweepers got wedged the other day and they broke his arm getting him out,' Moll was saying. 'This one is small enough to do as a replacement. But is that really what you want?' She made a guffawing noise. 'Less coin, more damage, and an early, painful end?'

'It'd be easier if he were a real girl, then... When I first saw him, I was certain he was nought but a beautiful dell and I'd have lour for life.'

'You're so lucky you came to me first, you ignorant little babe. Any other would cheat you as soon as speak to you. Don't you know what you have? A girl so pretty can become someone's favourite for a season or two. A boy so pretty is such a rare find that he can earn us enough coin to buy the New World!' She slapped him on the back. 'Oh, I should've worked you well, and got him in exchange for a tankard of ale by the end of the night.'

John stared at the hobgoblin, who gazed back at him with blue eyes that were a reflection of his own.

'You are too kind,' Jack was saying.

'I am. So share with me: what are you planning to do with your little sweetheart?'

Jack gave a heavy sigh.

'You are the expert on these things, and you tell me his value is in his rarity. So I'm thinking, won't he be worth more if we can hold onto him for a bit longer, keeping him safe and healthy? This time of year there are plenty of plump country things coming up to London, thinking their luck will be better than it is. Competition for our Fair One.' He paced up and down and spoke as if every thought was a tremendous idea just now striking him. John felt a twist in his stomach, hearing Jack use his nickname in such a strange way.

Moll rested the pipe between her lips and spoke from the side of her mouth. 'You may taste the trade, but you don't know it. Don't waste your chatter and charm on me; deal straight.'

'Moll, there's no game. I am asking your honest advice. If we waited, could we not get a better price?'

'With one like fortune's gifted you here, the value is in the freshness, and that'll last a week. Two at most. Take the coin while you can, and you won't be gnawing crow's bones in winter. You don't need reminding to take advantage of chances like this: you know you don't get many of them.'

Black Jack nodded, but his brow was creased.

'What you say is wise as ever. But with such a rare opportunity, is it not worth a little gamble to make the best of it?' He waved his arms as he spoke. 'If we get a good hit of plague, or the weather turns and ruins the crops, many will be looking for a fair face to cheer themselves up. And while we wait, I can make some bit out of him. He's formed for distraction, but he can also disappear when he needs to. I know how to put such a skill to good use.'

She tapped a finger against the end of her pipe.

'And, pray tell, do you have a plan how we keep him healthy, happy and innocent until we decide to sell?'

Jack's green eyes sparkled through the fog of Moll's smoke

and suddenly, he looked directly at John. The vines and branches crawled in on themselves, and John was staring at a plain, wooden door. The hobgoblin yanked him backwards to the hearth.

'Did he see me? It felt like he saw me? But it doesn't work like that, does it?'

The hobgoblin shook its head, its eyes blazing red flames.

John tried to stand naturally, putting his hands on his hips, hanging them loose by his side, folding his arms. He picked through the conversation the hobgoblin had shown him, trying to understand what it all meant. Black Jack had said, 'keeping him safe and healthy.'

But this seemed only a temporary state of affairs.

And there had been no mention of the theatre.

Jack strolled back into the room with Moll behind him, giving one of his wide, toothy smiles.

'Good news, Fair One, Moll is letting us stay with her for a few days while we find a suitable apprenticeship.'

'Thank you, Mistress Cutpurse.' John stared down at the hobgoblin sniffing at the dirty footprints. Moll said:

'Don't thank me yet. You'll be in the basement with the rats. People who work for their money get the better rooms.'

'I can work,' John said. The words of the overheard conversation tumbled through his mind. 'I can clean, sweep, and scrub the floor. I'll do anything you ask me to, Red One.'

Something flashed in Jack's eyes. John stood up as tall as he could, his back straight and his chin raised.

Moll looked him up and down.

'How is it that he seems to get smaller the more you look at him?' She patted his shoulder. 'How old are you supposed to be then, John, friend of Black Jack?'

'I don't know... I'm not a young 'un.'

Moll gave a great roar of a laugh.

'I'm not a young 'un either. How about you, Black Jack?'

'As far as I know I've never been a young 'un, Moll.'

Moll thumped Jack on the back, grinning wide, and John stared down at the stains on his stockings.

'Why are you looking sad?' Jack rubbed his cheek. 'Our good fortune continues. Moll isn't known for her generous heart, but she's taken a liking to you. I forget what a sensitive thing you are. Are your clothes upsetting you?' He turned to Moll. 'He needs some new stockings and some longer breeches. Have you got something suitable, or shall I go and see what I can lift?'

Moll clicked her tongue.

'He's too tiny to borrow any of mine, but you may be in luck. Little Mary is trying to gather the coin to bribe her man out of gaol and traded me all her son's garments.'

Black Jack and Moll chatted for a while about Little Mary. They both seemed to genuinely sympathise with the woman's situation, and moaned about the increasing greed of gaolers, but then Moll boasted about how cheap she'd got everything that Little Mary was trading, and Black Jack congratulated her on her cunning. It didn't make sense.

Nothing made sense.

Should you listen to people's words or trust how safe you felt with them?

When Moll left the room, Black Jack stretched out his arms.

'We're going to do well here. Just follow my lead and we'll get you settled in no time.'

'So... ' John swallowed, unsure how to explain the doubt in the pit of his gut. 'When will I meet the theatre people?'

'Don't fret. Now that we have a safe place to lodge, it'll give us the time to do everything we want to do.' Black Jack talked blithely about all the different people he was going to introduce John to, and John knew that he'd lost his chance to ask more. It was easier to listen to Jack's friendly voice and believe everything he said.

'Shorter breeches are more the mode.' Moll handed a heap of clothes to Jack. 'But I got what you wanted, longer ones.'

She looked pointedly down at John's legs.

'John doesn't care about fashion, and neither do I.' Jack thumbed through them and passed a few items to John. 'Put these on, Fair One.'

'Thank you kindly for these beautiful garments... Lady Moll Cutpurse. I will treasure and care for them in honour of your... graciousness.'

Moll and Jack bent double in laughter.

'All you have to do is wear them!' she guffawed. 'And I'm not giving you anything your good friend won't pay well for. Never mistake me for a fool—not like Black Jack, who does things out of kindness.'

'Do you need help with the dressing, John?' Black Jack asked with his slanted smile.

'More likely the undressing,' Moll chuckled.

Jack rolled his eyes.

'Don't, Moll, he's shy. More than shy. He's not like us.'

'I am like you,' John whispered. 'I am.' But Jack gave no sign of having heard him.

John balanced on the other boy's shoulder as Black Jack undid his boots and whisked off his stockings and breeches. When he was redressed in his new clothes, Moll took him into the other room, where she shunted some fabric aside to reveal a framed piece of metal polished to a shine.

Jack whistled. 'Long time since I've seen a mirror that grand. Is there anything you don't have in your possession?' He manoeuvred John in front of the mirror. 'Now you can see how pr... how handsome you are.'

John gazed at himself. He knew what the separate parts of him looked like—his hands, his stomach, his feet. Then there were the parts of him he'd never seen properly: his shoulders, his face. But the person staring back at him was entirely strange. He ignored the new clothes, the unfamiliar smell of Moll's pipe clinging to him. Instead, he studied his face.

There was something in the way he set his lips that made him appear bolder and more determined than he'd ever felt. His eyes were truer to who he was, he decided: they were wide and scared. But it wasn't himself he was searching for, he realised. It was Ma. He tried to soften his face with a smile. The bones of his cheeks vanished momentarily into roundness, but he still looked wrong.

Black Jack chuckled.

'You're pleased by the sight of yourself?'

Moll grunted. 'It does not matter how long you make the breeches, your find still looks more woman than I do.'

John swallowed. He didn't see a boy in his reflection either, but Moll's words still stung. He took the cap off, but Jack had pinned his hair well and most of it stayed in place.

'I need to cut it,' John said, even as he raised a hand protectively to his tresses. If his face wasn't a perfect copy, his hair was definitely Ma's. Could he really get rid of it so easily? Then he let his arm drop. No normal man wanted to look like his ma.

'I can sell that for you, if you won't let me put anything more valuable up for trade.' Moll cracked the knuckles in one hand and sucked on her pipe with the other.

Jack patted John's locks and gave a rueful smile. 'It's a pity to think of something so beautiful being used to stuff tennis balls. Does it grow back fast?'

John shrugged and stared away from his wide-eyed reflection.

Black Jack took the cap from John's hand and placed it back on him. 'I think you'll do as you are for now. Thank you, Moll. How much do I owe you?' Black Jack produced a coin from somewhere, but Moll waved it away.

'All I want is your word that when your senses return in a day or two, you'll not deal me false and approach any of those other festering stews. And in return I promise I will treat you both fair.'

'I swear it, Moll. The only festering stew I will approach will be yours.' Black Jack grinned and Moll nodded with a closed smile.

'I'm keeping you to that. I know you've been giving old Saggy Dugs in the city all your business due to your fondness for Kind Kate, but I trust you have no loyalty or obligations there and I'll not be hearing any of that while you're staying with me.'

Jack and Moll rambled on in voices that were friendly one moment; guarded and suspicious the next.

John stopped listening. He stared back into the polished metal. Oh, Ma. Beside her, everything else that had happened to him faded into pale winter colours. But he had said his goodbyes—that part of his life was over. It struck him now, like a new and raw pain. All he had of her was his own pale reflection, in a strange room, surrounded by strange people, far far from home.

Well, God give them wisdom that have it; and those that are fools, let them use their talents.

Black Jack tipped his head backwards, as if he was looking up at the stars. A small part of his mind did see them, loved their brightness in the dark night, but as always, most of his conscious thoughts were focused on his immediate plans and problems: That which could actually affect him was far more important than distant worlds. He'd never been able to believe that your fate was fixed by the position of the stars when you were born. The things that mattered when you came screaming into this world were: how much coin your parents had, how angry your dad got, and how ill your ma was.

But those particulars were long past his personal interest. If you wanted to survive, you lived in the moment. And if you were one of the lucky ones, you could plan for the winter. Right now, in this moment, he was one of the lucky ones. If he remained careful.

Only three people, all trulls, were close enough to notice him. They were the leftovers, the remnants that hadn't been picked up earlier, or who had finished off quickly and were out searching for another customer with more money. Not Anne though—she could do well enough with her round, friendly face and only lightly poxed skin. The problem was that she hated the work and tried to creep off to places where she wouldn't be found. She wasn't going to last much longer: a week, two at most, and she'd be gone. He'd tried to talk to her, but some people couldn't be taught how to survive.

Then there was Helena. She had no issue with her trade, but the trade had an issue with her. Every time he saw her she looked thinner, her skin sagging off her bones. She leaned against the wall, her eyes closed and her breath rasping.

The last was Bianca. The grey streaking through her hair and the wild look in her eyes made people think her older than she was—not that that mattered on a dark night. But it wasn't the years; she'd made the fool's mistake of loving her babes too much, and now her own survival seemed to enrage her. It was common knowledge that sometimes, when she'd crimped together enough coin, she'd buy the dead animals that were sold for spectators to throw at those caught in the stocks, or paraded through the streets, or hung at the gallows. Unconsciously, Jack raised his hand to his neck, snapping it back to his side when he realised what he'd done.

Grisly tales were told of what Bianca did with the animals—Black Jack had made up a few himself that were so popular, he'd often had them retold back to him. But he was unique in knowing the truth: she liked to take the little corpses outside the city walls and bury them where the wildflowers grew.

When times were good, Jack would sometimes secrete a few coins to those in need rather than those he desired—not a fact that was common knowledge, but good business in more ways than one. And today his kindnesses were being repaid by their discretion—each one of them pointedly ignored him. It was an unspoken rule of this life, cemented by coin: if someone didn't see you, you didn't see them.

Satisfied, he cracked open Moll's door and slid his body through, stepping over the creaking floorboard and pausing for a moment, listening, checking the shadows. Some looked only for movement, but he knew better than that: he watched for areas that were too still; shapes that weren't quite right. Eventually, he closed the door and made his way down to the basement.

He'd made sure Moll wouldn't be expecting him back all night, but he knew these random returns to the house were of little practical use. All it did was break up the hours when he was earning real coin rather than dreaming of future riches. It'd be pure chance if he happened to come back at the exact moment when Moll's patience had worn through and she'd chosen to deal with the treasure on her own. He felt like a miser, constantly checking his hoard of gold.

Nothing moved, not even the rats that were perpetually gnawing away at something or another. He edged across the floor.

Moll complained he was doing John no favours by taking him to people on the pretence of an apprenticeship. But nor had she implied that she meant to trade John in by herself. Not that she would. It was easy behind her bluster to forget how skilled she was. Which was, of course, the whole point. Moll was doing well at the moment. She was in a good patch with her fencing, not relying on the other side of her business too much. She would not risk losing his loyalty over quick coin. But still... if an opportunity arose, if she saw she could get an offer beyond her expectations, then he was just another gull who had let himself be cheated and deserved no better.

Jack felt forward with his feet. Nothing. And this was where the bedmat should be. He kept edging forward.

He cursed his stupidity. Right now, she was probably locked up in the back room of one of the cheaper inns, surrounded by all their acquaintances, telling the story of what a fool Black Jack had been. If she'd told him about such a clod, he would have laughed louder than anyone. He smiled wryly. Then he thought of John.

What would John be doing? Not laughing.

He kicked out at the wall, and his foot hit something soft.

A yelp. 'Da!'

Jack hunkered down, finding his hair. 'How are you so quiet?' he murmured. 'It is not a good jest, Fair One. I thought, oh, I thought bad things.'

He felt around the scrunched up figure at his feet. His treasure was fully dressed from cap to boots, huddled against the wall. He hadn't even put the sleeping reeds down.

'Doddypol,' Jack said softly. 'How much will I get for you if you catch a chill or have your ears chewed off by rats?'

John was still asleep, but Jack could see he had nudged him into a nightmare. Now he whimpered, his body jerking. Jack eased his cap off, pulling out the pins that fastened his hair and stroking it out over his shoulders. It was far too dark to see anything and Jack knew it was only in his imagination that the gold shimmered, but still, he smiled. Then he retrieved their sleeping mat from the chest Moll had lent them for their belongings, and set it in the centre of the room. He stamped his feet as he moved to scare the rats away, but the scuffling on the floor was only John's twisting and turning. The little thing was making those sad whining noises again.

He knelt again and removed John's boots, then rubbed his hands up and down John's stockinged feet until his legs stilled. Jack felt a strange, stupid pride at how he could soothe the boy. Of course, John would probably calm just as well if Moll held him thus. He leaned in to undress John for sleep, something he'd done for dozens of friends in the past. It was a common favour: no one wanted their outer clothes to get the extra wear or the stink of night sweat. But his hands hovered in the air. He shook his head. What was unsettling him so? In the end, he carried John to the sleeping mat, braided his hair to stop it tangling, and tucked a cover over him. He didn't undress him.

He touched John's nose.

'You'll be fine for a night. You never smell like other bodies anyway. You're... apple blossoms.' He laughed at his own foolishness—It was fortunate that the Fair One was asleep, and couldn't hear the rot he was talking. John's body curled towards the sound of the laughter.

'Did I do well yesterday?'

These moments when John was still asleep but spoke as if he were awake were far more disturbing than the crying and trembling.

'You were bene,' Jack whispered.

And he had been. John was a natural thief without being a natural thief. Garret's den had been perfect. Jack had pulled in a favour so they could practice alone on the complex wall that Garret had set up for his young novices, and John had danced around, taking every purse without making any of the bells ring. Soon his Fair One would be earning as much coin as any, and he had to keep reminding himself that this was only a stepping stone—that they had bigger plans for John. But not tonight.

His original plan had been to exchange the pretty thing for some quick coin from Moll and leave her to make the real money. He didn't have the interest or expertise to be involved seriously in that sort of trade. And yet here he was, breaking up his night's real work to check on his sleeping treasure. There must be something in the idea that John would sell for more if they waited for the right time or Moll wouldn't have agreed, but Jack was honest enough with himself to realise he had no idea when this mysterious right time would be. Except that it wasn't tonight.

'Rest now and dream sweetly. Your da's not here—only me, and I'll look after you. As best I can.'

Jack stroked John's hair a last time, then stood up. He climbed out of the basement, jogged back into the cool night air, and merged with the shadows.

I am not what I am

John's heart thumped; they were truly here! He'd been right to ignore the things that Black Jack and Moll had whispered to each other when they thought he couldn't hear. It was a wise decision to trust the redheaded boy and do everything he said, even if none of the people he'd introduced him to had ever glimmered with magic... He had believed in the goodness of his first-ever friend and now, Jack had been true.

'Fair One, I present, for your pleasure and enjoyment, the great, the glorious, the only entertainment worth paying for in all four corners of the world, Bankside's youngest theatre, the Globe!' Black Jack spread his arms, oblivious to the people swarming around them. The hobgoblin rose high over his head, spinning and twirling as it soared above the thatched roof of the theatre.

John giggled.

'You talk as if you built it with your own hands, Red One.'

'Don't mock a working man, country boy.' Jack grabbed John's hand and shook it. 'I may not build theatres, but the hard-practiced skills of my fingers keep us in lodgings. We aren't all blessed with faerie friends looking after us.' As always, Jack lowered his voice when he mentioned faeries.

John felt himself redden. But today Black Jack didn't take the jest any further. Instead, he continued in his normal tones:

'There is a fine story about how this theatre was built, though unfortunately I was not a part of what sounds like a great adventure. But I've heard it told enough to know it as well as if I was there.' He leant in, eyes wide, hands dancing. 'Twas one of those winter's nights where the air you breathe will freeze your nostrils into ice. Imagine it that cold, then imagine all the players sneaking out with their tools—hammers, saws, chisels, the works.'

John shivered, feeling the chill night on his own skin.

'And now you're curious, aren't you? What did they need all those things for on such a night, a night that was made for cuddling in front of the fire with a fair wench, not venturing into danger? I can tell you what they were up to.' He paused, hands clasped as if he'd caught something between them. 'They were stealing the timber from the old Theatre up by Shoreditch. Yes! Such a mass of wood to haul back over the river before they got caught. Then what did they do with that good night's lifts? Why, they built this grand building. Remind me when we have the time and I'll tell you all about it.'

'I think you just have.' Mimicking Jack's posture and voice, John said, 'In the midst of a normal summer's day, Black Jack explained yet another story of noisy, stinking London to his ever patient, kind, wonderful, tolerant, virtuous friend... '

Jack mimed cuffing John around the ear and they both laughed. Then Jack looked at him curiously.

'How is it day by day you become ruder with me and quieter with all others?'

'I think... I've been talking to Moll more. And I'm getting used to everything. All the people.'

'Come now, don't slip back into shyness, I did not mean anything. Perchance I like seeing sides of you that others don't.'

Jack's eyes were open and honest, and John found that he had to look away.

'I am truly grateful for all the gentlepeople you've been introducing me to and I'm sorry... I'm sorry I haven't been right for any of them... ' He glanced up at Jack from under his lashes, trying to read his reaction.

He didn't want to lie to his friend, but he couldn't tell him that he didn't need a trade in the way that Jack thought he did. But when Jack had questioned him about his skills and assumed he'd come to the city to get an apprenticeship, he'd made up all those stories of how he'd worked in the field with Da like every other boy his age did and how that was the only skill he knew. It was easier, even fun, to make up things about sheep and crops, rather than say he stayed indoors with his sister and Ma, cooking and mending and cleaning. And it was impossible to say what he really wanted to: that he just needed to find the magic and then everything would start to make sense and he'd know where he belonged in the world. Now, Black Jack laughed merrily and linked his arm through John's.

'Nay, it's them that have been wrong for you. But do not fret. Be merry. We will find the place for you. I know you've been pining to come here, despite it being bigger than all those buildings you're so afraid are going to fall down and squish you.'

John had not once mentioned his strange fear that the whole of London would collapse and he'd be trapped beneath the broken bricks. These moments when his friend seemed to understand him almost as well as he knew himself—at these times Jack seemed faerie-blessed too, and John found it impossible not to trust him.

'There's a sparkle around this place,' he said, looking sideways at Jack. 'Different from the grey mist everywhere else.'

Black Jack's mouth twisted.

'Sparkles? I should heartily like to see that. Describe it for me.'

'Are you mocking me?'

'Surely not. I only wish to see the world as you do.'

John gazed upwards. The building had appeared round, but now that he was closer, he saw it was formed from many angled lines, giving the illusion of a circle. He blinked and opened his eyes wide, catching again the flittering lights above the brown thatch.

'It's like a night sky, when it's got dark gradually, and the greys and whites and pale blues become a deep and eternal purple-black. Then a cloud moves, and you look up and see the first stars, pinpoints in the darkness. And you feel in your soul as if they've always been there, you just couldn't see them before. And they are both small, as if you could catch them in your hand, and bigger than you can ever understand.' John swallowed.

'I can imagine it.' Black Jack stared up. He squeezed John's hand, and when he let go, John felt as if it was a cold day and he was the one allowed to sit nearest to the fire. But even as he melted into the feeling, he felt his ribs shattering apart, leaving all the organs of his chest exposed. He swayed.

Apparently oblivious, Black Jack led him to the taphouse at the side of the Globe, nodding to acquaintances as they passed. He seemed to have the gift of finding as many, or as few, friends as he wanted to, wherever they went.

John's head pounded, his hand fluttering to his chest to confirm that his ribs were still there.

'When I look on the crowds in the street, it hurts my ears... and nose. I see something like a millipede, a head that is not much more than another piece of the body and lots of scuttling legs. What do you see?'

Black Jack glanced at him.

'I cannot tell it as prettily as you do, Fair One. It is not something I think much on, it is more... instinct... my nature, I suppose. But even when I have no plans to work, the first thing I see is always who would be a good draw, who to avoid, and all that lies in between. I spy if there are constables, or those that have a mind to feel moral and interfere with my craft. Those who may be a danger, usually men, oft drunk, or simply those who like to fight. Then I look for friends and the friendly... a healthy plump woman is ever a welcome sight...'

At the taphouse, the damp air smelt of cold pastry and warm beer. Black Jack bought ale and a pie, and they walked back to the Globe, John looking around for the hobgoblin, who had disappeared again. He waited as Jack chatted easily to a woman holding a clay pot at the entrance to the theatre. Black Jack held his hand over the pot and there was a chink of coins, but John knew the boy hadn't dropped any money in. The woman only laughed at whatever Jack was saying. Then they walked inside.

Jack was still talking.

'There was a gang of cutpurses here who claimed the Globe from the start and were mighty territorial. I did not care for the trouble of that, when there are plenty other places to find over-coined people standing around not taking due mind of their person. But in time it was clear that this gang were better at fighting than thieving. Last I saw, their leader was bruised and humbled after a turn in the stocks, and the rest dispersed between begging, gaol, and death.' He gazed about. 'And this may be the first time, nay, this is the first time, I've ever come out with the sole purpose of watching the entertainment. We can pretend we are rich and spend all our hours deciding what leisure suits us best.'

John heard him and didn't hear him. People stood all around with mouths frozen open, awaiting food to shovel in or words to spill out, but he could hear no sound except for his own breathing.

In the open space within the boundaries of the thatch edging, hundreds of faerie folk flew and twirled to melodies coming from somewhere beneath the stage—more faeries than he'd ever seen in his whole life. The sky-blue faerie from St Paul's was there, leaving rainbows of colour with its every movement. It stared at John, and a tremor went through him. Then he saw his own companion, spinning in circles faster than any other. It waved at him then stuck out its tongue and danced away. John rubbed his palms over his eyes, where tears were pricking. The faeries were still there when he looked again. All he could do was laugh.

'You like the sound of that?' Noise rushed back in, and John saw Black Jack smiling at him.

'Yes. Yes!' he cried, though he knew in some part of his mind that he was answering the wrong question.

'Maybe another time. You are a lot quicker than you look, and this is a good place to begin, but you're not practised yet. Hmmm.' Jack crossed his arms, balancing his pie in the palm of his hand.

Then the music stopped and a voice boomed above the rustling of the crowd.

'If music be the food of love, play on.'

John's attention snapped away from his friend again.

'Yes, play on,' he whispered.

Jack chuckled.

'The actors on stage are paid to answer, not you.' He began dividing the pie, but John grabbed his hand and held it. Now there was no pain; only the glow of touching his friend.

The packed crowd shifted constantly. Traders were calling out their food and others were buying, slurping on bones, and cracking nuts with their teeth. Some grazed past casually, eyes sharp, looking very like Jack: the pickpockets and cutpurses. If they could walk freely then so could he. John squeezed forward through gaps between bodies, tugging Jack along with him.

'Where are we rushing to?' Jack laughed.

John ducked under the wobbling arm of a round, rolling man, yanking on Black Jack's hand when his friend proved too slow and Jack shoved through, cursing cheerfully at those who shouted at them.

Eventually they were close enough, John decided. Maybe too close—craning his neck, all he got was glimpses: shapes winding across the raised stage and the distant curves of a canopy, painted with the sky.

Now he could hear different voices. One was a woman, bright and witty, filled with some magical charm so that she could speak softly, but still be heard above the rumble of the crowd.

'What does she look like?' he breathed to his friend.

Black Jack shrugged. 'I don't know, I was looking at you.'

'You can look at me any time, fool. Look at her,' John hissed, desperate not to miss a word.

Black Jack grinned.

'How about you look at her?' And he grabbed him with one arm, as if he was weightless, and lifted him up to his shoulder.

'Jack!' John protested, thumping the palm of his hand against his friend's back. A few children were also being held up, though none as old as him. He waited for someone to shout, or laugh at him, but the hubbub continued exactly as before. He looked around, his chest tightening. So many people. Sweaty, red faces. Grease dripping from flabby lips. Food tossed to the ground. Men relieving themselves where they stood. Why had he rushed to be at the front of this bog of stale, grimy bodies?

'Conceal me what I am.'

The voice from the stage reached out and wrapped around him. John turned, and fell slack in his friend's grasp.

In some indefinable way, he knew her.

He didn't need to understand her words to see it: he knew her loss, the loss that she couldn't grieve, not properly, not yet. There was no time or space for her to sit and cry. She was in a strange, unfamiliar world and to keep surviving, she had to disguise herself as what she wasn't, to protect what she was. And John didn't just see the girl.

Within her outline, her shadow, was a boy. He had the same facial features as her, an oval face with a small nose and chin, but his skin wasn't as white, nor his lips as red. His hair was cut short, the colour of tree trunks, and his body was slender, straight lines up and down. John could see the padding in the lines of the costuming to give the illusion of hips and a bust; he could see the layer of painting on the boy's face and hands; and the carefully curled and piled horse hair arranged over a wire frame.

John stared at the real and the unreal as they blended, blurring and separating in a repeating pattern. He was barely aware that there was another person on stage talking to the girl-boy.

When the scene changed, John was about to ask Black Jack to put him down, but then another woman-boy came on stage and he remained where he was and watched, spellbound. Then a little later there was a third, and sometimes all three were on stage at the same time. Only John's eyes moved, following each of their actions—from wild chases around the entire stage, to the smallest twitches of their fingers.

Occasionally, Jack hefted him from one shoulder to the other. He passed John food; bits of pie, and John held them for a while and then passed them back, or ate them unthinkingly.

During one song, John became aware of Black Jack humming a tune that almost matched the one on stage. He giggled, and for the first time looked down at the boy who had been holding him for so long without complaint. Standing close to his friend was the woman he'd met on the first day in London. He knew her now as Bess Porch, although each time John saw her, she looked slightly different. Today she was dressed in fine clothes, with an ornate feathered hat. John's ears sharpened to her words.

'Not much is required: just stall, and I'll do the picking. This mort has no more brain than stone. The world would not be a right place if she were left walking around with all those riches so brazen and no one to cloy them.'

She glanced up at John and smiled, though her voice was clipped.

'Tell your good cousin that this is a bene chance to catch a cony and make plenty of easy bit.'

Black Jack stopped humming and chuckled.

'Thou hast no need of me, Bess.'

'Devil take thee, Black Jack. What's your scheme in being here if not to foist?' She folded her arms.

'Watching a play with my boon companion. Why are you here, Bess? This is not your usual patch.'

She rubbed a hand across her forehead.

'The Rose has not had such good pickings; they say the rich and foolish are here now. If you'll just aid me.'

'You need more bit?' Black Jack frowned. 'Has it worsened with Nick?'

'Ask the poxy, whoreson, wormfood physician,' Bess snapped.

'Another time, Bess, on my honour, I'll be yours. Just not today,' Jack said.

'You're mistaking yourself for someone else, coz. We don't get to make choices such as that, we take opportunities, or we starve.' Bess turned and disappeared into the crowd.

Black Jack stared forward, his face blank and John leaned to put his mouth next to Jack's ear.

'Help her. Do not fret about me. I will wait here for you... or just outside if Bess keeps you longer.' He tried a wide smile, showing his teeth like Jack so often did.

Jack threw a nut in the air and caught it in his mouth, then reached up, put his thumb and forefinger on either side of John's chin and pointed his face back towards the stage. John didn't know what else to say, so he allowed the magic of the play to pull him in again, and he sank into a different world, where boys were girls who were boys, dead twins turned out to be truly alive, and people were happy being married to the wrong-right people who they'd mistaken for someone else.

The man called Duke Orsino was speaking. His had been the first voice to captivate John, though he had faded into the background once the women with their boy shadows appeared. Duke Orsino addressed the first woman-boy, the one who shone brighter than all the rest. She had started as a grieving sister, then pretended to be Orsino's page, Cesario. Now she was reunited with her brother and was Viola again, though she still wore male clothes.

Duke Orsino boomed:

'And since you call'd me master for so long, here is my hand: you shall from this time be your master's mistress.' Then he pulled her close and kissed her.

John's body was bathed in sunlight, his skin afire. He had to blink several times before the flames disappeared, and he was himself again.

But it wasn't over. Olivia, who had been adored by Duke Orsino and had herself been in love with Viola before marrying Viola's twin, Sebastian, ran up to Viola and said, 'A sister! You are she.' And she kissed Viola too, on both cheeks and then the lips.

John gazed at the male shadows laughing together beneath the faerie magic of the women they played.

Then he tapped Black Jack and waved to be put down.

'The best part's not happened yet, where the clown comes out and there'll be a jig,' Black Jack said. 'Do not fret, Fair One, I am strong and you are feather light, I can keep holding you through to the end. I want you to see it all.'

'Thank you... but I need to stretch out.'

But when Jack placed him back on the dusty ground, he was grateful that the other boy kept an arm around him. He leant his forehead against Black Jack's chest. Sweat poured from him and there was a pounding coming from somewhere: he didn't know whether it was inside or out.

'Are you ailing?' Black Jack asked. 'Shall we leave?'

'No, I want to be here.'

And he did, although all he could see now were the heads and backs of the people in front of him. He copied the rest of the crowd, cheering and clapping when they did, pretending that he was one of them. He glanced at Black Jack frowning down at him, and stuck his tongue out. 'Watch! This is the great, the glorious, the only entertainment worth paying for in all four corners of the world.' It wasn't his best mimicking of Black Jack, but his friend smiled. John twisted Jack's chin towards the stage, as Jack had done to him earlier.

John stared into the sky at the faeries whirling in a frenzy of orange, red and yellow. Only that one blue faerie, who hovered still, was looking straight back at him. Had it been observing him this whole time? His tongue flicked over his lips, his mouth parched. He felt like he'd sweated every drop from his body.

The music ended and John let Black Jack steer him through the crowd to the exit.

As they left, he stole a last glance behind him. Above the stage, the blue faerie was bobbing against the velvet sky, watching him as he left. And next to it hovered his own dear hobgoblin.

A shiver went through John's body. He tore his gaze away and hurried after his friend.

Let me be that I am, and seek not to alter me

Black Jack lay in the grass, gazing at the clouds crawling across the blue sky. How long had they stayed here? He dared not think of how many hours of work he was losing, or how much he'd have to make off of John to be paid back for all the time he'd invested.

He rolled onto his side and leaned on his elbow. John was on his back, both hands resting above his heart. For a while, Jack watched the steady rise and fall of his chest. Most people, when they relaxed, when drink or happiness loosened them, got louder, their bodies spreading out to claim as much space as possible. John became stiller, smaller, quieter.

He'd brought John out here beyond the city walls, thinking he'd divert him with some archery. He wanted John to remember how happy he was with Jack; to stop asking about the theatre. A plague on the cursed place—and he'd only taken him there because the boy had been acting so jumpy, and he'd thought it might distract him. Well, it had, but the boy seemed different now, as though he wanted to take care of himself, rather than leaving it all to Jack. Surely he couldn't have lost his country innocence so quickly? Yet Jack already felt like he was losing his grip on the Fair One. He had to keep reminding himself to watch, to work, to plan for all eventualities.

Right over there was an ideal group of lads: dressed well,

thinking they were better than they were, laughing and not taking anything too seriously. It'd be easy to act friendly enough. They wouldn't take offense at a little betting that didn't go their way—if, say, Black Jack suddenly proved to be better at hitting the target when money was at stake.

And then there'd be the fun of teaching John how to use a bow and arrow. Would he even be able to hold it? Or would Jack have to steer his hand; help him draw and nock? If the afternoon was to be spent like this, without much prospect of coin, it would have been bene to play at being John's teacher, having him gaze up with those eyes that could make a body feel like they were the cleverest person in the whole of England.

But the Fair One had ignored the boys, staring instead at the women pegging out their sheets. 'The beautiful rippling of the fabric in the breeze,' indeed.

Jack snorted.

John was happy, he could see that. As clearly as if he'd done a jig, or sung out that this was the best day of his life. Because that was another thing John did when he was relaxed: he started noticing how beautiful plain and boring things were. And then Jack looked at the same things and could all of a sudden see why they made the Fair One smile. So Jack had sat meekly down and let John be quiet as the afternoon ebbed away. And here he was, allowing his thoughts to wander again.

With a sigh, he rolled onto his front, resting his chin on one hand, while he tore clumps of grass up with the other and let them drift away on the breeze.

It wasn't just the time he spent with John; it was the time he spent thinking about John.

It went beyond mere practical concerns, like how much food and ale the other needed to stay pretty; how to take him out without meeting anyone who might ask awkward questions. There'd been too many occasions now; moments when he'd had important things to consider, when he'd been distracted by the boy. Like the way John had stopped an argument between him and Moll by mimicking them both. The sight of their coarse manners copied so delicately always made them both laugh until their bellies ached. Even now, he grinned at the thought. And there he was, getting distracted again!

He turned onto his back, raining a handful of grass down over his chest. He was going to have to sell his alleyway treasure, if he wasn't going to become as ridiculous as Moll teased him for being.

Not immediately, of course. He could take John on a few jobs first, earn some money off him that way. He'd seek out easy, low-risk work that John could assist with, things that would favour his smallness and silence. He wasn't delaying—it was just common sense to make the treasure go as far as possible before getting rid of it for good.

'Red One?'

Jack looked sideways with a smile and a raised eyebrow as John wriggled in, closer than was strictly necessary. When Jack did this it was to test people's boundaries, to intimidate, sometimes to be friendly, but with John, it was unconscious and shy. John always accepted Jack's hugs; allowed himself to be patted or held. Yet if he realised that he'd been the one to move in, his face flamed; he jumped away, and went through that little routine he had of squaring his shoulders, clenching his fists, sticking his chin out, deepening his voice, before he'd look at Jack again. A feeling fluttered through Jack's chest that he decided to interpret as a pleasant anticipation of wealth. There were none that could be taught the innocence that John carried naturally, and that meant more coin, when the time came.

'You got any more you want to say, Fair One, or you just fancied the sound of your voice after such a long silence? Which I am all in favour of. You should speak more. Sometimes I talk on so long that I even bore myself!'

Here, he noticed John was staring at a point to the side of Jack's head, his lips pinched in a determined line. Not a good sign.

Jack punched him lightly on the shoulder.

'You're supposed to flatter me and say that I'm the most amusing fellow you've ever met and that I could never, ever bore you.' The trick was to act merry and keep talking, as if he was oblivious to the fact that John was trying to say something. But maybe all this quiet was driving him to madness, for today he fell silent and let the other's voice ring out.

'Jack... I know you said not to mention it again... that there was no chance... but... ' John bit his lip. 'But I think the Globe...'

John's eyes darted between Jack and the thing that only the Fair One could see. Normally, John tried to hide his glances at his invisible friends (or friend? as Jack suspected, from things John sometimes said when he was tired, that he had only one special confidante). Did this slip mean that John was relaxed and trusting him more, or a sign of him sliding still further from Jack's grasp?

'I understand all you've said, about the theatre not being safe... but I think I need to try it.' John's eyes were wide, his cheeks pale, but dotted with two fierce pinpricks of red. 'If you are busy, I could... ' A pause for a succession of deep breaths. 'I could go to the Globe on my own, and find the right people by myself.'

Jack cursed himself. He'd been weak, weak. He'd followed his heart, rather than his head, too quick to offer kindness, and John must surely be the easiest person in the world to be kind to. The Fair One glowed with such gratitude at stupid things, like Jack going out for a minute to get him breakfast. And the other was already scared of so much; Jack had not wanted to add to it. But now here John was, talking about going off on his own.

It was Jack's fault: introducing him to good sorts like Bess and Moll, or Starving Robert, helping him talk to them, encouraging him to be more confident. Instead of gently easing John into his world, he should've shown him how harsh the city would be without Jack to protect him. On their trip across the river today, John had chatted away to River Robin with only the merest glance at Jack, and his skin had carried only the faintest tinge of green.

Now, there was a slight tremor in John's hands, but this was not the country gull Jack had rescued from the alley. That boy would have never stammered through to the end of the sentence. The fearful, quaking creature he'd been in those first days had been perfect for Jack's purposes; he should've kept him preserved like that.

Time to correct his mistake.

'John.' He drew the syllable out into a long, sad drawl. 'Don't make me tell you what the theatre folk will do to you. Because those are things that should not be dwelt on, especially on a fine afternoon like this when all I want to do is speak of friendly matters.'

'Sorry. I just... I don't know.' John twisted his hands together in his lap. 'Perhaps they're not as bad as you think. You've said before that it's not part of your world, that's why you couldn't help me, so you can't really know. And you've said before that rumours are lies that people want to believe. You've told me that I am scared of nothings. I don't want to be, any more. I want to be brave like you.'

The boy had the most cursed ability to remember every word Jack had ever spoken! With most people, Jack's arguments would leave them doubting their own name, but John had such a stubborn certainty about some things, and Jack knew better than to press.

Not yet, anyway, when he had other tricks to try first.

'And you said that you were going to earn coin and pay back all the kindness I'd given you. I also recall you saying, on several occasions, how much you liked being with me, and that you wanted to learn from me. Is all that forgotten now? I took you to one play, and you've decided that boys in dresses suit you better than I do?'

John's mouth opened and closed, his eyes darting around, his hands clenched desperately.

Jack found he could not look at John. Instead, he stared over at the boys hitting the archery targets. He needed to ensure his victory, make certain the other would be too terrified to ever wander off on his own. Jack forced himself to look back at those blue eyes, wide and pleading.

He gritted his teeth. He had more sense than this. And it wasn't pure selfishness, after all! John's beauty wouldn't keep him safe on the stage. His quietness and ignorance would get him used and turned into coin wherever he ended up. He was better off with Jack than with some strangers who'd leave him friendless and broken. And Jack would go to Bedlam rather than see any other grow rich from his treasure. Excepting Moll, of course.

But the things he could say to hurt John, to keep him close, to keep control of him, kept dancing out of sight. For the first time in memory, Jack realised he was stuttering.

'What I'm meaning, Fair One, is that... I need you by my side. You bring me luck and once I train you, you'll be a help to me like none other could be. You and I are good together, aren't we?' He stood up, stretched, trying to shake away his uncertainty, and offered a hand to John.

John paused for a long moment, gazing again at that fixed spot, off to the side. Then he slowly shook his head.

Jack's stomach constricted, bile rose to the back of his throat. John was so light, it'd be no effort to to drag him along, but then... the other slipped his small white hand into Jack's calloused one.

'We are good together.' He smiled, looking down at Jack's boots rather than into his face. 'I will be of help to you.'

Black Jack swallowed his moan of relief, turning it into a stream of words without knowing what he was saying, something about what a fine apprentice John would be to him. He hauled him up, and the boy leapt to his feet, jumping with the joy of living.

'I'll be my best for you, Jack,' the boy said.

'I know you will.'

He turned back towards the city, back to Moll's, and to whatever the future might hold.

'I'll make the coin I owe you, as quick as I can.'

'Ay, I don't doubt.'

'I won't bother you with questions about the theatre any more.'

'I'm sure we can go to a play again.' Never, he thought. 'But I still have to take you to the sea. I promised, didn't I?'

John giggled, covering his mouth with his hand.

'You didn't, you just told River Robin that you had.'

'See, that's a promise, isn't it? It doesn't matter when or how I said it, just that I am now bound on my honour to be the first one to take you, and you are bound on your honour to let none other accompany you before I do.'

He nudged John's ribs with his elbow, then carried on speaking, making the ocean sound like the most wondrous place in the world, and while he spoke, he truly believed there'd be nothing more precious than watching John's face as he saw the sea's eternal expanse for the first time.

But there was an ache beneath his skull, as if nails had been struck through the bone and into his brain. Things would change between them, and soon. It was the way it had to be, the way it was always going to be. John would change; it was impossible that he could survive, otherwise. And in all likelihood, when that change came, he'd not choose to go anywhere with Jack, ever again.

But that was tomorrow. Not today. And with his words, Jack could conjure up a place where he and John wandered across the sand, found crabs in rock pools, and paddled in cooling water, and for as long as he talked and John listened, it would be the only future that mattered.

Foolish curs, that run winking into the mouth of a Russian bear and have their heads crushed like rotten apples

The night city growled. The beast was pacing, snarling, wide awake.

Black Jack had been preparing him for an eternity; making him crawl in and out of Moll's windows while the moon and stars were all that lit the world; drilling him as soon as he woke and questioning him even as he fell asleep; playing a game where Jack had his back turned and John had to creep around behind him without being heard. Today, he had managed to touch Jack five times.

Jack had been pleased, but even more so when they'd worked the streets around a big market. Jack had left him on his own to search for potential targets, and the hobgoblin had suddenly appeared with a rainbow of faeries streaming behind it. In less than a minute, the faeries had laden him with purses. Before it disappeared, the hobgoblin tugged his hair free from his cap. Then it was gone, with a sharp-toothed grin.

On returning, Jack had stared at him, mouth agape. Then he shook himself, stowed the purses away on his own person, and hastened them home. All the way, he'd chatted breathlessly about how he was underestimating John, not challenging him enough; how, with John's skills and Jack's knowledge, together they could rule the world—or at least a few streets in London. Jack seemed carelessly happy in a way that he hadn't before.

John's mouth dried out when he thought about telling his friend the truth—that it was all the work of the faeries; that he still had no idea how to steal someone's purse without them noticing. Da had been asleep when he'd snuck away with his pouch, so that counted for nothing.

And he couldn't tell his dearest friend that his dearest wish was to merge in with the magic he'd found at the Globe. He'd promised not to mention it again, but he knew that the hobgoblin often returned there and his heart longed to fly alongside his faerie friend.

Now John glanced around, hoping the hobgoblin would be somewhere near tonight. He knew the faerie was cross; it had been very clear about wanting him to try his luck in the theatre. And John knew he should have pressed Jack harder—whatever it was he was supposed to be doing, he felt sure it wasn't this.

You and I are country beings, John thought, wishing the hobgoblin was there to hear. But Jack knows how to survive in this city. He knows what's right.

He balled and flexed his fists. Back at home, he'd always left the best morsels out in the hope that the hobgoblin would aid him in his embroidering, or teach him new songs and dances. Now he needed help in thieving from a stranger's house. Was this what becoming a man meant? Was it really what Jack wanted from him? Again, he found himself imagining Da's reaction—my so-called son. A common thief. Da was a man, and Da would've thought it shameful.

But Da had been wrong about other things.

John looked over at Jack, who was staring straight ahead, chewing his lip. He cleared his throat and asked lightly:

'Should I be wearing a sword? To look more convincing? Or one of those ruff things around my neck? Like other men do?'

'You do think of the strangest things, Fair One. Starving Robert knows you. Do not be worrying yourself about what he thinks of your appearance.' Jack rubbed the back of his hand briefly against John's cheek. It was a moment of warmth in the night air.

John was quiet again, his stomach twisting with knots. The darkness pressed down. He spoke again to try and distract himself, to hear anything other than the howls of the beast.

'At first he mistook me for your... woman.'

'Aye he did, didn't he?' Jack said. 'Tonight he'll see you're the same as me: a good lad who knows how to handle himself.'

John blushed. Could his friend guess the effect of his simple words?

'Can you go over what I need to do again? Just once more?'

'You can recite it back to me ten times over without mistake. You don't need me to... ' Black Jack stopped speaking, his eyes wide. 'Ah,' he murmured, 'This doesn't look good.' He pulled John close and hissed in his ear, 'Let me do the talking.'

John followed his friend's gaze. It was not Starving Robert who awaited them, but a different man, slouched under the eaves of a house. Nothing more than that. But when John saw him shift and look in their direction, blurring the shadows, teeth nipped at the flesh of his belly. He laid a hand on his own stomach.

Jack elbowed him upright and said in a bright voice:

'Richard, what are you doing in these parts?'

'Robert shared your schemes with me.' The voice was brittle and sharp, a knife on bone. John glanced at Jack, but his friend's manner was just as easy as ever. 'He mentioned you having some new young thing to train that needed a more experienced man than him. So out of the kindness of my heart, I volunteered.' The man stepped into the street, the moonlight glinting off his belt buckle. He grinned from one of them to the other. 'Why, Jack, you don't seem pleased to see me.'

'It is kind of you to take notice of our small concerns. And I am shamed to say your time has been wasted, for my friend has taken sudden ill. We'll wait for another night when Starving Robert can make it.'

John's throat burned with acid. He was suddenly sure that Jack was more frightened than he was letting on. They shouldn't have come—he'd known it, the hobgoblin had known it—so why had he let Jack bring him?

'I do not waste my time.'

The voice was somehow both cold and hot, though Richard smiled and smiled as though they were old friends.

'I'm fine... I'm fine. I can do it,' John said.

The sooner they got the whole thing over with, the sooner they could get back to Moll.

Stepping out, he saw the man properly now. His features

were regular, a plain, sallow face finished with a pointed beard. His eyes were dark and flashing, and when John looked into them, his heart thumped with the feeling that he was falling.

'What do you call yourself?' the man called Richard said.

It took John a moment to realise who he was speaking to. He glanced at Jack, who gave an almost invisible shake of his head, but he was already replying:

'My name's... my name... I'm John... just John.'

'And this is your first time, John, yes?'

John nodded. 'I... yes... this is my first time... I've never... '

The man's lips turned upwards in something that wasn't quite a smile.

'Well then, First Time John, I hope I can teach you something tonight.'

'We should be moving while the night is quiet.'

Black Jack glanced casually around. John could see the uncertainty coming from his friend in dark, red waves, though to look at him, you'd never know. John wanted to reach a hand out, to tell Jack not to worry—if they just stuck together, this would all be over and they could go home.

Jack said with a light laugh, 'Right then. One for watching; one for receiving the goods through the window. We'll have to help him: John is too slight and inexperienced to carry much himself, and as Starving Robert must have told you, we've hopes for a good haul.'

Richard made an unusual sound.

'Slight and inexperienced. An interesting choice of partner.' He made a sweeping gesture, ushering the boys forwards. 'Let's see if it's of any use tonight, shall we?'

Black Jack walked with an easy lope which John copied as best he could. They stopped outside a house with an open lower window.

No one spoke.

Jack had described everything to him before in great detail, and now, John clenched his hands into fists. He walked forward, waiting for Black Jack to lift him up, just as they'd practiced. But instead, the man called Richard stepped out, put his hands on John's waist and held him.

John forced himself to stay still. Claws dug into his skin.

Little hooks crept and multiplied all over his body. He stared down at the man's gloved hands glistening in the moonlight and tried not to shiver. Jack hovered behind Richard, looking at John with wide eyes that were obviously trying to tell him something.

The man waited a second more, then carried John to the window, his fingers digging into John's sides. Black Jack had told him time and again that they had to work in complete silence when they reached the house, but Richard put his mouth next to John's ear and whispered:

'Be quick, First Time John. I'll be waiting.'

John wrenched himself away and scrambled in through the window. He'd thought this part would scare him, but he collapsed down in the strange room with a sense of having escaped—although from what exactly, he wasn't sure.

It was a long moment before he took a deep breath and stood up. His eyes had always been good in poor light—as long as the world around him remained real and didn't shimmer away. Unconsciously, his fingers darted to the places in his side where the man had touched him. His stomach twitched.

He looked around, still half hoping that his hobgoblin would appear, but when it didn't, he swallowed and focused on hearing Jack's instructions in his head.

First thing, it is a job, that's all. Do what you need to do, and don't ever think about being in someone else's home.

Of course, all he could think about now was being in someone else's home. His chest constricted. How would it feel if he'd woken up in the middle of the night and found a stranger in his family's little house? Not that there was anything there that anyone would want to steal but...

If it'd only been Jack outside, and no man with the scraping voice...

John tensed his muscles and forced himself to concentrate. He knew what he was supposed to do. Sweet Maria worked here and had left the window open, had given Jack detailed descriptions, right down to which floorboards creaked.

John pictured Black Jack in the room with him. Jack squeezed his hand and pointed to where John should step, showing him the places he should avoid. When he reached the first cupboard, Jack stroked the back of John's neck and smiled, the whites of his teeth and eyes shining so brightly that they lit up the room. John saw exactly what he needed to take. A silver plate. He nodded. The plate was cold and light as air in his hands.

He followed the spectre of Jack back to the window, where the smell of blood blew in on the breeze. He kept his eyes low and stretched the plate out. Gloved fingers brushed his hand.

Imaginary Jack laid a gentle hand on his shoulder. John pulled away from the man's touch and went back for the next object, a heavy jug that smelt of sugary wine. Lifting was the easy part. It didn't feel like stealing, that was the rub: it was nothing like the shadowy gestures he'd seen Jack make on the streets. It was just moving things from one place to another. He realised he was smiling, glowing in the warmth that radiated from the ghost Jack's face. But each time he returned to the window, his legs trembled. Each time he wanted it to be the real Jack waiting for him, but it was the stranger with his pincer fingers.

John moved quickly and surely, even retrieving things off the higher shelves with Black Jack's hands on his waist, helping him balance as he reached up. Slowly, the claw marks washed from his skin.

When they had found everything and passed it into the waiting hands, Jack gave him a wink and a pat on the back.

John was about to climb out into the street, when one of the real Jack's instructions flashed into his mind: there was one last drawer that he was supposed to open. He turned back, but his Jack had disappeared. He was alone.

A shiver went through him. It was the middle of the night and he was alone, an unwanted stranger in someone's home. Smells he hadn't noticed before crept in: the beeswax scent of the furniture, and from deeper within the house, the savoury odours of the evening meal, vegetables and fish. Without meaning to, he glanced upwards. The people he was thieving from could be right there, in the room just above his head.

He bit his lip. His own da had been sleeping in the same room when John had searched out his leather pouch and stolen it away. And he was far more frightened of Da than he was of the strangers upstairs.

Without imagined Jack guiding him, John stared down at his feet and edged forwards, much slower than he had before. He glanced over his shoulder at the window. The real Jack would be just as proud, he told himself.

His footfall seemed to echo through the silent house, but he was almost finished. He'd been quick with the rest, so there was time in hand: he just needed to do this last thing. John pulled on the drawer. It didn't move. He put both hands on the handle and pulled.

The hobgoblin appeared, floating in the air in front of him. John had to put a hand over his mouth to stop himself from crying out loud.

The faerie flicked the drawer open with one tiny finger, and it shot out, crashing down on top of John. Silver knives clattered to the floor, louder than the bells in St Paul's. The whole house was noise: thumping started in the room above. Shouts and yells.

More than the upturned drawer, it was the clamour that seemed to pin him to the spot.

He heard Black Jack call out:

'Fair One! Run! Now!'

Jack's voice broke the spell. His body moved again, and John fled for the window, icy with fear.

Let every eye negotiate for itself

Black Jack licked his lips, heart thudding.

He realized what he was thinking. John is mine. Leave him alone. Don't look at him in that way.

This was all messed up. From the moment he'd seen the Butcher, he'd messed it up. And he couldn't work out how to fix it.

The Butcher positioned himself to take the things off John, then passed them to Jack, signalling where to hide the less portable objects, as if this whole venture had been planned by him, and the boys were mere servants. And Jack obeyed—what choice did he have? Running around like a schoolboy to barrels and bushes, and secret hiding holes in the ground, which were all too far away. Far enough to give Richard plenty of time to grab John before Jack could get back and—and what?

What could he really do, if the Butcher decided to take him?

He glanced sideways at the man. There was no knowing what he was thinking. Perchance the worst stories he'd heard were nothing but rumours made up by bored minds—perhaps the man had no interest in John at all. But Jack had seen the way he'd looked at the Fair One—there was no doubting that.

The hairs on the back of his neck stood on end, his skin prickled. This was more than fear of the Butcher. With instincts that worked faster than his thoughts, his body was tensing for trouble. With everything else, John had been quicker than he'd dared hope, but now he was taking too long.

The Butcher had taken a couple of paces away from the window. He'd noticed the same thing and was readying to run.

Good.

Even before the hellish racket, Black Jack was darting forward, two steps ahead.

'Fair One! Run! Now!'

John came through the window as if he truly was flying on faerie wings. There was no time to pause and wonder. Jack felt the heat of the Butcher close behind him, smelt his odour so densely that he tasted fresh blood and salt on his tongue. Gloved fingers brushed his upper arm and Jack kicked backwards, swept John up into his arms, and ran.

He didn't dare look back. Not yet. Get further away. Get safer.

He tried to think like he always did. He never panicked. He wasn't panicking now. His heart might be thumping, feet pounding, body sweating and his mind a mess, but he wasn't panicking.

John's racket would have woken the house owners. Even if they were the courageous sort, which most weren't, it'd still be minutes before they were out on the street calling for nightwatchmen. And no watchman would come: the only one that ventured near this way was being kept occupied by Kind Kate. All they had to do was make their way home without drawing attention. So why was he hurtling down the centre of the street with John in his arms? This was not how you escaped from a job gone wrong. Even his ignorant little treasure remembered that lesson—John was mumbling,

'Put me down, Jack. I'll slow you. We're supposed to go in different directions and stay quiet.'

He turned a corner, and set John on the ground, but grabbed his hand and carried on running.

This was his world. The shapes of the buildings, the changing aromas, the texture of the ground, the noises. Everything should've been familiar. But it was like he'd been trussed up in sacking that muffled his senses. He wasn't certain of anything beyond the sounds of his own body and the feel of John's hand, clasped within his own.

Were they being chased? He didn't know. He should know! But he didn't.

He wouldn't waste time by looking behind. As confused as he was, he still knew that life and death balanced in ticks shorter than seconds, quicker than the blink of an eye. He squeezed John's hand tighter. Zounds, what a mess.

The clever thing would be to leave John somewhere, hidden. No one would see him, he knew how to be silent and not be noticed. Yes, he needed to leave him somewhere... in the dark... alone...

No. He couldn't do that to John.

But he could circle around. That was one of his favourite tricks. They didn't expect you to double back on yourself. You could saunter right past. Could sometimes talk to the gull, sympathise, and express outrage about how wicked people are. Worked better in the day when there was a crowd to blend with, though. Not so good in the night when all the proper people were abed. Not so good when someone even trickier than Black Jack was about. When the Butcher was after them.

Or was he?

Maybe Jack was being too protective of John, imagining an interest from the Butcher that wasn't there. Richard could've swiped him up as soon as he saw them if that was what he'd wanted. He had the loot, so he wouldn't be distracted, wouldn't risk his neck for one pretty thing. Still, the way he had gazed at John.

Jack's feet slipped from under him and he flung his arms out to cushion his fall.

But he didn't fall. Next to him, John had stopped and held himself upright. He was so perfectly calm and unhurried. Sometimes, he seemed stronger than Jack himself. Fair One, have I taught you nothing? Use that toughness to look after yourself! He should say it aloud. Couldn't say it aloud. Had to save breath for running. Who knew how long this chase would last?

Without slowing, Black Jack calmed himself enough to look around. His eyes confirmed what his feet already knew: he had doubled back. He'd thought about it as a plan, dismissed it as foolish. And then his body had gone and done it anyway. He wheeled around too sharply, and his knee twisted. Again, John grabbed him and stopped him from thumping to the ground.

He had to get them back to Moll's. Who else could he ask to hide them? Even Moll was a push; but though she'd deny it, she'd become attached to John. But he couldn't risk it yet. If the Butcher was following—if—he'd guess where they were headed.

So they raced to Moll's, but in the opposite direction. With his knee throbbing, Jack was noisier than he should have been, his boots clattering on the cobbles. Beside him, John made no sound, like some creature of light. The boy ought to be on his own: he'd have more chance. Except that Jack had been so busy getting John to memorise and learn how to do this one botched job, he hadn't ensured John knew his way around the streets.

They had to stay together.

He stopped at a wall and hoisted John up, clambering after. For Jack, climbing was usually as easy as walking, but today, he struggled to find holds. His feet slipped and he grazed his hands. Small, slight, John was already at the top, leaning back over, reaching down for Jack. He ought to shout at the boy to stop being a fool: to get out of sight and get clear...

But he couldn't risk talking. And there was John, waiting for him, trying to help him, holding his slender arm out. Black Jack hauled himself up, then dropped down first and caught John. It was like carrying air. How easy it had been, lifting him up in the theatre so he could see the players. How John had smiled at him as if Jack had built the Globe himself, and written all the plays especially for John. Jack could have held him up to watch plays all day, every single day. Instead, he was scrambling up walls in the middle of the night with no promise they'd make it to morning.

Another memory struck him, seemingly from nowhere. A sickly male chick whose eyes hadn't opened, who should've been killed swift under a stone. But Jack had rescued it, kept it warm under his clothes, against his skin, fed it, until it was too big to go unnoticed: a proud cockerel that he'd carried everywhere. But when mouths were hungry and it'd been taken from him, it was blood and bone, just like any other piece of meat. And he'd cried even as he'd chewed through the gristle.

He forced himself to put John on the ground, then took his friend's hand and kept moving, telling himself to stop blundering and come up with a plan. What was their best route?

He slowed. Time to change tactic.

He did what he should have done from the start, and drew John silently into the shadows. John followed his lead with no need for words. Black Jack squeezed his hand tightly, thinking of how soft it was. How white.

Not that Jack even liked white. White was for the pampered and the rich; proof that they'd never had to work, that they'd never had to stay outside with the sun burning their delicate complexions. Jack liked healthy and robust. Jack liked a girl who drained a tankard and sang badly and danced until her legs gave out and she collapsed in a sweating heap on top of him. That was what Jack liked.

He pulled his companion into an alleyway. How similar this was to the day they'd first met. How different.

'Sorry,' John whispered.

There was a power in the simple word that sharpened Jack's mind. He was the one who should apologise, but he should worry about apologies later. For now, he drew the other into the darkest corner.

Jack breathed in the stink of human waste that pervaded the whole city. Heard animals crying out. Or perhaps it was others, screaming their madness to the moon. Felt John's body, trembling. He'd been so solid until now. But sometimes it went like that. It was easier when you were running; when you stopped, the terror set in.

Thanks to whatever power looked after broken thieves, it was having the reverse effect on Jack. He felt his heart still, and he wrapped his stillness around the other boy. After a time, John's limbs stopped shaking, his chest calmed.

There were no more stray thoughts, only the two of them hiding in the alleyway. Black Jack didn't think of the blunders he'd made, whether this was the right place to be or not. This was where they were, and now all he had to do was listen.

Closer, much closer than the animal sounds, he heard a footfall.

Slow and steady.

'Are you there, lads? Is this where you're hiding? Is this where you take your pleasure?'

Black Jack lowered one arm to his side, blade at the ready.

He felt John's fingers, tracing the line of his arm from the shoulder, down over his biceps and the taut muscles of his lower arm, to where his fingers were gripped around the knife.

Something skittered around their feet, scampered away down the alley and into the street. There was a stamp, a crunch, wet noises like a cleaver sticking into flesh.

'Codso! Rats, always rats, when all I want is one pretty little piglet...'

Black Jack remained still for a very long time. Finally, the footsteps moved on. In his arms, John seemed to have stopped breathing.

A few nights ago, calmed after a nightmare, John had sat upright, whispered:

'Are you only kind to me because you think I am pretty like a girl?'

Jack had replied, 'What a strange mind you have, Fair One.' The other said, 'I know,' and settled down, falling immediately back into sleep. Jack had lain awake with the question repeating in his mind.

Waiting for the Butcher to leave, he knew the answer now.

In nature there's no blemish but the mind;
None can be call'd deform'd but the unkind

John didn't know how long they were in the alley, nor how or when they found their way back to Moll's. Sometimes he was a faerie, flying around Black Jack, protecting him. Most of the time, he was a small, shivering boy and Jack was carrying him.

When they burst in, the front room was clean and empty. Moll was pacing up and down, chewing on an unlit pipe. She looked at John, her mouth falling open, but Jack spoke up before she could.

'John's taken a fright. The Butcher got to Starving Robert and came in his place.'

Moll cursed.

'How bad?'

'Not as bad as it could've been, but bad.' Jack set John's feet on the ground, but kept a grip on his waist, and the other leaned into him again—

'When things went wrong, the Butcher had all the lifts, but then he came after us. He wanted John.'

Moll spat into the dust on the floor.

John stared down at his feet. He could hear Moll and Black Jack talking, but he couldn't hear them. He was naked and a knife was cutting red lines across his belly. He watched numbly as his pale flesh transformed into a dripping crimson checkerboard.

Then he was clothed, and Moll was crouching in front of him. Her pipe had gone, but the air was thick with the bitter tobacco smell. 'Hear me now, John,' she said. 'You can stay here as long as you need to. He's just a man—I'm not afeared.' She patted the sword on her hip. John shivered, and Jack spoke:

'Moll, thank you kindly.'

Moll carried on.

'However much a dog barks, you don't show fear. If he sees you're scared, he's got you. Listen to me. On the morrow, go and seek him out and claim your share of the night, just as you always would. If he knows you're willing to give up all your rightful bit rather than risk John, he'll want the boy even more. Take the game away from him before it starts.'

Black Jack ran a hand through his hair.

'We're not talking about a yapping dog. It's a plaguey cur, Moll, foaming at the mouth.'

'So you have to deal with this right. He will not bother you once the heat of the night's chase has passed. There are enough pretty things around.'

'Maybe, but none like...'

John had heard enough.

He shrugged out of Jack's arms and climbed down to the basement. He undressed down to his smock, and sat with his chest on his knees. His fingers danced over his two pouches: Ma's one, and the one that had once been scented, but now smelled only a little of dry summer grass.

Da's was long gone, and he didn't know where.

After a while, he went and got the bundle of Jetta's clothes that were stored in a chest in the corner. Something had nibbled the edges of one sleeve. He lay down on the thin reed mat, and curled himself around Jetta's clothes. He must have slept, for it seemed only a moment later that a candle lit up the dim room, and he saw Black Jack sitting beside him.

'Did I disturb you, Fair One? I hoped you were resting, after the night we've had.'

John met his eyes for a moment then rolled over to face the other way.

'Your sister's dress. You've still to tell me about her, you know.'

John clutched the cloth tighter against his body.

'It was generous of Moll to give us a whole candle. I know it's not on my account; she's taken a liking to you. Or a liking to all the chores she can get you to do. I've never seen Moll's place so tidy.'

He chuckled, but it sounded tinny and strange.

John chewed at his lip.

'You did so well tonight. I always knew you were strong, and now you've more than proved it. I'd have been flat on my face a dozen times over without you at my side.'

The shadows flickered as Jack set the candle down.

'I was not sure if you'd be wanting my company. I left you alone as long as I could, but I needed to see you. Now I have, do you wish me to leave again?'

The beat of John's heart stuttered. Jack was quiet for a while, and eventually John turned back, to see if the boy had left as silently as he'd come, but he was still there, gazing down at him. His eyes were the dark green of leaves before they crackled into their autumn hues.

'Please, don't be angry with me, my Fair One.'

John's breath caught in his throat. Angry—him?

'Thinking on it now, I do not know what addled my brain into seeing the job through. As soon as I saw the Butcher, I should've got you out of the way. There are many ways I could've done it, many excuses I could've made. But in the moment I thought of nothing. I'm sorry, John, I truly am. I did not look after you tonight.' His voice was raw.

John thought of how often Black Jack had comforted him, how he'd held him in the alley when his body wouldn't stop trembling. Now, John knelt up and pulled Jack's head against his chest. It was something he'd never done before, to anyone, but Jack wrapped his arms around John, and John rested his cheek on the top of Jack's head as if this was how it always was between them.

But his body prickled with words, itching to get out.

'I've not been honest with you, Red One. I know you know that, and you don't mind like you should mind, but I want to make it right. I want to tell you everything.' John's voice was strong, but tears fell from his eyes into Jack's hair. 'I think Ma and Jetta liked me... Jetta is my sister... my twin, in fact... but before you... no one else ever did. I have not known, not ever, what it is to have a friend... nor to be a friend.'

Black Jack rubbed John's back.

'Do not say anything that pains you. In truth, I've started daydreaming since meeting you. I used to fill every waking second with scheming and planning and thinking of surviving. Now my last thoughts before I sleep are of you, and of wondering about you. I dreamed that you came from a beautiful place where everyone is well fed and sings and moves as prettily as you. And you are the most beloved of all your village, because how could you not be? But you heard of this grey, ugly city, and being so sweet-natured you chose to bring your light here and brighten up the world where it was most needed.'

John laughed a sad, short laugh. 'It wasn't like that.'

Jack gave him a squeeze. 'I know that, fool, that's why it's a daydream. You're unique in many ways, but you're not the first person to try and change the story of their past.'

John's tears fell harder, but he managed to swallow them for a moment. He looked down at his hands.

'The man. You called him the Butcher?'

'It's his trade. More the trade of his father before him, but still his official trade.'

'But there are lots of butchers in London, and you've never called any of the others the Butcher? He cuts people, too, doesn't he? Their stomachs.'

Jack audibly breathed in.

'Now how would you ...? No matter. Yes. When they want someone to do the cutting up of a body; when a wretched soul is hung, drawn and quartered, he's the butcher they ask. There are many stories about him and none of them nice.' His voice was quiet. 'I'm sorry, John, but it may be better for you to leave me. To leave London, I mean. To go home.'

John shook his head.

'You're my only friend. I can't leave you.'

Black Jack laughed. 'Mayhap I can walk with you some of the way, but you'll find me grumbling company. I fear the way I've been formed, I'm only worth knowing when I'm in the city.'

John pulled back from Jack and hugged himself, peering into his friend's face.

'You do not mean it.'

'I think Moll will let you rest in her bed this one time, and then we'll set you up for returning home. You'll make plenty of friends when you tell them of all your brave adventures. You'll be so happy. And you need never think on me again.'

John heard a whimper. He thought it came from outside himself, but then Jack started rocking him and making shushing sounds and he realised it was himself, crying harder than ever. He scrubbed a hand across his face. His eyes and nose were streaming.

'I can't go back, Jack. I never told you the truth about where I come from. I let you believe lies. I never worked in the fields. And Da hated me.' His voice came out in stunted jerks between his sobs. 'Boys younger than me were all breeched. Da said that he wasn't wasting fabric on new clothes for me until I... until I.'

He tried to take deep breaths but he couldn't calm his crying. Jack stroked his hair until he was able to speak again.

'Da said unless I learnt to be a man I had to look like a girl. Jetta was always bigger than me. I wore her old clothes as she was constantly growing. Da and his friends laughed at me. I was a bad joke, no more.' John raised his head and forced himself to meet Jack's eyes. 'I mostly stayed in the house with Ma and Jetta. Ma thought it was better if people didn't oft catch sight of me. I was good at sewing. And I cooked and cleaned and learnt about healing plants. I had lots of time on my own, see? When Ma and Jetta were out, or sometimes when everyone in the village, men, women and children were together working, or dancing. But Da never allowed me to go, and... '

'Was that when the faeries came and made friends with you?' Jack said, his voice encouraging. 'You've said enough to let me guess. You do not have to be shy with me. I do not speak others' secrets, but I can tell you that there are plenty who've had enough of this world and search for comfort in another. Tis not so strange.'

John swallowed. He could no longer hear Ma's voice, warning him not to tell.

'I... I do see faeries. Mostly, just the one. A hobgoblin. It kept me company and helped me with everything, and when I was alone, it taught me singing and dancing. Hobgoblins are normally attached to homes, but it came with me when I left, and guided me here. I thought it was leading me to the Faerie Queene. But... ' He smiled weakly. 'Things have turned out differently. It helped tonight. Or tried to. It opened a drawer that was stuck, and that was the noise. It's never usually so clumsy.'

The hobgoblin appeared as John spoke, as if he'd called it directly. It hovered in the air, stroking John's hair and wiping the tears from his cheeks. Jack said:

'It caused the crashing? But then, it did help. I think that distraction put the Butcher on edge enough for us to escape. If the job had gone smoothly, he might have just snatched you away.'

'I'm sorry I lied to you,' John said. 'It pained me to think you'd see me like all others do. I wanted you to see that I am what I'm supposed to be.'

Black Jack held him at arm's length and stared at him.

'Fair One, how can you be anything other than what you're supposed to be?'

'Easily, Jack, if you're born wrong.'

'There is nothing wrong about you.'

'There is.' John bit his lip. 'And I've been punished for it.'

'What do you mean, punished?'

John felt the truth, bursting to leave him like water boiling down a rapid. He could hold it no longer.

'Jetta and Ma... Jetta and Ma... they... they're...'

Something flitted over Black Jack's eyes. He looked down for a moment, then sighed.

'Yes. It follows. John, I'm sorry to hear that you've lost your kin, but I cannot pretend to be surprised. It is the way of this life. I've never counted up, but sometimes I feel I know more dead people than living ones. But you cannot truly believe that you're responsible. You're the gentlest soul I've ever met.'

John shook his head. A cold numbness had crept into him.

'No, it's true. I looked after Jetta and Ma. Or I tried. I tried so hard. But they ailed and died fast. So fast, Jack. And Jetta... Near the end... She screamed out how my herbs were making it hurt worse. The villagers said that... they said that... ' John crammed his fingers into his mouth, as though it could keep the words inside. 'The other villagers said that I killed my own twin and my own ma because I was jealous of them... they said I was evil...

that I was formed wrong, and jealous of those formed right... and I'd cursed and killed my kin for being real women when I was... when I wanted to be... but could only ever be...'

Black Jack prised John's hands away from his face. His lips were a savage line.

'John, look at me. I forbid you to get upset about what ignorant people say. They've got no choice but to live with their stupidity, but you are bright and witty and don't need to even listen to their petty words.'

'But Da... my father... he believed it as well. He didn't stop them when... ' John writhed free of Black Jack's arms and knelt on the cold floor. 'Maybe it was... maybe I am to blame. I sometimes wonder if I'm some sort of witch, that I hex people without meaning to.' He turned his drooping head to look at the other boy. 'None of the villagers even knew that I can see between the worlds... they just knew I was wrong by looking at my outside. That I'm not normal.'

Jack crawled over to John and wrapped his arms around him again, squeezing him furiously.

'No, you're not. And you shouldn't wish to be. Normal people are ugly in their persons and their souls; they hurt others without even thinking about it. You're better than normal people, heartily better.' He rested his head against John's shoulder.

Both of them were silent. John's mind felt empty. He tried to conjure Ma's voice and couldn't. It was as though by telling it, he'd thrown his past into a river and watched it wash away. Could it really be that simple? He had always half-expected Da to appear one day and drag him back to the village, back to his misery and his memories; but after all, why should he? Why should Da come and bring him back when he had never really wanted him in the first place? The thought made him heavy with sadness, but there was also a sense of freedom. Was it really possible to just... let things go?

Jack sighed.

'We can't send you home, Fair One. That is clear. Maybe you would like to go to another village, perhaps a small town? Somewhere quiet and green with faeries?'

John shook his head.

'Small places don't trust strangers. Someone like you, who

can talk and smile and make others laugh, you might get past that. But someone like me. Jack, I think London is my only chance to be right.'

'That's ever the way, isn't it? I, who am constantly thinking of how to steal and cheat, can get folks' trust; you, who want only to have friends, are feared and chased away. Prithee, say that your faerie world contains more justice than this one.'

'I don't think I fathom it enough to know. It's more something you feel rather than understand.'

John put his hands in his lap and gazed down at them. His face tingled as if it had been blasted with icy water. When he spoke, though, his voice was clear and ringing. 'I do not want you, or Moll, to be troubled any further because of me. I thought I'd come to London and the Faerie Queene would be here waiting for me with her magic and I'd be safe. I never dreamed that I'd meet someone as good or kind as you, but I'm so glad I did. It'll not aid me, running again. There's nowhere for me to go. If you think this Butcher man will continue to bother us, then let me go to him.'

John saw the knife slicing down the centre of his belly and felt his skin being peeled open. He shook the image away.

But Black Jack laughed.

'I will never let you do that. And do you know why? It's not because I'm good or kind. It's just that being with you makes me so.' Black Jack shuffled around so he was kneeling opposite John. 'Now can I tell you something?' Behind his smile, his friend's face looked sadder than he'd ever seen it.

'Of course. Anything.'

'My dream. My own secret hope, has always been that I don't have to do what I do forever. I didn't want to always be a drigger, a thief; it only ends in one way. I wanted to be a sharper, at cards, dice, even bowling; anything where the gentlemen come of their own free will and you don't have to be risking the streets.'

'So why didn't you?' John asked.

He remembered when Jack had first mentioned his dream, that day when they'd met, and John had thought this stranger was the most wondrous creature he'd ever encountered. He'd pictured great plans, out of this world dreams that someone like himself couldn't even fathom. To learn that his friend's hopes were so simple and humble pained his heart.

'I don't know. Too young, too set in my ways. Maybe I was afraid of failing. But then you appeared. And now—I don't know. I feel I could do anything. You've made me better, John. So of course I cannot hand you over to a beast like the Butcher. We'll lay low for a bit, and that creature will forget about you soon enough. I'm sure of it.' He didn't sound sure, but John let his words soothe him nonetheless. As he stared into Jack's eyes, their dancing green light made anything seem possible.

'Jack. You know all about me and you know all about this world, so it might be a fool's question, and I know I said I wouldn't ask again. But is there any chance that the theatre life could be for me? I truly felt I belonged there.'

Black Jack grinned, and suddenly he was fully his old self again. He pursed his lips mischievously.

'Perchance there is hope. Me and my ilk, see, we live and die without any taking notice. I've told you many stories, haven't I? That first night we met, didn't I tell you about the original Black Jack, who disappeared? And no one asks or cares. But if you were to become someone that people will ask after, someone people remember, the Butcher wouldn't dare touch you. No one would.'

John held his breath. The hobgoblin tilted its head towards Black Jack, its eyes fizzing with sparks. John smiled at it stupidly.

'Is that a yes? It is possible?'

'Hark now. If you only ever place in your heart one thing I say, let it be this: you mustn't let your life be shaped by people who are too stupid to appreciate you. Only listen to those that care for you. But sometimes even they get it wrong. At the end, John, you can only trust yourself. The trick to life is knowing when you need advice, and when to follow your heart. This is what you knew was right, and mayhap I did too, but I was selfish and wanted to keep hold of you for myself. But now I can see that letting you go may be the best way to save you.'

John couldn't breathe. He pressed himself into his friend, breathing in his apple-y scent and listening to the beat of the other's heart. He wasn't sure if he spoke them aloud to Jack, or if the words remained a river, shining in the sunlight and flowing through his mind, but he knew that in this moment, they were all that mattered—for both of them.

I trust you.

Here's ado to lock up honesty
And honor from th' access of gentle visitors

John shifted on his mat, reaching out and searching with his arms. Where was Jetta? He didn't remember falling asleep. He didn't remember when he'd last been awake. Was he late stirring?

He couldn't hear Ma or his sister moving about, nor smell the wet animal scent of their home. Where were they? Had Da beat him? He couldn't remember that, either.

He rubbed the crustiness from his eyes and forced them open, pushing himself upright.

A boy, sparkling with red fiery light, smiled down at him, his eyes shining with the fresh green of new spring buds.

'Sleep longer, Fair One. I needs go out, but I'll return as soon as possible,' the Faerieboy said.

'You're going to see the Butcher, like Moll suggested.' He knew it was his voice speaking, but he didn't feel connected to it, or understand the words his own tongue uttered.

'It is the best way to find out how things lie,' the Faerieboy said.

John struggled to his knees. With numb, prickling fingers, he took the ribbon of Ma's protective pouch from around his neck and stretched out to knot it around the Faerieboy's. The moment it touched him, the long-dead flowers danced into life with new, white blossoms that glowed from within. The threads of the ribbon unwound and remade themselves, in colours of sunlight and dead night and all shades in between.

The Faerieboy laughed. He tucked John's hair behind his ear, and settled him back down to sleep. He laid a warm hand over John's eyes, and they sank closed as though weighted.

'Dream sweetly until I return,' the Faerieboy said softly.

'I will try,' he replied.

But the world was chill and empty. The Faerieboy had left him alone. And deep within his chest, John understood that somehow the faerie had got it wrong: he would only be able to dream sweetly when Jack returned. Until then, all would be darkness and nightmares.

John's eyes flicked open. Had he been asleep? The light in the basement varied little between night and day, but there was a slight difference in the shadows that he recognised as morning. His body was crunched up and aching. Something had touched him. The hobgoblin?

He leaned up on one elbow and peered around the basement. The sharp claws of a rat pricked over his bare feet as his movement sent it scuttling away. He yanked his knees up tightly, heart thumping. Black Jack and Moll were always laughing about stories of hungry rats nibbling people's toes off as they slept. But neither of them paid any more attention to the rats than they did to the smudgy birds everywhere, ready to sweep down and scuffle with the rodents over scraps.

John put a hand down and felt his toes, wiggling them one at a time. Then he worked his way back, checking them again. Satisfied, he stretched his legs out and sat up fully.

Moll had left out a clean smock for him, and he wriggled into it, then paused. Instead of pulling on his normal clothes, he went to the chest in the corner. The shapes of the room were familiar to him now; just like the slimy feel of the floor beneath his feet. His fingers moved, counting and recounting the days since he'd last seen Black Jack.

Three days. And there was no sign of the hobgoblin, either.

In the darkness, he creaked open the chest and found Jetta's garments, stroking the material. Last time he'd touched them, he'd imagined they had the scent of home: Potage and straw. His sister's wet hair. But now, he smelled only mould and death.

Quicker than he'd ever managed his breeches, he dressed in what had once been Jetta's clothes. Then, he smoothed down the skirt and went to find Moll.

She grunted when John opened the door, but didn't look up. In her hand, she turned a book, her lips moving wordlessly.

'I shouldn't've accepted this poxy rubbish as payment. Black Jack's softness is a stinking, spreading disease. Zounds if I know what a thing like this is worth.' She tossed it to the floor with a curse, then turned to John. Her eyebrows rose, but only for a moment. She twisted her mouth, beckoned him closer, and walked around him.

'I do not think that'll do, John. The Butcher will know your face and eyes.' She stopped in front of him and shook her head. 'If you want to disguise yourself, you'd be better picking up some scars and bruises'

John opened his mouth, but his tongue remained wordless.

Was he in disguise? Was that what he'd intended?

Truly, he didn't know why he was wearing his dead twin's clothes.

An image from the play he'd seen flashed before him: Viola dressed as a boy, being mistaken for her brother.

Moll twisted his chin left to right, inspecting him with sharp eyes.

'Black Jack is wretchedly incapable of doing what's necessary.' She put her hands on her hips. 'It'd be far better to cut you myself, and hang the coin we could've earned from your looks.'

Her words were like different birds, all chirping out of chord. Of course, he had known in his heart that both Moll and Jack had planned to make money off him. But to hear it spoken so openly reminded him that he had had no part in the decision; even as he also knew, that something since had shifted. They all knew it

She was talking to him, stretching out something with a silver handle and sharp prongs. He closed his eyes.

'Still, if that is to be your look for today, you may as well perfect it.' He opened his eyes again and saw Moll holding out an ornate comb.

She smiled at him.

'Come now, I'm not your mother. I will not dress your hair for you.' She threw the comb and John caught it. 'You can wait for Black Jack to return if you like; I'm sure he'll play at that with you.' She laughed, and did not stop laughing for a long while.

It was a long, dreary day. Moll's head was throbbing, and she wouldn't venture out. When they heard the cries of the food sellers and water carriers in the street, John offered to go and buy, but Moll shook her head. So they ate some crusts, and drank the remnants of a sugared wine she'd left from the previous day. John watched how quickly she devoured the food and he took from it as little as his willpower would let him.

She gave John some sewing, and kept him beside her, sitting at her feet. Once, she said:

'Folks do not always look down. If there is trouble, use your smallness, keep low and get gone.' But mostly she chuckled and blew pipe smoke down at him. When he'd finished his embroidery, she had him comb his hair out and watched with twinkling eyes. 'Perchance Moll Cutpurse deserves a pretty pet to look upon for just one day of her life.'

And that was that. The day was over. And still no Black Jack.

Moll climbed up to bed, and John went slowly down to the basement but he did not get undressed. He lay down, and after several eternities had burnt themselves into cinders, he climbed up to the front room and sat with his back to the door. Now and then, he looked down and saw frost imps dancing over his fingers, their teeth sharper than any rat's. Then he rubbed his limbs and forced himself to move around before settling down again to wait.

Late morning next day is when the knock came.

Though John's limbs were numb, he leapt to his feet and rushed forward so fast, he almost ran straight into the door as it opened.

Black Jack caught him and held him for a moment. Then

he took John further into the room and closed the door behind them.

'I've missed you.' John clung to Jack.

'Have you? I think none have ever said that before.'

John pressed his cheek against Jack's chest and breathed in, wrinkling his nose. He gazed up into the freckled face with its dancing green eyes. No changeling could copy Black Jack's sparkle, but something was different.

'You smell strange.' He sniffed. 'Stale ale... and freshly slaughtered meat... and something that's not you.'

'Do you mean that stale ale and freshly slaughtered meat are part of my customary smell?' Black Jack laughed.

John shook his head.

'You're always apples, hot apples.'

Jack's brow creased and he held John at arm's length, looking at him seriously. 'If a body did not know you, perchance they would be afeared of you. There was a story once told to me of one that cared for me before I could care for myself, and they were as honest as the poor can ever be, and made bit from selling coddlings. I, being a useless nothing, would curl up amongst the freshly baked apples and ruin them all. But I was told she never minded.'

'Your ma?'

'No.' Jack stared upwards for a moment then laughed again. 'But that is a boring tale. There are plenty more. I'll share them all one cold night when you're having trouble sleeping and need something to dull your mind. Now, enough of me. Let me look at you.'

John felt his cheeks grow hot. He'd forgotten that he was still wearing Jetta's clothes. Jack gazed at the skirt and the loose hair, motioning for John to twirl. John shook his head, so Jack circled him appraisingly.

John spun on his heel to try and stay facing his friend. 'I did not like looking at my legs all the time,' he mumbled. 'After spending so many years not having to look at them, I suppose... ' His voice faded away.

They met each other's eyes for a second, and Black Jack threw his head back with a guffaw. John smiled too. Then he said, 'How fared it with the Butcher?'

Black Jack sighed.

'I will not bore you with all the particulars. I said enough to send him in the wrong direction if he is of a mind to chase after. But I do not think he is, not any more.'

John tried to focus on Black Jack's voice, but the world had started shimmering around him. Now the two of them were in a different room, with four white walls, and a floor speckled with blood. There were no doors or windows. In the centre of the room was a hollowed-out cow carcass. The Butcher stood in front of it, pulling out ropey intestines, cutting out the blue-veined heart, slicing the thick muscles.

Another Black Jack stood talking to the Butcher, joking, rolling his eyes, waving his hands, as if they were great friends. But John spied the almost invisible beading of sweat on Jack's upper lip, and smelled the change in Jack's scent; the salty fear that was never normally there.

'You should be on stage, you're a better actor than I'll ever be,' John said to the Jack next to him.

His Black Jack grinned.

'You are aware, Fair One, that this is not real, just a dream of your mind? Even Richard does not have a room like this, and if he did, you'd not catch me in it.'

'Your fear is real,' John said.

The Black Jack talking to the Butcher chattered on.

'Our acquaintance was chance, and he did not offer the opportunities I had hoped. I cannot decide if he is too cunning or too stupid for me. Either way, with all the bit you and I made, I'll be relaxing in Kind Kate's arms for some long and pleasant nights.'

The Butcher grunted.

'You should have more sense and taste than that. Embracing those poxy trulls is kissing death.'

'If so, it is one of the better ways to die,' Black Jack grinned.

The man wiped his bloody hands on his apron, and nodded. 'It's not worth my time, chasing after street rats. But that boy trusts you. Next time you chance upon him, bring him to me. I'll pay you more coin than you'll get elsewhere. Understand?'

The room vanished, though the tang of blood hung in the air. John looked down at his trembling hands.

Jack was still talking.

'So, all is done. And now the fun starts. I have someone waiting to meet you. Someone I think you will like.'

'I need to get changed.' John felt his lips moving, heard his own voice, but part of his mind was still in that room with its blood-caked floor. Had it really been that easy for Jack, or was there something his friend wasn't telling him; something the faerie magic refused to show him?

'You're perfect as you are.'

'But my hair... '

'....will suit the one we're meeting better than I could've foreseen it.'

'Should we not wait to say goodbye to Moll?'

'Our sort do not deal in goodbyes, Fair One.' Jack linked his arm through John's. 'All done. It's time to go. This'll be a new adventure, and luck willing, our best.'

There was no point in pressing Jack further. He kept his own counsel more closely than most, when it suited him: no doubt he would concoct some fantastical story about his dealings with the Butcher for a later time.

John looked around Moll's room, then followed Jack out into yet another new world.

What's to come is still unsure
In delay there lies no plenty

They had not walked far from Moll's, when Black Jack stopped and faced John.

'You're such a kind one, to lend me your charms. But you need all your luck today.'

He removed the ribbon from around his own neck and tied it back around John's, tucking the pouches under his clothes. Then he winked and continued as if there had been no pause.

John trotted beside his friend and was aware of the constant hum of Jack's voice, but his mind was distracted. He had an urge to pull the pouches out and see if they now held Jack's apple-y scent.

He also had another urge, to ask his friend more about Kind Kate.

Jack was generally happy chatting on and telling stories about all the people he knew, and he'd mentioned Kind Kate a few times, so surely it wouldn't seem odd if John was curious about her? But John couldn't think of the right question to ask, or even what he actually wanted to know.

All his other thoughts disappeared as he realised Jack was guiding him into a tavern. John felt his heart begin to race, his skin becoming clammy as it always did when they entered these booming, crashing places. But as he pulled back against his friend's hand, he caught the light of his hobgoblin, dancing around from drink to drink. The faerie turned to John and waved, before returning to its business: splashing ale in the face of a gentleman every time he tried to take a sip. Even from across the room, John felt the faerie's lightness touch him and he straightened his shoulders and followed his friend.

The victim of the faerie's jest had shoulder-length brown hair, a pointy beard, and a hooped gold earring in one ear. Something seemed familiar about him and John recalled the man he had glimpsed in St Paul's, but immediately dismissed the idea that they were the same. This man didn't have the aura of someone followed by faeries. His large hazel eyes had droopy eyelids like he'd just woken up. He sighed and wiped the ale from his nose with a look of resignation.

Jack squeezed John's hand.

'He's here already. That's a good sign. I knew his reluctance was all for show. He must be eager to meet you. Follow my lead and remember everything I said to you on the walk here.'

'Jack, what did you say to me? I was lost in a... ' John rushed the words out, but Jack was already striding ahead, over to the table where the hobgoblin was creating mischief.

'Thank you most kindly for meeting us! This is John Flaxen, the fair young actor I was telling you about who is desperate to become an apprentice to you. And John obviously knows who you are. What an honour it is for us to be in the presence of the great actor, Master Edmund Shakespeare!'

Jack stepped to the side and shoved John into the seat opposite the man.

'Greetings, gentle sir, I am John... Flaxen.'

He looked to Jack for confirmation, drowning already. Completely unsure of what was expected of him. Why hadn't Jack told him who he was going to be meeting? Or maybe he had, but John had been too lost in his own imagination to pay heed.

Thankfully, Black Jack didn't seem to require anything more from him than to sit opposite Master Edmund and stay silent. As ever, his friend's words made worlds spring into being and swirl before his eyes. A world where John was completely enchanted by the stage presence of this stranger; where the hobgoblin danced to Jack's words as if they were music. John's stomach clenched at the enormity of the lies.

'Every single day he's begging me to take him to the theatre, just to see you. He even misses half the action, and does not care for the jigging or music, his whole focus is on the magic that you bring to the Globe.'

'Hmmmm.'

The man looked into his tankard, but did not pick it up. The hobgoblin hovered by his shoulder, eyeing the ale with a toothy grin.

'My brother has not yet given me a role large enough to suit my talents. Thus, as you must have discovered, there's always a long wait between my appearances on stage.'

Black Jack held a hand to his lips in what seemed to John so obviously mock horror, he couldn't believe Master Edmund drank it down.

'No, I have not met the gentleman, so it is not my place to debate, but surely your brother cannot be jealous of his handsomer, younger sibling, and is deliberately holding you back?' Jack scratched his chin and then his face brightened. 'Of course, that cannot be the case. He is a clever man, proudly displaying your skills in smaller roles that others would wither in. He knows how you give power to every word you speak.'

The man sat up straighter, but his brow creased as he said:

'There are those who think that I am a route to my brother, and the power he holds within the company.'

Black Jack drew in breath and pulled back as if shocked.

'How can that be? You are well spoken of as the heart of the renowned Lord Chamberlain's Men. Who would not seek your company for its own sake? You are a famed actor. What is it your brother does? Scribble a few words?'

'He acts too. And I am also a playwright. Not that any of my plays have been performed yet, but... '

'But you are living with hope that you'll find a raw actor ready to be instructed and trained to a high enough standard to be worthy of speaking your fine lines.' Jack patted the top of John's head. 'Pray, are there many roles in your plays that require such rare beauty that it leaves the most oafish and coarse of men breathless?'

He put a finger under John's chin and pushed it up.

Master Edmund coughed.

'I understand your thinking, but it was not well thought out to wear a costume to meet me in a public place. If a constable... '

'Any who saw him might look twice at his prettiness; but not for one moment would they believe he was anything but an uncommonly lovely girl. And be assured, this is no false hair and clever painting.' Black Jack licked his finger and drew it down the side of John's face, then showed it to Master Edmund. 'See? And no reddening here, either.' He pressed his thumb on John's lip, hard enough to send a sharp tingle down John's neck. 'And look at this hair, as real as yours or mine.' Jack tugged on a lock and pulled it across the table for the man to do the same.

Master Edmund's hand hovered in the air before he returned it to his tankard, though he didn't drink.

'The look is indeed very convincing. Especially if no artifice is involved.'

John knotted his fingers under the table.

'And see how prettily he blushes; that is a frequent trick of his. Someone as talented as you can surely write a part in one of your plays inspired by John's natural skills, Master Edmund? His appearance was made for the theatre, but he'll only meet his destiny if you agree to be his master.'

Suddenly the man addressed John directly—in a different voice, more like the one John had heard from the stage.

'Pray, young John, you're very quiet for one that aspires to the great profession of acting.'

'I am sure you must be well accustomed to your apprentices being struck dumb in the presence of a great master such as yourself,' Black Jack said. 'And now that you've seen John, you'll surely make him your apprentice. What a waste it would be, if he didn't train with you and lesser actors fought over him instead.'

The man smirked.

'I agreed to one meeting, but I have an important part to play in the company; the others look to me for leadership. I cannot be seen taking on street children as apprentices, out of pity. There are standards to be met.'

'Exactly! That is the demand for perfection that John immediately recognised when he saw you. Now, let me get us some more drinks so we can arrange the details.' Jack winked at John as he turned away to search out the barmaid.

'Your friend is very wise,' the man said.

John nodded, then blushed and looked down at his own hands, wishing he could slide under the table and hide.

'Are you enjoying life in London?' Master Edmund gazed over to where Black Jack was laughing with the barmaid. John stared in the same direction.

The hobgoblin poked him between the ribs and jabbed its finger at Master Edmund.

'You were asking me? About London? Yes, I love it. All the noise... and all the people. It's just what I always imagined and wanted.' John's voice got quieter with every word.

Master Edmund nodded curtly.

'Anyone with any ambition needs to be in London. It is the centre of the world.'

The silence returned like a stone wall between them.

John chewed his lip, cursing his shyness. What else could he say? He'd been in Jack's company for long enough; why hadn't some of Jack's easy manner rubbed off on him? Jack could talk the evening away with no greater subject than the tavern table. He'd spin it into a tale of fights and adventures that would make everyone laugh and huddle closer. He tried to imagine what Jack would say.

Instead, he heard the Butcher's voice. 'Little pig, little pig, I'm going to eat you up. Cut you into morsels, and gobble you with a snap.' He shivered and the other said:

'An actor needs to be fearless. Audiences are not always kind. I think an ugly boy with courage will make a better apprentice than a pretty one who is scared.'

The man spoke off to the side, rather than to John. He seemed bored, as though he'd had enough of the boy's company for one night.

John gathered his courage.

'Master Edmund, good sir, you are clever, so of course you see who I am. I'm sure a great actor, with all your vast bravery, finds it hard to understand. But in truth, I find the city... difficult.' John twisted his hands. 'I don't like the noise; all the clamouring and clattering scares me. Part of me, the part that feels most like me, still wants to run away from all the strange faces. And I miss the greenness and fresh smells of my village...' He swallowed. 'I'm sorry. You do not want to waste your time listening to all this. I do not often speak this much. Only to Jack.'

Master Edmund was looking at him steadily. Then he rubbed his eyes and cleared his throat, putting on the theatre voice again.

'I imagine London can be lonely. I have never felt like that personally. But being an actor, I am accustomed to put myself in other people's minds. Perhaps I can see a little of what you mean. Perchance I can be of some help to you.'

He tapped his fingers on the table.

The hobgoblin jumped in rhythm to them. John's mouth opened, but his throat was dry. He wasn't sure what had happened—had Master Edmund agreed to something? If so, what?

Now Black Jack returned, slamming a jug down in the middle of the table with a loud laugh as if it was the punchline to a joke he was in the midst of telling them. The hobgoblin snickered and leapt up onto Jack's shoulder, and Jack absentmindedly scratched the place where it had landed.

Master Edmund rummaged about his person, and while the man was busy, Jack hunkered down next to John and whispered:

'You've charmed him, Fair One. I knew your ways'd suit him. I am heartily happy, though I will miss you. Work hard for me, because I do not have the patience to wait long before I can see you on stage.'

Before John could reply, his heart a whirlwind, Master Edmund thrust a piece of parchment across the table.

'This is the part I need to learn for Romeo and Juliet. I have the central role of Friar John. Try reading my cues to me.'

The parchment glittered as if it was made from gold, and John's fingers trembled as he touched it. But the faerie magic didn't extend to the words themselves, which were still as meaningless as ever.

Black Jack's knee knocked against John's under the table.

'Mayhaps I could have a look at your lines?' he said. 'I've never seen an actor's cue sheet; it is a thing of wonder indeed.' Jack put two fingers on the page and edged it closer to him, away from John.

'The wonder is in how an actor says his lines. Hark now.' Master Edmund put one hand on his chest and the other in front of him as if he was grasping out for something and then shouted out, in a voice that made even Jack jump, 'Holy Franciscan Friar! Brother, ho!' He relaxed his hands and smiled at the boys, evidently pleased with their reaction. 'It is a good entrance, is it not? Now read the cue for my next line, John, and I'll continue.' He raised his hands back to their previous position and opened his mouth wide as if he was about to scream.

John widened his eyes at the hobgoblin. The faerie stamped up and down on the paper several times, but still the words danced before John's eyes. Black Jack leaned over and poured ale into Master Edmund's tankard. In a voice that was barely a breath, he said, 'Or, if his mind be writ, give me his letter.'

'Or, if his mind be writ, give me his letter?' John repeated.

Master Edmund relaxed his posture.

'It's not a question, boy, try again. And in a loud voice like mine, that all can hear.' He returned to his former expression.

Under the table, Jack squeezed his knee and in front of his face, the hobgoblin blew its stomach and cheeks out, and mimed a deafening shout.

'Or, if his mind be writ, give me his letter.' It was loud for John, but not particularly loud for anyone else.

Master Edmund paused, frozen for an eternity, then boomed out his next lines. The hobgoblin shone in rainbow colours and turned a somersault.

While Master Edmund declaimed, Jack pressed his body so close to John's that there wasn't a sliver of air between them. 'You're going to be heartily busy, but when next you're free, we will go to the sea as I promised and celebrate this victory properly,' he whispered in the same quiet voice he'd used to give John the line.

But John's heart was still thumping.

He tried to push the paper closer to Black Jack—there wasn't even need to, they were sitting so close together and his friend had sharp eyes. It was a useless, nervous gesture and Master Edmund saw it.

The actor stopped mid-sentence and frowned at them.

'Forgive John's rudeness. My dear friend is too kind, showing me your cue sheet when all he truly wants to do is watch and learn,' Black Jack said with a dig in John's ribs.

But at the same moment, John burst out in a voice that now, impossibly, was somehow much louder than Jack's, 'I'm sorry to waste your time, but I cannot read, Master Edmund. Jack reads for me.'

Master Edmund's eyebrows shot up and his lip curled.

'An apprentice who cannot read his own lines. Yes, that is very suitable for me. To play teacher to a village fool.'

Jack started explaining about John's incredible memory and ability to mimic others, but Master Edmund interrupted. 'Let him talk, then. Prove this remarkable skill. Repeat the lines I just performed.'

It was a simple task that John knew he could perform easily, but his throat felt frozen. He forced himself to speak clearly and boldly.

'Master Edmund, I have no home.' He took a deep breath. 'I have no kin that care for me. People in my village never liked me because of how I looked. But if you were kind enough to train me I could—I could belong somewhere, for the first time in my life. Please, Gentle Sir, please.'

Master Edmund sat back in his seat and stared at them. Then he sighed and shook his head.

'You do speak prettily. And you look the part. But all would mock me if I took on an apprentice who can't even read.'

Black Jack leaned across the table.

'This is an opportunity for you, not just us. You'd be a fool to turn down the gift that I am offering you!' There was a note of rough desperation in Jack's voice that John hadn't heard before.

John gazed at his friend and suddenly remembered the conversation he'd seen between Jack and Moll when they'd first met. It seemed so long ago, he'd pushed it from his mind and forgotten it. But now it flashed before him and made his spirit lighter, even though things weren't going well with Master Edmund. It was a warm sensation, separate from the reality of everyday life. A boy who'd chanced on him in an alleyway was now his best friend, putting all this effort into making John safe and happy.

Jack quickly recovered his manners and spoke on, in his most charming voice:

'What I meant to say, Master Shakespeare, is that you have a discerning eye that surely sees the potential in him.'

But Master Edmund was already standing, dismissing them with a wave of his hand.

'I'm done with you both. I have no need to listen to anything your sort say. My family has a coat of arms; I'd be surprised if either of you even knows the names of your parents.' He gathered up his parchment as John sat, too stunned to speak. How had it all gone so wrong?

'Edmund, that is unkindly done.' The voice came from beside John, just out of his line of sight. It was a rich, gold and blue sound, that hummed in his ears like the chorus of early birds signalling the beginning of a summer morning. John's mind whirled with colours brighter than any he had ever seen. The Butcher's last few whisperings scampered away into the shadows; butterfly wings fluttered through spring blossoms and merged with bees buzzing with the happiness of finding sweet summer pollen.

Master Edmund was stammering:

'William, I did not expect to see you here—I, I believed you were still working on your new poem? Nay, I was not being unkind. Would you believe that these two ask to be apprenticed to me? They have dreams of acting with us in the Globe.' He gave a high bray of a laugh.

The hobgoblin was back, looking pleased with itself, beckoning the newcomer forwards, and the deep, gilded voice cut through Edmund's bluster.

'You've done well finding them, brother. I've been waiting to see if they would return, but little did I imagine they were your friends. Settle the terms of apprenticeship without further ado, then get them home. There is no time to waste.'

'Yes, yes, of course, I was about to... ' Edmund's voice trailed away.

John shivered thinking of the way the blue faerie had gazed at him when Jack had taken him to the theatre. He turned. There was no one there, but a blue shimmer stirred the air. He moved his hand through it and for the briefest moment, he was standing on top of a snow-peaked mountain looking down on an infinite world. It seemed magnificent and eternal. But then there was a faint breeze and it all blew away into tinier and tinier fragments, particles of dust

—each a world itself.

And he realised deep in his soul that everything he thought he knew was, in the end, just airy nothings.

John blinked several times.

He returned to the tavern.

Jack and Master Edmund were still talking.

The hobgoblin was skipping gleefully across the table, leaving little frothy footprints behind it.

It was real. It was all real.

He looked at his friend. The tavern had crept its way into his clothes and he smelt of the hot food and the smoky, ale-soaked scent of the room.

And the blue shimmer was still there, hovering just out of John's reach.

He was careful not to look at it directly again.

We know what we are, but know not what we may be

The room smelt of ink and old parchment and blood and dreams and butterfly wings and red thornless roses in winter. Even after they'd cleared all of Master William's things out into a smaller store room, the heady aroma remained.

John wanted to hold onto Black Jack's hand and be still for a long while, but silence and stillness didn't come naturally to Jack. Since leaving the tavern, he had been engaged in a continual argument with Master Edmund.

The air buzzed with their words, and John picked out the same things repeated, again and again.

'But it's only John who wants to be an actor, how many times do I have to tell you?'

'My brother clearly said 'them' and not 'him.' Need I repeat myself again?'

'You made him think we were both trying to be apprentices. Mistakenly. All you need to do is tell him your error.'

Eventually, Master Edmund left them with a flustered command. 'Stay here until William decides what he wishes to... I mean, while I plan out the exact terms of your apprenticeship.'

Black Jack strode up and down the room. The space could barely contain him and John stood with his back against the wall. He ran his hand over the surface.

'Red One?'

Black Jack stopped pacing.

'Ay?'

'Is this truly happening?'

'I believe so.'

'Then why are you not happy? Do you not wish to stay here with me?'

Jack sighed, and slumped against the wall next to him.

'Of course I would love to stay here and live the easy life of an apprentice with you. But even using all our coin I can only pay for your apprenticeship: one, not two.'

'Am I costing you much money? I'll pay it back one day. I never want to be a burden to you and... '

'You could never be a burden. You're ever my treasure.' Jack linked his hands on top of his head. 'But to the present point, I cannot even argue properly with Master Edmund for fear of destroying your opportunity.' He looked down at John with a frown that turned into a smile. 'Ah, but forgive me, dear friend.' He put his arms around John and pulled him in for a hug. 'It is but a minor problem that should not draw away from the joy of our fortune. Let me make amends.' He backed away, holding John's hands, and pulled him into a jig around the small room that was to be their new sleeping quarters.

John giggled and allowed himself to be spun around. Jack's dancing was often lumpen and out of time, and he usually tried to copy his friend's heavy movements, but today he darted and twirled the way the faeries had taught him, skipping his feet in and out of Jack's to avoid being stomped on.

'You are so light and quick when you are... working... How are you so clumsy when you're dancing?' John teased.

'Clumsy, am I?' Black Jack grinned. 'But still as strong as you are small.' He lifted John up and whirled him around by his waist. John wrapped his arms around Jack's neck and let his legs swing out behind him. They wheeled faster and faster, until they tumbled to the floor, laughing.

Black Jack got his breath back first and stroked the strands of John's hair that had stuck to his forehead.

'The London folk do not deserve you. It's strange thinking of them all, going about their lives, entirely ignorant of the bright beauty that is going to light up their lives forever, the moment they see him step out on stage.'

A little of John's dizzy merriment vanished at Jack's words and he stopped laughing.

'I wish I were the person that you imagine I am,' he said, looking down at where Jack was twisting a lock of his hair around his finger. The colour seemed strange against Jack's work-hardened, freckled skin. 'You've done all this for me and I am still in terror that I'll disappoint you. My heart is racing.'

'Nay. Your heart is racing because you've been flying. Have your faerie friends never told you how exhausting it is?' He pulled John close and said softly, 'Master Edmund is blessed to have you as an apprentice. And I've never had a stroke of fortune as great as meeting you. You will be the fairest actor that's ever been, or ever will be, and I will work every day in the Globe, doing bad trade as I impatiently await your scenes, and then doing no trade at all as I stand useless and enchanted.'

John relaxed his body and closed his eyes as he listened to his friend speak.

'Mayhaps you are right. Or part right at least. Master William said he was waiting for us, so the blue faerie must have told him to, and the faerie would not guide him wrong.'

'Of course it wouldn't. You belong here.'

John gazed up at Jack.

'And you, too? Can we make it so? That we stay together?'

'If you want it so, then it must be made so.'

'Thank you.' John's eyes drooped shut. 'Do you think I can sleep for a moment while we await Master Edmund?'

For answer, Black Jack hugged him a little tighter, and John fell into a flickering sleep.

Master Edmund exhaled heavily.

'I chance that William has never considered me for a romantic lead before, but if we get this right, John, it could change everything for me.' He made a noise at the back of his throat. 'And you, too, of course.'

Jack rummaged through the piles of parchment whilst

Master Edmund shook his limbs out and made 'brrrrrr' sounds. John sat still. A strange feeling prickled in his stomach.

He wasn't familiar with Romeo and Juliet beyond the few lines Master Edmund had said at their first meeting, but he'd overheard a conversation when some of the actors had come to the house. John had recognised the voice of Viola ringing out, making the others laugh: 'The play failed today because no one believed that Romeo would ever leave Juliet's bed after I kissed Thomas like that.'

Would Master Edmund expect John to kiss him as part of their practice?

Jack offered some pages to Master Edmund, but the man waved them away.

'I have all my brother's words locked safe, right here.' He tapped his head and chest.

Black Jack sat on the floor next to John. He held the piece of paper between them and laid a finger at the top of the page, waiting for Master Edmund to speak.

John squinted at the words.

Were any of them 'kiss'? All the letters paired up and embraced each other. Why wasn't his reading improving? Maybe because he and Jack spent too much time like they had yesterday, making each other laugh with stupid impressions and silly conversation. These days, whenever Master Edmund found the two boys together, he would puff out his chest and boom that they were being 'idle.' It seemed to John, if they were both considered apprentices, he seemed to be of a different sort than Jack: Master Edmund was always calling for John and demanding that he recite his lines at a moment's notice.

Now John licked his lips. Master Edmund looked down at the boys, pulling on his beard.

'This won't do. Juliet is supposed to be speaking from a balcony. Stand on the desk. But be sure not to touch anything. Fortunately, William is much more organised in business than he is in writing. Well, somewhat more organised. At any rate, he has a good instinct on when to move to avoid taxes and debts.'

Black Jack lifted John on to the desk.

He balanced on his tiptoes, staring down at his feet to avoid knocking any of Master William's work.

'No, no. You must gaze at me for it to be in any way convincing. Look at nothing but me.'

John checked his feet again, then raised his eyes to Master Edmund. He felt as if his clothes were shrinking, suffocating his skin.

'Not good, but better. You look like you're expecting me to kill you. We're lucky that very few of the audience will understand the subtleties of facial acting, so all we really need to do is get your voice nice and loud.' Master Edmund tapped his fingers together. 'This isn't right, though. You shouldn't be on the desk yet. I don't see you at first. So you will hide behind Jack and then he'll lift you up on the balcony and we'll both pretend that I haven't seen that happen. Jack will act the part of the wall of the Capulet house. Now I will prepare privately while you, Jack, school John in the scene.'

Master Edmund marched out of the room. Jack caught John's eye and nodded at the door. Through it, they could hear Master Edmund doing his 'preparations,' which seemed to mainly involve repeating 'I am an actor' in various different voices and volumes.

Black Jack helped him down and John gulped:

'Jack, quick! Please, what do I do if Master Edmund tries to kiss me?'

Before he could reply, Master Edmund came back into the room, bellowing, 'He jests at scars that never felt a wound.'

Black Jack lifted John onto the table, but it was not fast enough for Master Edmund. He made them repeat the entrance four times before he was satisfied. Even then, he only recited two lines of the speech before moaning that John looked like he was standing on a gallows rather than gazing out over a garden. Jack suggested that he run out and buy some flowers to help John's imagination—In the end, they settled on some marjoram found in the kitchen to at least give the scent of a garden.

When Master Edmund left the room again, Jack picked up the marjoram between his thumb and forefinger and sniffed it, then dropped it on the desk, chuckling:

'If only he knew the things you see, hey, Fair One? He wouldn't make such a fuss about creating the right atmosphere.'

John pressed his lips together. Did Black Jack's merriment

mean that there was no kissing; or that John was silly to be worried about the kissing; or that he'd forgotten all about John's question?

Master Edmund marched back into the room and shouted out his first line. Black Jack was swift lifting John up, and after all the practice, John could place his feet without needing to look down. He gazed only at Master Edmund, and as Master Edmund boomed through the speech, he tried to think about moonlit gardens. But his hands unconsciously clenched into fists and his stomach twisted...

'It is as if you're not listening to a word I am saying. When I say, 'See how she leans her cheek upon her hand,' do you not think it would make more sense if you were leaning your cheek upon your hand?'

John put both hands up to his face.

'No, not now; when I say it. Actually, it should be before I say it, otherwise why would Romeo say it, if Juliet wasn't already doing it?'

John's head drooped.

'I'm sorry, Master Edmund. Let me try again.'

But he didn't get better. His memory failed him so that he couldn't even recall his first words, the simple, 'Ay me,' without Jack repeating it.

Finally Master Edmund sighed, his shoulders slumping.

'I do not think we will be able to present this to William after all. I fear all our work has been wasted—if anything, you seem to have gotten worse. Perchance I am not as good a master to you as I hoped to be. I do not like to say it, but maybe I should talk to William about moving your apprenticeship to another person who may be able to...'

Black Jack put a hand on his arm.

'You are right, as ever, Master Edmund. I do believe that your natural talent combined with your powerful voice is intimidating to Fair John. He is nervous acting in your great presence. Maybe I should familiarise John with the part alone so as not to waste your precious time, and then when he is ready he can perform the scene with you.' As he spoke, Jack guided Master Edmund out of the room. 'By the morrow, John will be ready to receive your most excellent advice on how to be a fine actor like yourself.' Black Jack closed the door on Master Edmund and turned back to John with a half-smile. The other trembled.

'I thought for a moment you were going to tell him he should be rid of me.'

'Don't be a fool. You're having a bad day; it happens to everyone. And you know the beautiful thing about this new life of ours? When you have a bad day, the only result is that Master Edmund is a little disappointed that he can't show off to his brother. And tomorrow he'll be even more pleased when you are back to your usual perfect self. Indeed, he'll be heartily proud and believe himself to be the best teacher in all of London.' He looked over the sheets of paper. 'Now, you stay up there in your balcony, fair Juliet, and if you can use your imagination and do without me playing the wall, I'll be your Romeo.' He gave an ornate bow.

John smiled. 'I think you're better as the wall than I am as Juliet.'

'Let us see about that, shall we?' He scanned the lines. 'I cannot be bothered to say all these long speeches, all that'll do is give me a sore throat.' He prodded his finger at a page, and held it up for John to see. 'Although this one captures you, Fair One. 'She speaks, yet she says nothing; what of that?' ' Jack laughed and continued reading to himself.

John felt his cheeks burn.

'Stop jesting and tell me what this play is about. All I know is that Master Edmund's character shouts a lot, and mine... ' His blush deepened down his neck, and his mouth went dry.

Black Jack arched an eyebrow and stared at John with amused, questioning eyes.

'You do know that Master Edmund is not a good actor? Romeo is not supposed to yell like that.'

John swallowed.

'Master Edmund is a fine actor. Master William cannot give him the best parts because the other actors aren't talented enough to recognise his skill and would accuse... '

'Yes. Yes. You are a very loyal apprentice. But... ' Jack shook his head. 'It is of no matter now. Just forget about Master Edmund for a moment and start fresh. Romeo and Juliet have met and fallen in love with each other and everyone thinks it is wrong.'

'Why do they... '

'Don't fret the details yet. Focus on love, focus on it being thought wrong.' Jack flicked between the pages. 'Your perfect memory isn't working so well today, so what say we learn it bit by bit and then put it together. This is an easy few lines to start off with...'

He rushed the words out, slurring them together and speaking in his thickest accent. 'Mybounty is asboundlessasthe-sea, Myloveasdeep; the moreIgivet thee, ThemoreIhaveforboth are infinite.'

John spoke in the clear theatre voice that Master Edmund was teaching him.

'My bounty is as boundless as the sea.'

'And the rest.'

'My love as deep... '

Instead of vanishing, the words hung in the air; John watched as they grew and blossomed into a chain of flowers between his chest and Jack's.

'Very good, but admit you need me to repeat the rest.'

In his own, old voice, the one he fell into when he was tired, the one his Da had tried to beat out of him, John said softly:

'My bounty is as boundless as the sea,
My love as deep; the more I give to thee,
The more I have, for both are infinite.'

He closed his eyes. When he opened them, the words had gone, and Black Jack gazed up at him with a smile John had never seen before.

'I'm fine now,' John said. 'You can teach me the scene in the usual way, from the beginning, pointing out all the words on the paper. I will learn to match them up with the letters one day.' He looked down at his hands. They were clenched together, the knuckles white. 'You didn't answer me before. The thing that was making me so nervous... is there any kissing in this scene?'

There was silence. Then Jack's voice, soft and light. 'No. There's no kissing.'

John felt his shoulders sink with something—with relief, of course. For what else could it have been?

Behind the stage at the Globe, Jack and John stood at the edge of the milling crowd of actors. It was hard to imagine how all these plain-looking people could transform into the magic John had witnessed. Today's performance was a play by Master William Shakespeare's friend and John wondered if Master William had sucked up so much of the faeries' powers that there was none left for other playwrights, or if this was what it always looked like backstage?

The area was packed with people in various stages of undress and make up, half in ordinary street clothes, and half in finer costumes. They were like bread being left to rise, John thought, before it grew from sticky dough into something wonderful and nourishing. The air was heavy with a smell that was a somehow not-unpleasing mixture of male bodies and flowery perfumes. John couldn't see where the flowers came from; it must've been some faerie magic.

'Everyone, if I can please have your attention. These are my apprentices, John and Jack,' Master Edmund called. None of the people rushing around the tiring room so much as paused to glance at them.

John looked down at his feet and watched them edge closer to Jack. He'd soon be standing on his friend if he wasn't careful. His faerie was around, but there was no reassurance to be found there. The hobgoblin was amusing itself the same way it had been for most of the day; floating around Jack's head and flicking his ear until Jack unconsciously swatted it away, spinning it through the air with a wide grin on its face. John was intrigued—on some level, his friend could sense the faerie, even if he couldn't see it. But right now he was too concerned with himself to worry about Jack and the faerie. It felt like a whole flurry of magical creatures were pounding at his ears as he tried to listen and watch and keep track of the people darting about.

Master Edmund stood where he was, gazing around mutely. His leg jittered, and his tongue flickered over his lips.

'Mayhaps, you could tell us what they are called, Master Edmund,' Jack suggested.

'Yes, yes, of course.' Master Edmund pointed to people and began to reel off names. 'There's Ezekial, I have no idea why he is wearing that donkey's head. I'm almost completely certain it does not appear in today's play. Those three smoking and drinking when they should be checking their cues are one of the Edwards, Old Thomas and Young Tom. The boy called just Thomas doesn't appear to be here yet. He runs late so often, I don't know why anyone puts up with it. I am always on time.'

John nodded dutifully as he tried to figure out which man might be Edward, which Old Thomas and which Young Tom, when all three had identical mouse-brown beards and wrinkles.

'Thomas's good friend Nathan over there is much more reliable. And you can see Samuel, Joseph, Toby, and Henry, together as always. Creating trouble for everyone else I have no doubt. Kendred and Augustin are already in full costume, which is good to see. They like to think they're more important than anyone else, but they're a burden, to be honest with you. Obviously, you know William, and the man he is talking with is Ben, Ben Jonson. I'll approach them on my own for now. Ben, I'm afraid, can be quite harsh; it is said that he killed a man, and he'll be vexatious today. Be careful around him.'

'Master Edmund, could you please repeat the... ' John's voice died away as Master Edmund strode off. '...names.'

Jack slapped him on the back. 'No fear, Fair One. We will have more fun finding out for ourselves.'

John watched Master Edmund for a moment. He hovered behind Master William, coughing ever more loudly as Master William and Ben leaned in to each other, whispering. Poised by his shoulder, Master William's blue faerie stretched his large wings and Master Edmund stepped back as if to give the faerie more space, though he looked down at his feet with a frown as he did so.

The man called Ben glanced for a moment at John, then gave him a nod of acknowledgment, as if they were already well acquainted. John found himself curtseying before he quickly corrected himself, but the man was already looking away, nodding attentively at whatever Master William was saying.

'Do you think Master Ben Jonson has really killed someone?' John said.

Black Jack shrugged. 'Most likely, it's nigh impossible to have a gathering of any number without a few scoundrels, murderers, and thieves being present. I should know.'

As John continued to watch, the beautiful blue faerie made the slightest movement of its head. An azure glow surrounded the hobgoblin and it was yanked off Jack's shoulder by an invisible force and hauled across the room. The hobgoblin snarled in the direction of the blue faerie, and beckoned John sullenly with its clawed fingers.

'I think we are supposed to go in this direction.' John went to take Jack's hand, but tugged on his sleeve instead.

The hobgoblin stopped above the head of a young man applying make-up. John blinked several times as the actor's outline sharpened. His heart thumped and his tongue felt like a lump of meat in his mouth. He remembered how enchanting the boy-girl's presence had been on stage; how she'd brought both loss and hope to life.

Words tumbled out before he'd even decided what to say.

'It is an honour to meet you. You are beautiful, wise, brave and intelligent, Viola.' John half-curtsied, half-bowed.

Viola turned with a coquettish smile, but became more man than girl on seeing John. He rolled his eyes. 'Oh, you're Edmund's toy. I'm sure you're very amusing, but this is my space and my time. Piss off and annoy someone else.'

John's face flamed, but Black Jack was already sliding between John and Viola, bristling with anger.

'John is an apprentice at the Shakespeares' house, and you'd do well to respect him. The minute he steps on stage, no-one is going to notice you again.'

Viola's face flushed and there was a brief flash in his eyes, but suddenly he was a she again, laughing a girlish laugh.

'Oh, I like you. Very much.' She leaned backwards, rocking her chair onto two legs, to peer around Jack and address John. 'Tell me exactly what I need to do to get one for myself.'

A portly man with grey whiskers who happened to be passing put a hand on the back of Viola's chair and straightened her up.

'You get on with your painting. No man's going to fall in love with you half done.' He gave John a nod. 'And you—don't look so worried or you'll wrinkle before your time. This one is all mouth and is entirely incapable of stealing your friend away from you.'

Here Viola gave a long speech all about the qualities of her mouth and its ability to steal whoever she wanted away from anyone in the world. The people around listened and laughed, even as they talked over her.

Viola created a merry circle around her, and John and Jack seemed to have been included without asking or being asked. Men clapped them on the back and introduced themselves, promising to talk properly at the alehouse, after the business of the play had finished. They stared unabashedly into John's face and joked about the bets that had been laid about what Master Edmund's apprentices would look like.

Black Jack sparked with all his normal, easy charm, but he watched Viola with a wary smile. John stood on tiptoe and whispered in his ear.

'How did you know that being cross with Viola would make everyone like us?'

Jack's eyes gleamed and he grinned.

'Experience, my Fair One. I can't give you all my secrets at once.'

An argument burst into life on the other side of the room and suddenly the air was heavy with curses. Jack put a hand on the small of John's back and leaned in. In a lower voice, his lips barely moving, he said, 'In truth, it wasn't a play. It was a slip of my emotions. I didn't like hearing her speak to you in that manner. I'm sorry. It is only your constant luck that made it turn out fine. But stay alert with this sort.'

John looked around at all the bodies moving around with purpose. Normally, he would have feared the noise and bustle, the strangers, but to John it seemed nothing like the taverns and streets with their stinking, festering crowds. Even the ongoing dispute was not as loud or fierce as the market traders outshouting each other for customers. He would have to ask his friend later why he'd felt the need to warn him against the theatre people—especially when they'd been comfortably living with the Shakespeares for so long.

His attention snapped back to Viola. The actor had finished talking to the crowd and was hastily trying to finish his preparations, but the hobgoblin kept knocking the lotion out of his hand. John bent down to retrieve it when it fell on the floor, and so knocked into Viola, who was doing the same. Viola swore under her breath, but in a hushed voice and with her eyes on Jack, rather than John.

Head bowed, John was about to pass the pot to Viola, when an image of the actor with peeling skin and hair falling out in clumps flashed before him. He closed his eyes and when he opened them, Viola's hand was held out—beautiful, yet with patches of green peeping through the porcelain skin. He snatched the pot backwards as Viola tried to take it.

'You shouldn't use this. It's poison.'

Viola pinched the top of her nose.

'Which bush were you found under, country boy? I need the ceruse to whiten my skin.' She pronounced 'boy' as if it was supposed to be an insult.

'I can make you an ointment that will enhance your beauty far more than this, and it won't hurt your skin.' His voice came out strong and clear, though his limbs were weak.

What was he doing, arguing with her like this?

'What, right now? Can you magic this miracle salve of yours onto my face before the performance?'

John shook his head at Viola and reluctantly passed the actor the pot.

'Thank you most kindly,' Viola said with an exaggerated bow.

John turned to see if Master Edmund had noticed how badly he was doing, but it was Master William who was staring at him. As their eyes met, the playwright smiled and John was transported into a summer meadow, where he lay by a trickling stream watching a pair of swans sail majestically past. Then John blinked.

Of course, Master William was not looking at him, but was still deep in conversation with Ben Jonson.

It had only been a second, John felt sure. But somehow, next to him, Black Jack was now in the midst of a completely different story. And Viola had finished painting her face, and was dressed in a gown and wig.

'Andrew! There's a tear in my skirt! What kind of fool are you to give it to me in this state!'

A man at the far side of the room who was fiddling with another costume shouted:

'It was fine when I dressed you. If you've damaged it with your clumsiness I swear it's coming out of your wages.'

'I am not clumsy!'

Viola cursed at him across the room, and Andrew cursed cheerfully back.

John realised he was smiling at the sort of stand-off that would normally have sent him scurrying to Jack's side.

The hobgoblin pointed to the rip and handed John a needle and thread. John dropped to his knees and began sewing, the faerie making his hands quick and delicate. The fabric was dyed in rich colours and more expensive than any he'd touched before.

And then, John was home with Jetta, the smoke from the hearth twisting around them, the scents of Ma's cooking in the pot above the fire. Jetta didn't speak but she didn't need to; he understood his twin's gratitude as John repaired her clothing before Da got back. If John failed, Da would be angry and yell at Jetta for growing too fast, forcing him to find coin to buy new fabric. Then he'd like as not beat John for not growing at all. But the hobgoblin helped him so he wouldn't fail. For tonight at least, he and Jetta would be safe.

John looked up when he finished, hoping for one of his sister's rare smiles. But it was Viola who stared down at him. Some part of him understood that Viola had been ranting at him, demanding to know what he was up to. But now the actor appeared merely bemused.

'In truth now, what are you?' He called over to Master Edmund, 'Well, have you checked that your boy apprentice is actually a boy?'

Laughter rippled around John, and a shiver went through him. It wasn't a vision. Just memory overlaying memory: Eda and her friends singing songs as they passed his home; the wide-eyed excitement of the other children when they managed to get him pinned against a wall; the adults walking by, not-caring or approving; Da, glaring at him.

But this wasn't the village. Da wasn't here. And, John told himself, he should be thankful for that. For what would Da think, seeing him now amongst these painted strangers?

Black Jack pulled him to his feet.

'Don't even think of coming near John in that manner,' he

said in his roughest accent. Then with a wink, he added lightly, 'Unless you want to be driven to Bedlam with jealousy. For not only is he a prettier woman than you can ever make yourself up to be, he's also more man than you could ever dream of.'

The laughter rolled on, and Viola joined in.

'Oh, I think we all know who's jealous here. And don't presume to know my dreams. I can dream pretty big, Red.'

Voices that John's spinning mind could not attach to individual men were merrily chastising Viola.

'You haven't got time for your games; why don't you make sure you know your cues for once!'

'Give up teasing your replacement. You're still too young for bitterness and envy.'

'He has to put up with Edmund; try and show him that the rest of us are better than that. Let's make the boy welcome.'

'I am making him welcome,' Viola protested. She pouted at John. 'Tell them I am making you welcome.' Then before John could reply, she smiled in a way that somehow made John glance at Jack, standing next to him. 'I'm not working tomorrow, but come the day after that with your special ointment and I'll let you put it on me.'

John opened his mouth to speak, but he was already being pulled across the room by the dresser called Andrew.

'I don't know what is going on at this company; it is all madness. The way you stitched that fabric, clearly you should be my apprentice, not Edmund's.'

John looked back over his shoulder at Jack, who motioned for him to follow the man, while he remained talking to Viola. The hobgoblin danced alongside John, grinning and picking at his sleeves. The man leading him grumbled on.

'But no, why do the sensible thing? Old Andrew is left to fare on his own, no one thinks of me.'

Old Andrew was slim, but his face was round, and from the light growth on his lips it looked like he was just starting his first beard.

'I can help you?' John said.

'Yes, you most certainly can.'

After that, John was too busy following Andrew's instructions to even think about Jack. He sewed and fitted costumes before, during and even after the play, while Andrew was ensuring that everything was returned and no actor wandered off with clothing that belonged to the theatre. It was easy, joyous work, as if he knew all these people and had been doing it his whole life. But he had the hobgoblin guiding his fingers; he had his calming memories of his sister; and even if he didn't have time to check, he knew Jack was there, somewhere, watching over him.

That night, Jack and John gazed out of the window of their room, at the stars. This had become their habit of late, before Black Jack disappeared out on his own; or, as was much more frequent recently, they lay down to sleep together.

Sometimes they made up stories about the shapes and patterns of the stars, but tonight, John could only talk about one thing. He knew he was repeating what he'd said on the walk home from the Globe, and during their meal, and while they had gotten changed for sleep, but he couldn't help himself.

The words danced through his soul.

'Andrew said I had the most skilled hands he'd ever seen, and of course it was all the hobgoblin, but I couldn't tell him that, could I? I can't, can I, Jack? I only told you because you're you. Even though the theatre is surrounded by magic, I don't think any of them know about it. Apart from Master William: I've never seen a faerie follow someone around like the blue faerie follows him. But they are all magical people, aren't they? When I first saw them, I thought they all looked ordinary, but they're not. It was the first time they'd all met me and they treated me like I was their friend. And Viola is so beautiful, isn't she? She was so beautiful in the play, but having the honour to stand so close to her... '

'I heard Ben Jonson say that Viola's performance was flawed and that she had no rhythm.'

'Maybe Master Jonson meant compared to Viola's normal perfection? And what about Master Edmund? He did really well, didn't he? He told me that it was one of his best roles.'

'He was indeed mightily proud of the way he delivered his two lines.'

'I wish I could've watched the play, but Andrew kept me so

busy. Did you see much of it, or did they keep you busy too? Do you know that Andrew never watches the plays? He says they're boring and that bowling is the only good way to spend your free time. He says that if I continue to prove useful, he'll take me one night. Have you ever been bowling? I don't think it can be anything like the theatre, but it might be fun to try. Sorry. I've been talking all the time, haven't I?'

Black Jack gave a half smile.

'You've a right to. I bore you oft enough with my constant chatter.'

'I'm boring you? You never bore me.'

'Because you're lost in some far off faerie world where my voice can't reach you. But no, you're not boring me. Let me comb your hair out and I will listen to you talk about your theatre folk every night to eternity.'

John lowered his head, hoping that Jack wouldn't see his blush in the moonlight.

'They're our theatre folk.'

'Ay. Mayhaps. If you like.'

Despite what Jack had said, John didn't talk any more about the tiring room and the people they'd met, but sat quiet and still as Jack stroked his hair down over his back and started to comb it.

'I don't know why you always want to comb my hair. I do it much faster than you.'

'Yes, you do it too fast... Anyway, I hardly ever ask.'

Outside the window were the normal animal sounds of the city: dogs howling, cats yowling, and the snarling-purring of the night beast that only John could hear. But in their room was nothing save the kiss of the comb and Jack's hands, sliding softly through John's hair.

It's just like when I used to plait Jetta or Ma's hair for them, he tried to tell himself.

But he knew it wasn't like that. It wasn't like that at all.

Black Jack and John peered through the doors' gap and watched the noble party that milled around in the huge room, waiting for their private performance.

The ceilings were painted with vines and fruit, which made John's heart yearn for the real thing. He knew he should be in awe of the building they were in, Whitehall Palace. Black Jack and Master Edmund certainly were: In fact, almost everyone in the company had joined in to point out particulars, tell different stories all at the same time, and relish each detail as they explained it to John. They were all aglow with the honour of being asked to act here, and he nodded in the right places and made the right sounds of amazement, but later, when they were back alone, he told Jack how his pleasure had come not from seeing a painting of a long-dead king, or staring up at the architecture of the high ceilings, but somewhere deeper, more personal.

He wasn't scared of this new place.

His heart didn't thump, his hands didn't get clammy, his legs didn't tremble. He didn't walk every step terrified it was all going to collapse on him. Jack was the only one who could understand how significant this was, and John imagined his friend's eyes sparkling as he told him.

And though it was harder to explain, he also told his friend how it felt odd performing a play indoors, however grand and important the building. The magic belonged outside, where the words could fly free, up to the faeries dancing across the sky. Performing inside was like putting a deer in chains. But that was all for later. Now he spoke quietly to Jack, admiring the fine embroidery and handsomely dyed fabrics the gentlewomen were wearing. Occasionally, he tried to comment about the gentlemen's fashion so as to appear interested in that too, but Jack only shrugged.

'I'm afraid all I see is goods that can be turned into coin, and my mind busies itself working out which parts I could lift away. Would you rather Andrew were here to converse with you about all these costumes?'

'I think Andrew would dress all the actors in sacking for the ease, if he could get away with it. He actually asked Master William if he'd ever considered having his characters naked, as it'd represent much better what man really was.'

He expected his friend to laugh, but Jack only said:

'Your Viola, then? That one definitely likes fineries.'

'Nay, I only want you here... if you don't mind me talking on so.'

'You surely know I like the sound of your voice. I remember how silent you were when we first met, how heartily I wanted you to speak to me.'

It felt as if Jack had more to say; that if John listened hard enough he'd hear the unspoken words. Instead, he whispered:

'We should return to the others. We've been away too long. Andrew will want my help.'

'It's Master Edmund, not Andrew, you answer to. You work harder than any 'prentice I know, managing to get yourself a second Master, when most are busy cosying up to their Mistress, or doing me a favour ganging up on the streets, calling Clubs, and keeping the constables well occupied.'

There was a sad tone to Jack's voice, and John gave him a sideways glance. Perhaps it was unfair, always expecting his friend to be happy when the world was so sad. But Jack's way of sauntering through life made John feel safe. He coped with the Butcher's shadow in his dreams, and the nightmares from his previous life, because he could open his eyes and know that Jack was there.

John pushed his worries aside, keeping his voice light.

'All the time we've spent together, and I still can't understand half that you say. Is calling Clubs even a real thing, or have you just made it up?'

Jack grinned.

'Don't flatter yourself so much, Fair One. Though if I had conceived of making up a whole language just to impress you, I might well have done it.' He pinched John's knee and went on. 'Perhaps with all the time we've spent together, it's me who gets confused—thinking by now I can talk to you like I would any normal person, rather than this simple, faerie-seeing, Bedlam-destined country gull.' As he spoke, Jack poked John in the ribs, under his arms, beneath his chin. John batted Jack's hands away, covering his mouth to muffle his laughter. 'Master William clearly made a mistake allowing you to come today. You're still more used to sheep than fine folk. Look, the Queen is coming and you've got the giggles.' Black Jack stopped tickling and pointed through the gap in the door.

John expected a trick; as far as he could tell, Jack hadn't even been glancing in the right direction. But there she was, amongst elegant attendants—a woman in a huge, white gown, heavy with jewels, walking stiffly towards a large, gold chair at the front of the room. Jack and Master Edmund had given him such lectures about what you could and could not say and do regarding the Queen, with Jack recounting the grisly punishments that awaited if you spoke about her in the wrong way. Now that he was here before her, John hesitated to speak at all. She was so different than what he had been expecting. Shorter. More human? But of course, he told himself, this wasn't the Faerie Queene. The Faerie Queene, if indeed she truly existed, would never live in such a city. He'd long ago accepted that he wasn't going to find her in London. Indeed, it was strange remembering that his whole purpose in running to London had been to find her. How little he'd thought of her since he'd begun working in the theatre.

'She looks better than last time I saw her. Not that I was paying much mind: I was working the crowd while she was doing her yearly procession. You think I don't notice these things, but I do. The wind must have been blowing the wrong way, because the air was full of her stink. Rotting just as badly as any of us.'

John frowned. Surely Jack was teasing?

He squinted at the distant, elegant figure, and the world shimmered. Then suddenly, they were on a dirty city street. The queen wore tattered rags; her jewels were stolen, her eyes sank back into her skull, her hair had fallen out. Nothing was left of it but a few grey wisps, and her skin had melted into poxes and scars. She bared toothless gums and yelled a single battle cry in a voice like rusty iron. 'Attack, my Boys, attack!' The Roaring Boys in all their sickness appeared around her, running forwards with a speed that defied their ailing bodies. The city fell to their stench.

And now, the queen sat on a throne of squirming rats and bones.

John blinked, but didn't return to Jack's side. He floated in the mist above the Thames. She was there with him, but a young woman now, dressed in nothing but a smock and pearls. He recognised his own embroidery around the hems of her garment. Her hair was the same red as Jack's, blown around her face by a wind whirling from all directions. The skin of her face was freckled in exactly the same pattern as Jack's, but where he was sunbrowned, she was pale. And her eyes were dark and old like Master William's.

'Do not linger here with me.' Her lips did not move, but the voice was hers, the same one that had shouted out the battle cry. 'You have a gift, John, to be wherever you need to be. Go there.'

He opened his mouth to say that he needed to be with her; that he'd run from his home, and travelled through cold nights to find her. But the mist whooshed down his throat before he could speak. It condensed into droplets of water. Freezing wetness surrounded him. Was he drowning? No. Warm hands on his waist lifted his head above the surface.

Black Jack was grinning at him.

'How's my little mermaid? I told you there was nothing to fear; that I am the best Master in the world. See, I've even taught you to swim.'

On one side, water stretched out forever, until somewhere unreachable, the green-blue sea merged into the sky. On the other side, white-tipped waves caressed a sandy beach, and crabs with gleaming shells darted sideways among the rocks. The sea. Just as Jack had described it to him. He put his arms around Jack's neck.

'Your merboy learnt to swim, despite having you as a teacher, because he is most wondrously clever.'

'I cannot argue. My merperson is indeed most wondrous in every way.' Jack tilted his head towards John.

John closed his eyes and his lips seemed to part of their own accord. He smelt spice, and apples, and felt Jack's breath.

But it was Da's voice that he heard, as close as Jack himself.

'I knew you were no man. And now I know what you really are, a...'

'Fair One? Please speak. Are you ailing? I cannot tell if it is one of your ordinary blushes, or if you are flushed with illness.'

John hesitated to open his eyes, but when he finally did, they were back where they had always been, standing outside the doors.

'I'm sorry. I... it overwhelmed me for a moment... the Queen.' He glanced at the doors; the gap between them had closed. The play had started: The Merry Wives of Windsor.

He tried to shake himself free of this unsettling feeling of unrealness.

'We should get back. Master Edmund'll want to see us before his part. I'm glad Master William asked him to be first servant instead of second servant this time.' He lowered his head and turned away, unsure where to turn, where to walk.

'It was heartily generous of him. Especially after Master Edmund dropped the hamper last time and tumbled Thomas off the stage and into the groundlings.' Jack linked an arm through John's, looking at him strangely. 'Are you certain you're not ailing?'

'I am... bene.' He leaned up against Black Jack. They started ambling along the large, wood panelled hall. 'I know Master Edmund was secretly hoping to play Falstaff... '

'Yes, he did mention that secret hope a few times, didn't he?'

'But if First Servant goes well, perhaps he won't be disappointed in the end.'

'The only way to avoid disappointment is to hope for nothing.'

'You have to hope for something, Red One. Hope is life.'

John listened as Black Jack tried to explain why Master Edmund would be laughed at for all the wrong reasons. Now and then the world dimmed and silence rushed in; and John would glance around, certain that they were being watched. But only the empty eyes of the portraits stared back at him.

We cannot hold mortality's strong hand

Jack held an oyster to John's lips; John tilted his head back and swallowed it without thinking. It was only as he watched the other toss the empty shell to the side of the street that he remembered how special it had felt when Jack had given them to him for the first time. He moved his tongue around his mouth, capturing the remains of the taste. It wasn't something he could explain even to himself, but it seemed essential to always be aware of how precious everything was. To savour every moment. To balance becoming used to oysters with the stink of the street.

The noise and stench of the London crowds no longer plunged him into terrifying visions, but he still walked close to Jack. A habit he'd picked up in those early days of fear and had never broken. He glanced at his friend, watched Jack spread his arms wide: He was in the middle of a particularly animated speech, trying to convince him why today's brutal Titus Andronicus was better than the romantic misunderstandings of yesterday's Much Ado about Nothing.

'You can't deny the satisfaction of everyone being punished who needed to be punished, Fair One. It happens so rarely in real life, it's bene to spend an afternoon pretending to believe things work out how they're supposed to.'

'Jack, it's too much pain, far too much! It's much nicer to

spend an afternoon pretending that people never do anything that deserves such punishment and that everyone ends up happily with the person they love.' John's stomach tightened just thinking of how palpable the tragedy had felt today. 'When Viola had to act her tongue being chopped out and... '

Jack laughed.

'Ay, that was a good bit. Imagine that one never being able to say another word.'

He thumped Jack's arm.

'That's not funny. It was horrible, and it made me feel sick, even knowing it wasn't real. You can talk as much as you want, but there's no argument, comedies are much better than tragedies.'

Jack wrapped an arm around John's waist.

'Where've you hid the one who thinks I'm the wisest person in all of London and agrees with everything I say?'

The question was light, and John paused, unsure whether to answer it in kind, but he'd barely opened his mouth before someone else had captured Black Jack's attention. His friend gripped John's arm and turned them back the way they'd come. It took John a moment to recognise the finely dressed lady they walked behind. She turned them into a tavern that seemed far too rough for her garments.

'Bess.' Jack muttered, followed by a curse.

'Bess?' John smiled. 'We see all the theatre folk now, but none of your friends anymore. I miss Moll and would... '

'Well in my world, people don't visit each other without a reason.' Black Jack cursed again. 'But the problem isn't Bess, it's that she spied us and I didn't notice until she wanted me to.'

There was no more discussion as they entered the tavern. Bess sat at a table facing the door, as if she'd been sitting there patiently waiting for them for hours. The only other person at the table was her friend, Nick. John had met him a few times since that first day when Nick had begged off of him, but today, the man's face was so contorted, he didn't recognise him.

Jack sat opposite the two and greeted them as if nothing was amiss. Bess replied in a warm voice.

'It's been a while, Black Jack. A long while.'

John stared at Nick with dismay, barely hearing the chatter, as Bess and Jack carried on in their mysterious cant—

'You don't look well,' John whispered to him.

And the other smiled, 'Ay, I don't.'

Bess tugged on a lock of Nick's hair.

'Don't lie, you old cur, you know you're as handsome as ever and can break a poor girl's heart with a single look.' She sighed and something changed in her expression that made her look as pained as Nick. Bess turned back to Jack in a heavy tone. 'You and I wouldn't have got this far, if we didn't know how to live in this world... And yet here I am giving all our coin... and more... away to men who call themselves healers, but they're the same as us, just tricking and lying. I know the game well, but I listen to them go on about their special leeches and how the bleeding that's always made Nick feel worse will now suddenly make him feel better. It's my stupid heart, overruling all sense for a scrap of hope. Even if it only lasts for a small time. Until the latest poxy physick has worked his way through all my coin and suddenly has no more need to talk about miracle cures.' She shook her head and her normal expression returned. 'But you don't have sympathy for a weak woman's heart, do you, Black Jack? You're far too canny to ever let yourself fall in love!'

She laughed, Nick made a croaking sound that might have been a laugh, and a beat later Jack laughed too.

'There's nothing weak about you, Bess,' Jack said. 'Don't try playing that old trick of the damsel needing rescue with me.'

Bess exchanged an affectionate look with Nick. 'Far too canny,' she repeated.

They laughed again, resumed a light banter, but John couldn't concentrate. His ribs felt cracked and broken, though he didn't know why. He hadn't been pulled into one of his violent visions. It was Nick whose eyes had a distant look, as if he was slipping between worlds.

Yet watching him hurt John. Not just seeing another human in pain, but the memory of Ma and Jetta, who'd both had similar expressions near the end. His heart thumped painfully. He looked around, hoping that the hobgoblin would show and either reassure him or warn him away from what he was about to do.

But nothing.

And thinking of Ma and Jetta should have frightened him away, but his eyes still flicked to Bess.

'I can help,' John said carefully. 'I don't know about leeches and bleeding, but I know the best leaves and flowers that can calm pain. Jack can help me gather them. We'll have to go outside the city, the ones people sell inside the walls are useless.'

Almost short of breath, he listed the things he'd need and the type of places they grew. All three stared at him: Bess with interest, Nick with unfocused, cloudy eyes, and Jack with something he couldn't identify. He hoped he sounded confident and in control. His mind was threatening to undo him with memories of how Da had been after Ma and Jetta died.

Would Bess be the same if he couldn't help Nick?

Would Jack?

Did everyone have that much rage and hate hidden deep inside them?

The need to make others hurt when they were in pain?

No, he didn't believe that. He knew better than any that Da had been angry all the time, and that the death of their family had merely given him a reason to not hold back. Bess wasn't like Da.

And even if she was... it didn't matter. Someone was in need and if there was any chance that John could ease Nick's suffering, he had to take it.

Bess's focus on him made him want to crawl under the table, but John kept on talking and explaining what he could do. His voice grew hoarse.

When he finished, Bess clapped her hands together, then entwined her fingers as if she was preparing to pray.

'Tell me more,' she said. 'Tell me everything.'

Black Jack was unusually quiet as they walked back to the Shakespeares'.

'Are you cross with me?' John asked.

'Why would I be? For committing us to days of work going around collecting all your magical leaves when you should be concentrating on your apprenticeship? For giving Bess false hope? For making Nick feel he has to endure more treatment for the sake of Bess when all he wants is to rest?'

John bit his lip.

'I... I... the faerie will help me... .' He took a deep breath. 'Even if it doesn't, I know enough. Viola keeps saying how much she loves the new skin lotion I made for her and I know healing herbs better than I know... I'm sorry, I should have spoken with you before I said anything.'

Jack squeezed his hand.

'Ignore my grumbling. Just be confident like you were in the tavern and you'll make me heartily proud of being your friend.'

They walked on and Jack chatted like he normally did.

The topic now was a cheery questioning of why the rats ran off the boats fine, but sailors wobbled as if they'd never walked on solid land before.

'Now who do you think is supposed to be the more advanced creature of the two?'

John laughed and listened as Jack rambled on, and he didn't mention the agreement he'd made with Bess and Nick again, or ask the one question that was sharpest in his own mind.

Neither a borrower nor a lender be;
for loan oft loses both itself and friend

Black Jack sat on the bench beside Bess. In the room above them something crashed followed by a scream. A shrill argument about money had been going on since him and John had arrived and it seemed to have finally reached its violent conclusion, but the only one to acknowledge the clamour was John. He gazed upwards, then at Jack, over at Nick. Then turned his attention back to his leaves and unguents. Jack watched him, thinking:

You can't save everyone, Fair One. Which was a sign of how much he'd changed. Once upon a time he would've said, 'You can't save anyone.' Bess poured them ale from a cracked piece of pottery. Stumps of bread lay on the table, but neither of them drank nor ate. They looked without looking at where John was tending to Nick.

Jack had hoped that a single visit would've got this itch to help out of John's system, but no, this friend acted as if it was normal to keep returning to a lost cause. Didn't they have enough to do to ensure their own survival? And for reasons he couldn't begin to fathom, Jack was indulging him.

Maybe an old attachment to Bess? He preferred the idea of an old obligation: it was more solid, less dangerous, could be repaid and forgotten. Before he'd proven himself, she had seen the potential of his quick hands and quicker tongue, and got him included in jobs at a time when everyone else viewed him as just another indistinguishable urchin who would live and die their brief little life without notice or care.

Not that many would notice or care much now, but...

His eyes stuck on John's delicate hands tending Nick's cracked, angry wound, and he was grateful for the sudden interruption of Bess's voice. It stopped his thoughts from meandering further.

'Do you understand any of what your John does? Nick sounded the liveliest he has for an age when he told me to stop fussing and let the angel do his work. Didn't he sound like his old self?' For once, Bess's whole face smiled, so different from the usual practised expression of people in their trade. They knew how to move their mouths to create the right impression, but if you looked at their eyes, those never changed. Always guarding. Always watching.

'Nick does appear to be having one of his better days,' Jack replied.

'Your John truly is an angel. After all the hard years you've been through, you've been blessed by Fortune to secure such a... '

'No one's an angel.' His voice firmly stopped her, while a secret, undisciplined part of him glowed as if the Queen herself had paid a compliment. And the same part of him chuckled back the answer he would never say out loud: John's no angel. He's a faerie-seeing, bound-for-Bedlam, oyster-guzzling, soft-hearted country idiot, who happens to have a future as the finest actor in London. And he's also my one true friend.

He didn't know what Bess's reply would have been to that, but her response to his harder tone was exactly what he expected.

Bess dropped into her lower working voice, lips barely moving as she turned her face away.

'What payment do you want?' she asked.

'He won't want anything.'

'Maybe. But you will.'

'When times are better for you.'

Jack looked up at the ceiling. A continual trickle of foul-smelling water dripped to the floor below. Mould crept across the wattle—the whole place was dank with the cold. He'd lived in much worse places and been grateful for the shelter, but

John belonged snug in the comfort of the Shakespeare lodgings. He shouldn't even be walking past such dirty, diseased houses, let alone spending time within them. He ached for the money he could've made from selling his treasure. At how hard he'd worked to set him up in the theatre crowd. If John caught ill here, it would all be for nothing. He needed to get him out of here quickly and not come back. But he'd had the exact same fears last time and here they were again. Jack ran his tongue over gritted teeth. Perhaps the Fair One truly was magical; wielding the power to render him stupid.

Take now: He realised that Bess had been talking to him and he had no idea what she had said. In a less friendly place, a slip like that ended everything. However tired he was, however long it had been since he had slept, he'd always managed to stay alert to everything. But that was before John.

Bess was sharp enough to sense a change in him, she was uncharacteristically, openly studying him, and Jack forced himself to concentrate on what she was saying.

'You're aware there's someone asking after the pair of you?' Her eyes darted to John for the briefest moment.

'Yes.' He'd known about the Butcher's enquiries for a while now, but had chosen not to mention them to John.

Why give him even more to fear than what already plagued him?

'Do you have any particular way you want me to misdirect? A rumour you need spreading? You're so quiet these days, most seem to believe you've left the city one way... or the other.' She mimed a noose around her neck. 'I was surprised to see you, all told ... but I did see you, so others will have.'

'Are there many that think we're still in the city?'

'There's a story of you taking control of the trade at the Globe. And another that you are playing the long game with some noble gentleman, but no agreement. I don't think any take it seriously. You know how people like to talk. And of course, there's all the usual chatter, including that you've run off with Kind Kate, even though she's seen working oft enough. Sometimes they say you've got a fair woman with you, sometimes a boy, sometimes a whole gang of country children. The tales are different enough to muddle any truth.' She touched him with the lightness of an expert thief, the tiny blade secreted under her thumbnail for cutting purses caressing an old, forgotten scar on the palm of his hand. It was a sign between them that had once meant it was time to start working a mark, but with time and use could now signify anything, from celebration to a warning. 'What are you doing? Are you in trouble or fortune, Black Jack?'

'Right now, I can be of no more help to you than I am already—bringing him and his herbs to heal Nick. I don't suppose it'll do any good, but it cheers them both in the moment.'

'You underestimate your friend. That's unlike you. I don't understand what the boy is doing, but Nick is faring well with him. He's far better now than after any of the overpriced whoreson, clotpole, wormfood physicks I foolishly paid for. But that was not what I asked you.'

'I cannot answer what you asked.'

They sat in silence listening to the soft murmurings as the boy looked after the man.

The night was quiet and cool after the stink of Bess and Nick's lodgings. Jack took them on a twisted, turning route back to the Shakespeares', telling himself it was for safety, but he knew: He was indulging in the simple pleasure of walking through the empty streets with John at his side. He remained as alert as if he was working: listening and watching, aware of every twitch of every starving thing huddled up in the shadows. But he was also conscious, beyond all else, of John's voice as a lulling melody that would be too easy to get lost in.

Who could have guessed that inside that trembling little alleyway mouse was someone with so much to say? All John had needed was someone to listen.

Jack grinned at the idea that he, the greatest rambler of nothings, had turned out to be this fated listener. Without changing his pace, or looking down at his friend, Jack said, 'Fair One, for once I am speaking both completely serious and entirely true. I hope you always know that you are most wondrous in every way.'

John stammered out some soft sounds, gazed down at his feet, and if it'd been daylight, no doubt Jack would have seen a rosy blush on his cheeks. It was his usual reaction to any compliment. But then he raised his head and laughed, taking Jack by surprise.

'Yes, I am wondrous, aren't I? Or rather, we are wondrous. That's what you mean, isn't it? I never thought I'd heal anyone again after Ma and Jetta, but with you I can do anything. You got me an apprenticeship. You taught me how to talk to people. And now you've trusted me to help with Nick.'

Jack wanted to echo John's words: We are wondrous together. But there was a tension in his stomach and a prickling down his spine. What had he been thinking, bringing them such a roundabout way home? He knew the Butcher was still asking after them; indeed, he could barely put it from his mind.

He protected John from his new theatre people, but it was a different kind of protectiveness, based for once, on something other than pure survival. Wouldn't that be just how life worked, if he most excellently shielded his innocent friend from Viola's harmless jesting, but then left him vulnerable to an attack on a night street, just for the pleasure of walking out with him?

He linked his arm through John's and hurried him home on a much more direct route. They were both quiet for the rest of the journey. And when they lay down to bed, they curled up together and lay like that for some time before John fell into the slow breathing of sleep.

Jack remained awake a little longer, waiting in case the other had a nightmare. He tried to think through the day and the things he needed to do tomorrow. He tried to plan ahead. But his usual quick mind seemed to have left him. He was becoming soft, dull, he thought. It was this easy, comfortable life that John had drawn him into.

At some point, he'd have to help Bess. He hadn't raised it with her tonight—he'd let himself be distracted by her talk of the rumours about him and John. But he'd heard that she was running with people who weren't good at their craft, and taking risks that one with her skill truly shouldn't need to. How to word it, so as not to offend her? And would she even listen to him, now that his life was so changed? That would take some careful consideration.

Moderate lamentation is the right of the dead,
excessive grief the enemy to the living

John sat on the floor in the corner of the shop with an open book in his lap. The printed letters jumped up and down, doubling the weight of the tome on his legs. He'd squinted at them so long that his eyes ached, and whenever he thought he'd made out something meaningful, it always turned into a story about Black Jack. However ignorant he remained about so much of the world, he was certain that scholars didn't waste their time writing about him and his friend...

He smiled, thinking though, that perhaps they should—it would make learning to read a lot easier. His mind floated away and he wondered idly if Black Jack would return home while he was out, and fret over where he and Master Edmund had gone. Why Master Edmund believed that sitting here staring at things he didn't understand was supposed to help him any more than sitting at home staring at things he didn't understand. Well, it was just another mystery of his new life. The words on the cue sheets, written in Master William's hand, were far friendlier than all these printed ones. But there was a warm smell to the shop that John liked.

Master Edmund had told him the bookseller was a friend of Master William's; that they both came from Stratford. John pressed his lips closed just before the question slipped out: so wasn't he a friend of Master Edmund's too? But maybe one shouldn't make the mistake of assuming that living with people made them your friends. Again, he found himself thinking of Jack. A shiver passed through him, and he shook it away.

Master Edmund seemed full of nervous energy today, pacing up and down, talking about Master William, and repeating the same things over and over. 'I got the ear ring before William, it was him that copied me,' he was now saying to the bookseller.

John mouthed the words along with Master Edmund as the man continued to talk. The hobgoblin, wracked with silent laughter, waddled after the man, mimicking his pompous gestures. John tried not to giggle.

'And I grew a beard first; it is mere chance that his happened to show before mine, but still, prating fools say that I'm trying to look like him. If it'd been different, if I'd been the oldest child, he would have followed me to London.' He stopped in front of John and tapped his foot. 'And I would have been a lot more gracious and generous to him. I would write him parts in particular to suit him. I would read all he presented to me and do all I could to aid him in his art.'

John liked to tell Jack whenever he picked up a new snippet of information, but the only knowledge Master Edmund would pass on today was that great talent was always neglected, especially by older brothers; and that all people were unappreciative idiots and undeserving fools.

Now he imagined Black Jack holding his belly and laughing as John mimicked one of Master Edmund's long lectures. He glanced guiltily up at his Master, who was still tapping his foot as the bookseller murmured some noncommittal reply.

The letters in the book pulled apart and changed into red and green shades, and when they merged together again it was into the image of his friend. His face was sad, and John pictured him arriving home to the empty lodgings. He realised he was suddenly, unaccountably afraid.

'Shouldn't we go home now, Master Edmund? Jack... Master William may... will surely be awaiting our return? I think I have learnt a lot this morning, with your help.' John bowed his head, while the hobgoblin spun and grinned, chattering its teeth.

With sudden certainty, John knew what Jack would say in

this situation to make Master Edmund do what he wanted. But did John dare? He cleared his throat.

'Master Edmund? When Master William said he did not need you at rehearsal today, as your part was so unimportant... do you think... mayhaps... that he wanted you to have a rest? Perchance because he sees how hard you're working both with me and at the theatre?'

Master Edmund frowned down at him.

'Why wouldn't he say that outright, if that was the case?'

'Because... because he knows that a hard working person like you would never take a rest if it was offered to you directly as you are so... hard working.' He continued through flaming cheeks. 'He tried to be cunning and pretend he didn't need you. He hoped you wouldn't see through him and would... do something to amuse yourself, for once.' To his own ears, his voice sounded hesitant and untrustworthy, but as he spoke, a cat of black ink materialised in the air, purring and rubbing itself around Master Edmund's feet.

Master Edmund glanced down for the briefest moment as if he could see it as well, then boomed in his theatre voice:

'I was waiting to see when you'd realise that, young John. Seeing true motives is an essential part of becoming an actor. It took you longer than I expected; now we must rush back across the river and help William in rehearsal—for he surely does need me.'

John's cheeks were truly burning now. As he replaced the book on a shelf, he tried to say that Master William had wanted Master Edmund to have a rest, not to meet him at the theatre, but his words were half-formed and Master Edmund dashed out of the shop as if it was on fire. John followed and the bookseller nodded as he passed, eyebrows arched. Jack'd once told him that the secret of good conversation was in knowing that the vast majority of people only heard what they wanted to hear—and no more. John realised he had some way to go before he achieved Jack's mastery of the technique. But at least he'd got what he wanted. His feet itched to return to Jack; his heart was fluttering.

'Do you have any siblings?' Master Edmund asked, as John jogged to catch up with him.

It was rare for Master Edmund to show interest, and John

felt another lie growing in his throat, but he swallowed it and simply answered, 'None alive.'

'That is a pity. An older brother can prove to be of huge benefit.' He patted the peak of John's cap. 'No matter, you have me and William and Jack, and no doubt countless others will care for you during your life. I'm afraid that growing up does not mean you no longer need to be looked after. Indeed, it seems to me that as we age we need more care than ever.' He turned away from John, who was barely listening as his gaze darted around the street. He didn't know what he was looking for, but every nerve of his body was sharp and bristling.

Suddenly the hobgoblin appeared, quivering in front of his face, its skin ash grey and its eyes a shade shimmering between all colours and none. It plucked frantically at John's sleeve, and pointed up the street, where a cloud of blackest storms and fresh-drawn blood swirled around two figures. It was Moll and Jack. Something was wrong.

'Master Edmund, I must—' He ran without waiting for a reply, darting through a gang of boys; under a cart that was blocking the road with one wheel off, half wedged in the rutted tracks; around the traders shouting out their wares... He could not see Jack any longer, but he ran towards the place where that red mist still sat like a thundercloud. John opened his mouth to shout a warning, but before he could say anything, gloved hands gripped his upper arms and he was dragged backwards into an alley.

He was grabbed tight, his back pressing into a big, round belly. The smell of the streets' grime and the grease of lank hair liquified his stomach—

Then the vision of Jack surrounded by that black-red mist flashed into his mind. Jack needed him. John struggled and spun around to look at his captor, nails already reaching for eyes. The man's shoulder-length brown hair hung out from a dirty cape, and his face was splattered with dust as if he hadn't seen water for months. And his eyes... his eyes...

Sparkled faerie green.

'Fair One! I'm glad to see you can kick out like a wild pony when you need to, but I could do without any extra bruises.'

John hugged him fiercely. Then he gave him a robust kick in the shin. 'What are you doing, frightening me like that?'

Black Jack rubbed his leg.

'The important question is what are you doing running about on your own in this part of the city? You should be safe at home, or at the theatre with Master Edmund. What if it hadn't been me?'

John looked around the empty alley, lacking the words or patience to explain his vision, or indeed, how he'd come to be in a bookshop on this side of the river.

'Where's Moll?'

Jack frowned. 'Why do you ask?'

'I saw you speaking with her.'

'Ay, I did, but that was hours ago.'

'Is she... '

'She is bene. But the news she gave me wasn't.'

'Oh, Jack—what is it? What's wrong?'

Tendrils of red still clung to his friend like a disease. They crept into the lines on his skin and streaked his face like tears.

'She'll keep low and drink and smoke for a few days. She is no faint-heart, but she wants no part of what I need to do today. I want you well out of the way, too. But is there time? Have you heard any call out the hour lately?'

John shook his head.

Black Jack leaned against the wall and breathed out heavily. Staring up at the sky he said,

'It is of no matter. There's no choice. I know full well there's not time to do both. I'll take you home: that is how it has to be.' His eyes were red, and John realised it was not a vision, not the red mist, but the mark of real sorrow.

Jack headed back to the street, his shoulders stooped. He brushed by the hobgoblin, bobbing at the entrance to the alleyway, its skin sallow and grey. Its eyes were screwed shut, but it reached out a knotted hand to touch Jack as he passed. He paused, shivered, and looked over his own shoulder.

John ran forward and caught Jack's hand.

'Don't treat me like a helpless child. I've told you things I have never been able to tell any other. I see things in my visions that make me think that death and nothingness would be a release. There is much I don't understand, but I do understand suffering. We are friends. We share everything important. So, tell me.'

In a flat voice, Jack said:

'Bess Porch is to meet the gallows today. I never thought she'd get caught. But it has happened. She's needed help for a while.'

'But Nick—I mean, he seemed better.'

'I mean a different manner of help, Fair One. And I didn't give it because I've been constantly by your side.'

'It is my fault?'

Jack wrapped his arms around John, drew him back into the shadows. 'No, no, no. I did not mean that. It is me who chose to be with you. It is Bess who made a mistake and was taken.' Jack put his hands on John's shoulders, smiling with his lips but not his eyes. 'It's not that I'm trying to protect you.' John started to protest, but Jack shook his head. 'I—I don't like you to see me this way. With life weighing so heavily on me. That's why I want you away from my side, safe with Master Edmund. And here I am, wasting time, when I need to get you home. Perchance I can still make it to Tyburn in time to see Bess off right.'

'I won't waste your time. I'll come with you to say farewell to Bess. She's our friend.'

'It is not a sweet farewell, John. It'll not suit you to see a woman hang. There'll be too many people, all of them thinking it's a fair day out and good jest. They will be laughing and cheering and grabbing at Bess, fighting to get themselves a scrap of her clothes. Tell me true, is that something you want to see?'

John swallowed but held Jack's gaze.

'No. But neither do you.'

He could not read Jack's expression: sad, wondering, and hopeful all at the same time. Eventually, Jack took his cape off and put it around John's shoulders, pulling the hood up over his head. It hung large and heavy on John as if he was trying on Da's clothes. But it smelt of Jack, and John drew it around himself.

'Keep yourself covered. Do not let any notice you. And promise to do as I say.'

John nodded and they left the cover of the alleyway. Walked in silence. Black Jack set a fast pace and John tried hard to think of nothing but keeping up with him.

The crowd they arrived at seethed and boiled. John made a grab for Jack's sleeve before remembering that he was here to offer strength to his friend—not the other way around. He let go, making do with walking close to him instead.

It was much like being in the Globe. Anticipation sparked through the chattering people; food sellers shouted out their wares; and John's practiced eye could see the cutpurses and pickpockets working their way methodically through the noise.

But no faeries danced here.

Black Jack pushed through towards the front and John saw him signal to three other boys in the crowd who were also moving gradually forwards. The signals were quick—a tapping of the nose or pulling of an ear—and as incomprehensible to John as the letters on a page.

When they were near, John asked:

'What are you going to do?'

Black Jack stared at him as if he'd forgotten he was there, which chilled John more than anything else so far.

'Whatever happens, stay still,' Jack said. 'Unless the crowd gets raucous, then do what you must to protect yourself. And do not fret: it may take time, but I will always find you, wherever you run to.'

'Do not worry about me.' John hoped that his voice did not betray the racing of his heart.

'Here's one of the great sights of the city, then, Fair One: the Tyburn Tree, where you can view many a cove dancing a last jig to rival any of Will Kemp's famed performances.' Jack sounded formal and strange; his words rehearsed, as though he too was playing a part.

John looked at last at the thing he'd been trying to avoid. It hulked over the crowd: three timber posts, joined by a wooden triangle at the top. Plain enough to forget what it was for.

'I'm afraid there's only the five nooses today. I haven't witnessed it myself, but I have heard tell that on some days, they've used the space to string up twenty at once.'

John's hand flittered to his own neck as he looked at the knotted ropes. Jack glanced at John, then looped an arm about his waist and pulled him close. Held him for a moment, then lowered his mouth to John's ear.

'You do not belong amid the muck of this world, so close your eyes if need be—don't let it haunt you. '

'I've seen death before, Jack.'

'I know you have. Although I am thinking now that I must be sure to teach you how to bribe a turnkey and the hangman, so that when my turn comes, it'll end quick. Like we'll do for Bess.'

John opened his mouth, but could think of nothing right to say, nor how to ask what exactly he meant. Instead, he asked about Nick. Was he here too?

'Nay, Bess wouldn't want it. Some say it makes the end more difficult if you can see the faces of those who love you. And Bess was proud. Once you see a body jerking on a rope, you may forget the way they were before. She won't want him thinking of her like that.' John trembled, and Jack looked back, over the heads of the hoard behind them. 'Sometimes it may take hours for the cart to arrive. It depends how riled the crowds along the way are. Perchance there might still be time for you to leave this place and wait somewhere safe.'

John dared not speak, for fear that the frailest part of him would plead for Jack to take him far away from this place of death. He breathed deeply and squeezed his hands into fists. He would not weaken.

Black Jack was quiet, but John could feel the other boy as if it were only the two of them standing there. He heard the quickening of Jack's breath, and felt his body stiffen, as something louder and more real than the diverse chatter of the crowd gradually solidified into one low rumble.

Looking back, he glimpsed a cart coming through the mass of bodies. The ground vibrated, as if a dozen horses were racing towards them rather than one old, slow carthorse. He realised the pulsing came from the mob, stamping their feet and pressing forward. Beside the cart, men with long guns walked, carrying their weapons casually, as if it was mere chance that they were holding them. They allowed a few people to dodge past them and lean in close enough to touch the cart, before shoving them away. They were like indulgent parents, gently chastising their spoilt children.

'It's only an oddment of thieves today—nothing to work anyone into a frenzy,' Black Jack said. 'You'll be fine if you stay here.'

The cart creaked to a halt under the gallows. The prisoners stood up and the crowd thrummed. A man called out the name of each one, in a ringing voice as if they were being celebrated for their crimes. Even standing near the front, John found it difficult to identify individual words with the crowd roaring behind his back. He knew Bess Porch because there was only one woman, but he did not recognise the simply-dressed girl as the elegantly dressed lady he'd met on his very first day in London. Her hair was bedraggled and her skin dusty. She looked no older than John himself.

Alongside the stink of bodies, the air sweltered with the metallic smell of blood and flesh. For a moment, John looked around, sure the Butcher must be standing somewhere near; then he realised what the crowd was hurling at the gallows: animal entrails, cats' heads, and dead rats. Only a few actually reached their targets: most fell short, bursting open on the ground or splattering among the crowd. When a prisoner was hit, triumphant shouts went up.

Beside him, Jack stood rigid as the nooses were hooked around the prisoners' necks. Bess was last, and she stumbled before the rope was set in place. A guard caught her and pushed her upright.

John's mouth was dry, his heartbeat light as a butterfly.

Bess brushed the guard's hands away from her and in a merry voice, as loud as any actor's, cried out:

'Don't be trying to get thy thrills from me! Go to a stew like any honest gentleman, or if you lack coin, at least have the decency to wait 'til after I be dead.'

The guard led the crowd in howls of laughter. Bess squared her shoulders and gave a wide smile. John looked at Jack, and saw that his face was wet, but that he was smiling too.

Her eyes were scanning the crowd. Would she recognise them, him in the cape and Black Jack disguised? Jack gave a nod so quick and slight that John only saw it because he was watching so carefully. Bess kept on looking around as the noose was slotted around her neck. Had she seen them? He could barely breathe as the horse was led forwards and the cart was pulled out from under the feet of the prisoners. They fell like dolls.

Jack bounded forward before John was aware of him moving. He gave a cry, reached out a hand to stop him, then remembered he had promised to stay put, and forced himself to stand still. The three boys Jack had signalled to were there at the same time, quick as lightning. Two of them shoved themselves between the crowd and the gallows in a fighting posture, while Jack and one other ran to Bess, grabbed her legs and hauled down. John could only gape. What were they doing? Surely they didn't hope to rescue her?

The air reverberated with a crack. And suddenly John knew what the boys had done.

The crowd brayed, and John could not tell if they were cheering or jeering. Everything spun around him. He was nowhere and everywhere. He saw the shadowy, timeless tendrils of Death reaching through the future and the past. He felt hunger spreading over the world, seeking a satisfaction it knew it would never find. But its hopelessness gave it its power. It would keep going forever because there was no end.

John returned to his body, and found that it was standing squarely next to Black Jack.

On the gallows, Bess's body hung limp and empty of all that had made her human. Her arms dangled in the wind, or maybe with the movement of the still-living people around her. He remembered her hands brushing against him on his first day in London. Now they would touch no one. He thought of Nick, alone, and blinked rapidly. He entwined his fingers with Jack's.

Jack's three companions stood guard. One other prisoner was also dead, but the others gasped and gurgled out frantic breaths as they swung, their feet kicking uselessly through the air.

John closed his eyes. How much better it was to be a faerie, and race through the skies with eternal grace. A hobgoblin would shake with laughter if anyone tried to hang it dead. It would dance a jig and sing a sweet tune rather than struggle for breath. Then, when it grew bored, it'd vanish into air and leave the crowd to find some other amusement.

The people around them shouted out a mixture of obscenities and encouragement. John's head ached, trying to work out whether they wanted the prisoners to die quicker or fight harder for their last moments of life.

Did it matter?

Did these, the final voices the prisoners would hear in this world, make any difference to their last battle?

With a final jitter another man died, leaving just two, croaking and twitching.

'Is there... any chance?' John asked quietly. 'Would they have mercy and cut them down—if they live for long enough, I mean?'

Jack shook his head.

'Then why... why do they... keep going?'

'Well, there's none that survive to give testimony, but I reckon it's just a body's instincts. You fight for so long to stay alive, you can't judge when it's time to stop.'

'But... the others...'

Black Jack put his hand in the middle of John's back and steered him out of the crowd. 'I've seen that things went right. My friends can take care of her now. Let's get you home, and help you memorise another speech to practice with Master Edmund.'

'We don't have to leave. I'm fine. You can help the others like you helped Bess. Make it... faster for them.'

'It doesn't work like that, Fair One. We only paid the bribe for Bess. If we took others out, they'd charge double and make it more difficult next time.'

Next time. John looked over his shoulder with a shudder.

'Forsooth, the true trouble goes beyond the guards. Who knows when the people will turn. They could've turned on us for taking Bess out quick, and the guards might not have been of a mood to step in. We had a bit of fortune, and you know as well as I not to push Fortune too far. With those two holding out for so long, there'll be gambling going on; some will already think we were deliberately rigging the game, taking the woman out. It was worth the risk for her, but not for ones that I do not know so well.'

John jerked his head around.

'But you do know them? You know the others being hung alongside Bess?'

'I know many faces and names, especially when their trade overlaps with mine.'

As they came to the edge of the crowd, Jack took the smaller boy's hand and pulled John along more quickly.

'What about Nick? What will he do without her?'

'Please. John. I'm grateful you came with me, but I do not want to speak about it any more.'

John lowered his head.

He remembered Jetta dying in his arms. The sweet wet straw smell of her. He'd held her until she went cold. For once, even Da's fists couldn't frighten him. The silence and loneliness had gone far beyond any physical pain. It was selfish; he should've been relieved her pain was over, like Jack, making things shorter for Bess. But he couldn't let go of her.

He touched Jack's back.

His friend moved closer, so their arms were touching.

'I've seen many die,' Jack said, 'And I find it works best to keep moving and keep merry. And not to dwell. The best way to honour your friends is to live as well as you can and not waste time grieving for them.'

'Is that right?'

'I don't know.' Jack rubbed his brow. 'But it is what I have to do.'

They didn't take a boat, but walked the long route back, over the bridge. Black Jack told his stories about everything they passed, including the tarred heads on spikes displayed at the Bankside entrance. John turned away from them. He almost asked what would happen to Bess's body—if there'd be a burial they could attend. He kept his silence, though; listened to Jack talk about ghosts that would never haunt either of them, and he didn't mention Bess's name at all.

What shall you ask of me that I’ll deny

It was early. The sun was still low in the sky, and they were far out east enough that there were only fishermen and boats bringing in foreign goods and rats. But nevertheless, he couldn’t help giving John sideways glances. His friend’s hair was down, he was wearing his dress with no stockings, and he had taken his boots off to dip his toes into the river.

This was good. It was not that long ago that John’s skin had blanched yellow every time they were in sight of the Thames.

This was bad.

If they needed to run—and a body should always be ready to run, (or fight, but that wasn’t so much of an option when John was your companion)—John’s feet would get scratched to pieces and Jack would have to carry him.

It was stupid to let him do it. Stupid, like running them both wretched, tracking down Nick, just because John had been fretting about him. Like approaching people they’d have been much better to avoid—and after all the care he’d been taking to try and find out who had been asking about John without giving away anything himself. He’d found Nick, and had ensured he was as well as he could be for a one-legged, heartbroken beggar. He had no new notion of the Butcher’s game. And now, instead of doing something sensible about that problem, here he was wandering along whilst his friend, a boy in a dress, dabbled his dainty toes in a dirty river.

John turned his head and smiled at him.

'This was a bene idea, Red One. Watching the sun rise over the river is exactly as beautiful as you described it.'

Jack winked, a standard response that covered all sorts of situations.

A slight morning breeze blew John's hair around his face, hiding the faint blush that rose to his cheeks, (from the wind? Or some embarrassment that Jack couldn't even guess the cause of?), and he moved the hand that was holding his clothes out of the water to tuck his locks behind his ears, just as the tide came over his bare feet.

'Your skirt is getting wet.'

John giggled and pulled it up higher.

'Is this like the sea? Like the waves you described?'

'This is just the toing and froing of the current. It's nothing compared to the sea.' He began telling stories of the great ocean to John, while the main part of his mind watched his friend and took stock of their environment. And a small part of his brain, which he couldn't silence, considered whether John looked finer in women's clothes or men's.

He'd first seen John wearing his sister's dress after the Butcher, when he'd used every charm he knew to flatter Master Edmund into seeing his friend. He remembered how John had insisted on his boy garb back when they'd first met. Despite never seeming comfortable in it. But that was before they had moved in to the Shakespeares'.

No, before they had met all the actors properly in the tiring room. No. He'd only started wearing dresses regularly again after Bess had died.

To Jack it was obvious. A lot had changed since that hanging. His friend may always be mouselike, but no more a mouse—he'd stopped fretting so much about who he thought he was supposed to be. Started to let himself simply be. Once upon a time, how John had tagged in his shadow; now it was John's turn to stretch, to cast an umbra. But also, to make room. As if he was afraid that if he didn't make room for his friend in the theatre, that one would float away...

'Red One... if you're not too busy... my hands are hurting. Would you help me please with the mending of this bodice? It needs to be finished by tomorrow, but my hands are so tired.'

And then, 'I knew your quick hands would be good at embroidery. No, I mean it. It is really good. I'll just... perhaps... just strengthen this tiny bit here.' Before discreetly unpicking it all and redoing it.

The surreptitious attempts at teaching him how to sew were at least more subtle than the tricks John tried around the other actors.

'Master Edmund, my throat is a little sore today. No, do not fret, I am not ailing, but perhaps Jack could practice the scene with you for a while? He knows all the lines far better than me... and you can do one of the great roles immediately with him, as he can read far faster than I... Yes, I know I am learning well, but Jack doesn't need to learn, he can read anything, including foreign languages, and all Master William's most hurried handwriting.'

Then in the tiring room with his beloved Viola (there surely was some magic dust trapped in John's eyes that kept him from seeing her for the sharp, rat-featured thing she actually was).

'Jack, you're so strong, much stronger than me, could you pull this corset tighter please? I can't get it as tight as Viola likes it.'

Viola, missing nothing (for surely if luck hadn't landed him in the theatre he would have been a perfect thief), licking his lips and saying, 'What a good idea. I'm certain Jack can do things exactly as I like them. Are you planning to teach him how to be my personal dresser, John?'

All that and its ilk was endearing and sometimes amusing, as when Jack pulled Viola's corset so tight the actor could barely speak, but was too proud to admit he wanted it loosened. And of course, Jack understood his friend's desire to protect him. It was—well, it was sweet.

Harder was the panic that came over John when Jack left the house alone. The Fair One tried to cover it, but there was a squeak in his voice when he asked when Jack would be back. Wrung hands, whitened skin, blinks so fast it was hard to see his eyes. A dozen nervous twitches, as if he could barely contain himself from throwing his arms around Jack's legs and begging him to not go.

He wished he could tell his friend that what had happened to Bess wouldn't happen to him.

He ought to speak to John seriously, to make sure he understood that no one stayed in each other's lives for long; children became apprentices and never saw their parents again; men were mustered away from their wives and got stabbed through on battlefields in different lands. Friends grew up and their lives divided; one shone their light on the stage, the other remained in the grime and made what coin they could out of the pockets of others.

But John knew this. He'd seen his own family die. He'd left his village. He knew the impermanence of life as well as Jack. So why did Jack feel like—

'Jack? What are you dreaming about? I'm the one who goes wandering in other worlds, not you. You have to be firm and... tethered.'

John was smiling. In the morning sunlight, Jack could easily believe that his friend would live forever.

'I was not dreaming, I've been talking to you all this time, describing in wondrous detail... '

'You may have been talking, but you haven't been here.' John leapt about, mimicking Jack at his most animated.

They laughed together.

'If you do not like my conversation, then we can do the work I brought for you.' Jack produced the parchment he had chosen yesterday from the pile of papers Master William had given him for reading practice. 'It's not a theatre speech, this time. I know you listen to all the actors constantly, and with your memory, well, you need to be tested on something you haven't heard before.'

He gave John the paper and carried his boots as they walked along beside the water's edge. John read. His voice faltered over some words, but was clear in the morning air.

'When in disgrace with fortune and men's eyes,
I all alone beweep my outcast state,
And trouble deaf heav'n with my bootless cries,
And look upon myself and curse my fate,
Wishing me like to one more rich in hope,

Featured like him, like him with friends possessed,
Desiring this man's art, and that man's scope,
With what I most enjoy contented least;
Yet in these thoughts myself almost despising,
Haply I think on thee, and then my state,
Like to the lark at break of day arising
From sullen earth, sings hymns at heaven's gate;
For thy sweet love rememb'red such wealth brings,
That then I scorn to change my state with kings.'

John twisted his head to look up at Jack.

'Did I read it well? Shall I try again?'

'Did you understand any?'

'Haply I think on thee,' John replied. 'I know what that means.'

'Me too, Fair One, me too.'

They meandered back and forth. Jack explained the words that John didn't know with words that he did, until the sun rose higher and it was time to return to the Shakespeares'.

As they walked back, Jack reflected that the time they spent alone together seemed more and more like an impossible dream—and that it was becoming harder and harder to return to the real world.

I'll fight, till from my bones my flesh be hacked

The swords clashed against each other with a jolt that rattled his bones. John leaped back, gasping. Time had vanished; he could only guess at the hours they'd been fighting, but he couldn't give up, no matter how much his body ached. He gripped the hilt with both hands, one on top of the other, holding so tightly that his knuckles were white, and raised the sword above his head. He took a breath that filled his lungs and pushed his chest out, then ran forward with a yell.

His opponent took two steps backwards before dropping his own weapon and fleeing the room with a yelp of terror. John couldn't stop as his legs carried him forwards, and he skidded into Black Jack, who caught him in his arms.

'Oh no! Get Master Edmund to come back! This is the funniest thing I've ever seen, don't stop yet.'

John sighed, untangled himself from Jack and picked up Master Edmund's toy sword from the floor.

'This is an important part of my training, not a jest.'

'But when Master Edmund crawled under the table and you tried to poke him out, it was… '

'You know an actor is supposed to be an expert at swordcraft. Why don't you help me instead of cackling at poor Master Edmund, who is only trying his best to tutor me?'

'Yes, you're right, that probably was his best.' Tears streamed down Jack's face.

'And I wasn't trying to poke him out. It was practising fighting, in, in different conditions. Master Edmund is a perfectionist. He wants me to be prepared for every situation.'

'I understand. Girls with fake swords are a constant source of unrest and rioting on the streets. You must be ever vigilant.' Black Jack's head was thrown back, his hands clenched to his stomach, his breath coming in gasps.

John slumped against the wall, letting his feet slide forward and his back slide down until his rump bumped the floor. Jack came and sat next to him.

John looked away. He knew he was pouting, but couldn't seem to stop himself. 'Did I really look that foolish? You called me a girl.'

Jack rubbed his arm, but John still didn't look at him. 'When did I call you a girl?'

'You said it just a moment ago. Girls with fake swords. Meaning me.'

'Now, what's so bad about that? You're going to be playing a girl, so the fact I said it without thinking shows how well you were performing your part. That is all!'

'You mean that I looked weak and useless, trying to fight like a man.'

'You're looking for insult where there is none. Why would you think being a girl means 'weak and useless'?'

'You know that's not what I meant; it is just me that is... '

'When you've been in as many tavern brawls as me, you will know the truth of that! The worst punch I've ever received was from a girl. Though there's no doubting I deserved it.' Jack rubbed his cheek, as if the wound was fresh.

John leaned against the cool wall.

'Jack, tell me true, did I look ridiculous?'

'Not you, as such, it was the two of you together. I know you have a fighting spirit in you when you need it, but your nature is too gentle and tender, and it was clear that you did not want to risk giving Master Edmund so much as a splinter. Yet Master Edmund danced around as if he was facing off against a rabid hound.' Black Jack chuckled. 'You would have laughed to see yourself. You will, later—when you're not so worn from the effort of not hitting Master Edmund with a wooden sword.'

John tried to smile but failed. He rested his head against Jack's shoulder.

'Will you be cross if I tell you something?'

'Never.'

'Before I even met you, on the road when I heard a stranger speaking beautiful words which I didn't even know were Master Shakespeare's, I yearned to find more of that magic. Then when you took me to the Globe for the first time to see Viola... '

'To see a play. I would never take you to see that one,' Jack grumbled.

John took a deep breath and continued.

'What I'm meaning to say is that I dreamt of being on stage, but I wonder now if it was only ever meant to be a dream. I've found the magic and that is what I should be content with, not wishing for more. I think Andrew is right—I am more suited to be his apprentice than Master Edmund's. I am not loud or bold enough for acting. But I am good in the tiring room. The hobgoblin doesn't even help me as much any more, it's too busy dancing with the other faeries, but my hands are still quick, and everyone compliments me and sometimes they ask for me over Andrew.'

'Your Viola does?'

'Yes, Viola has from the start, but others too. Even Augustin wanted me to help with... '

Jack took his hand and squeezed it.

'You're meant for acting, Fair One. It hurts my heart to hear you think otherwise. When we say lines together you are more wondrous than I can express. Those are the moments I look forward to above all else.'

John felt the heat in his cheeks, but didn't let himself be distracted. 'It is easy with you. We're alone. Even with Master Edmund I fail; I cannot shout or move the way he asks me to.'

'Nor should you,' came a voice from behind them.

John jumped, his hand darting to his mouth. But it was Master William who had appeared in the doorway, not Master Edmund. The blue faerie hovered in front of the man. Today it glowed so bright that its eyes and mouth were barely distinguishable from the rest of its body.

The effect was blinding, and John was glad to turn his gaze to the master of the house instead.

'I saw you and Master Edmund at play. Jack was correct in all he said. Your timing is better than any youth currently in our company.'

Black Jack chuckled.

'See, John? Perhaps you will listen to the truth when it comes from wiser men than me.'

Master William's eyes were laughing. 'I was inspired to write a new scene in Twelfth Night for when you perform Viola. Which you will.'

John wanted to say, 'Viola plays Viola', but his heart fluttered. He could not disagree with Master William; nor could he quite dismiss the idea of playing such a role—for, even if it frightened him, it thrilled him too. Besides, in Master William's presence his mind had gone blank: he couldn't remember Viola's real name.

'Our John is having doubts. He doesn't think he's good enough to act.' Black Jack grinned as if it was a jest, rather than the deepest worry of John's soul.

'I've many roles to write for you. Some are fully formed, many are still wisps that you must inhabit to give them life. Boy actors age. Time cannot be stopped. But not you, this I know in my heart. Time will mature you and increase your beauty, but it can never wither you.' Master William was already walking away, but he called back over his shoulder, 'There is none at the Globe right now. Go and act on the stage. One speech will be enough.'

John pulled his knees up and rested his head on them. 'What did all that mean?'

Black Jack twisted his mouth, then sprung to his feet with his habitual grin.

'It means that he likes you, and doesn't want you hid away in the tiring room. Let me check the streets, and if all is bene we can go to the theatre as he said.'

'No,' John stood too, dusting down his clothes. 'There is no need for you to search for people who may mean me harm. We'll be safe.' He couldn't voice to Jack that it was spiders itching under his skin the way Jack always went first and had to search for some danger he never named before John was allowed out.

He still didn't know whether Jack truly believed in his visions. Sometimes he was sure he caught Jack glancing at him as if he thought his friend was mad. Perhaps he was. But then there were those other moments, moments between sleep and waking, or when Jack seemed half-aware of the touch of magic; moments when he was certain that Black Jack was faerie blessed and as much part of the other world as the hobgoblin itself.

Today Jack's eyes narrowed, but he nodded, and didn't insist.

Even though it had been his idea that Jack didn't do his usual checks, John's skin prickled as they walked the streets to the theatre.

In the tiring room, as though fate or fortune had always intended them to find it, was an expensive gown that should never have been left unattended. It glowed with a light beyond the rich dye of its fabric. John didn't think he'd ever seen an object sparkle with so much faerie magic before.

'Do you think he meant it for you?' Jack rubbed a sleeve between his thumb and finger.

'I do not know... I was going to read Viola, since Master William mentioned it... not that I think I am good enough for Viola... but if I try her... well, then she is dressed as a boy... and doesn't need... doesn't need to... '

Wear the dress.

His mind formed words, but the command had come from deep in a place far beyond human language.

'Will you help me put it on?'

As they worked together, undressing him from his everyday clothes and redressing him in the finery, John said, 'I'd be happy with this life, doing this for others, helping the actors. I do not need any more.' He lifted his arms as Jack fit the padding around his waist. 'What about you? Do you think you could be happy with a place in the company?'

He hoped it sounded casual, but he held his breath for the answer. Jack was silent for a moment.

'Jack?'

His friend sighed, theatrically.

'It seems to me that certain people are formed for certain things, and if they are fortunate enough to make coin doing those certain things then they have an obligation to be happy, as respect to all the other people dying miserably in the dirt.'

John exhaled, a half laugh, half sigh. 'What a Black Jack answer!' He tried again. 'If you could be any of Master William's characters, which would you choose?'

'One that survives.'

'Lots of them survive, that's no choice at all.'

'Lots of them die. Or are in such a state they'd be better off dead.' Jack dropped the locks of hair he'd been twisting around on top of John's head and instead smoothed them over his shoulders.

'I'd be... '

Jack pressed a finger against John's lips. 'Viola, I know.' His smile faded. 'Because her twin is still alive.'

They walked out on stage together, arms linked, the empty theatre belonging solely to them. John gazed around the Globe as if seeing it for the first time. The way the late evening sun was lighting it, it did feel like a different place today; the stage bright as if it existed separately from the dark shadows where the thatch overhang protected the richer patrons from the worst of the weather. He shuffled a little closer to his friend, licked his lips and tried to think of which of Viola's lines he should try saying.

But Jack jumped away and down into the area where the groundlings squashed and shoved during performances. Even without the crowds, it normally smelled of bodies and food, but today the air was full of summer fields and Master William's ink and parchments.

A crowd of faeries were there already, dancing high in the air, his hobgoblin at the centre. It swooped down to him, its eyes green and almost as bright as Jack's.

'Can I be Viola?' he said, almost to himself. He looked around the empty stage; surely it was growing, and he was getting smaller? 'No... no... this is such stuff as dreams are made on, like Master William says. It is not meant to be real.'

'Little One, Master William just told you you're an actor.' Jack spread his arms and in a voice as rich as the company's finest players, shouted, 'Be Viola, this once, only for me, my fair maiden.'

The hobgoblin swooped down until it was a breath's distance away, and with a lurch, John felt something enter him. His body swelled and twisted into something new and strange, his own flesh filling the dress as if the padding wasn't there. He was no longer a shy boy, despised by his village, bereaved of his sister and his mother, hated by his father. She was a brave, resourceful girl, dressed in boy's garb purely for survival in an unknown land. Her twin brother was missing, but she did not mourn him, because he was strong and the stars would surely pull their fates together again. He might not recognise her immediately, as her heart beat differently now and her womanhood had bloomed. In truth, she had fallen in love with a man who could not possibly return her affections; however, he kept her by his side and offered her warm and honest friendship. This bittersweet pang sung out in every word she spoke, though only those who knew how to listen would ever hear it.

Viola gave her hobgoblin a small smile. Then she gazed down at the tall boy grinning expectantly up at her.

'If I did love you, I would
Make me a willow cabin at your gate
And call upon my soul within the house.
Write loyal cantons of contemned love
And sing them loud even in the dead of night.
Halloo your name to the reverberate hills
And make the babbling gossip of the air
Cry out "Jack!" Oh, you should not rest
Between the elements of air and earth,
But you should pity me.'

In the beat after the last word, the hobgoblin soared up into the sky, and Viola vanished. John stood alone on the stage. He could hear Jack clapping loud enough for a thousand spectators.

John stumbled forward, trying to clamber off the stage. His whole body flushed, but the other spoke as easily as ever:

'I'll have to find myself a new name—saying 'Jack' rather than 'Olivia' broke up Master William's rhythm, and we know how long he spends balancing even the simplest words.' He took John's hand, making no mention of his trembling. 'If you are to be Viola, then I need to make myself into Duke Orsino, do I not?'

John swallowed.

He wished he was still Viola; she'd have a quick and witty reply.

'Are you saying you'll become an actor alongside me? That you won't do... other things? But what about your dream... the dream... of becoming a dicer?'

'It isn't that simple. But mayhaps I do dream your dreams now, filled with all sort of mischievous faerie folk. And I can put up with their trickery if you are there too.'

They gazed at each other. There was nothing in either the faerie or real world besides the two of them. John didn't know if he was lost or found. He opened his mouth to speak, but before the right words reached his tongue, Jack took a step back, grinned and tapped John on the nose.

'I heartily hope there will be no more of this foolishness about hiding in the tiring room.'

He didn't trust himself to give the right reply, so he walked back to the stage in silence, listening to his friend chatter on about how Shakespeare would be able to charge ten, nay twenty, times as much once London realised that the Globe was home to the most beautiful and talented actor that could ever be imagined.

As flies to wanton boys are we to th' gods,
They kill us for their sport

Viola ran her fingers over the strings of John's bodice, though it was fastened perfectly.

'Have you memorised all your lines? You don't want to make a mistake in your first role. Or are you such a good apprentice to Edmund you wish to copy his career?'

She raised a darkly inked eyebrow.

'I don't have any lines. I'm your silent handmaiden.' John steadied his fingers by folding his hands over his stomach. 'And I would be very proud to act half as well as Master Edmund.'

Master Edmund had no role in today's play, but John hoped he'd turn up anyway. John had wanted his first role to be in one of Master William's plays, but one of the other apprentices had fallen ill, and John had been volunteered to fill in. The two playwrights of this work were lecturing Augustin about his part. They were dressed in matching clothes and finishing each other's sentences. He was both disappointed and relieved that they had nothing to say to him.

Viola smiled and leaned close to John, but spoke loud enough for others to hear.

'Have I told you those two share a bed and a wo... '

'I don't have any lines. Do I?' John's cheeks burned.

'No. Of course you don't. And no one will even notice you—

you're only on stage twice and always at the same time as me. So stop worrying. You don't look so pretty when you're scared.' Viola pursed her lips into the mirror, and caught his eye over her shoulder. 'Unless it's not your first experience on stage that is frightening you. Where's that red-haired rough thing, your gallant knight? Have you two had a falling out? Did he do something you didn't like? Or fail to do something that you do like?'

John swallowed and Viola smirked.

'You have such an open face—you really need to learn how to act. Tell me everything. I won't tell anyone else. I'm sure it will be too boring to retell, in any case.'

'He said he'd be here for me.' John stared down. 'He promised.'

'So where is he now?' Viola didn't try to hide her delight, and John's body prickled with a heat that started deep in his belly. He looked around, as if Black Jack might suddenly appear beside him. Which wasn't that unlikely, was it? He and Jack liked to play at sneaking up and surprising each other, and Jack was much better at it than him.

His hobgoblin was nowhere to be seen, either. But here at the theatre, the faerie was always disappearing to dance with its own kind. It probably didn't care, or know, how important today was for John. But Jack knew.

'I'm going to get some air,' John said.

Viola smiled with her painted red lips.

'And perhaps you'll find a tall boy while you're out there? Don't be so glad to see him that you mess up your face. I won't do it again for you.'

As he hurried away, Viola called.

'John, I was only teasing, you can't go out in your costume!'

But no one stopped him.

The street rumbled with activity, as it always did before a performance. Crowds formed around the food and drink sellers, although there would be plenty on offer inside. Some were already shoving their way into the Globe. Those who were more interested in the people than the play cried their wares loudly; others slid through unseen, taking what they wanted without giving anything in exchange.

It was not so easy to convince himself that he was only here to get some fresh air when he realised he was staring at every thief to see if it was Jack in disguise.

He noticed that several of the cutpurses were looking back at him. Of course—his dress. He ought to be in the tiring room until it was his time to step on stage. In the theatre, he was an actor. On the street, he was another easy mark.

He glanced back at the Globe, but instead of returning, he picked up his skirt and pushed onwards through the crowd.

There had to be a good reason for why Jack wasn't here yet. Because if there wasn't a good reason, then there was a bad reason. John knew he'd not be calm enough to walk out on stage if he didn't find out. But if he hurried, he'd still have time to get to Moll's and back again. If anything was amiss, Moll would surely know. Indeed, Jack was probably at Moll's house right now, telling her to come and see John today. Just yesterday he'd been saying how he wished everyone he'd ever known could come and see John.

Two men on horses stopped in his path; one gazed down at him with hungry eyes. A memory, not quite a vision, flashed through John's head: being chased just after he'd left the village. Hiding in a thorn bush. These were different men—and yet they were the same, nevertheless.

His heart thumped, and his muscles tightened, but he darted around them and hurried onwards.

'Jack. Red One.' It was an unconscious murmur. For the first time, he almost wished that he was back in his tiny village where you knew everyone and no one could ever be lost. But no, he could never wish to be back in that place. This was his home now; this place where all the houses looked identical; where he never quite knew where he was.

But was that true? After so long, was he still the same village boy who saw all these rows and rows of houses as exactly the same? He couldn't be lost, could he? He must have walked this road a hundred times at Jack's side. And that was the thing, of course—he was always in the company of someone else leading the way.

He sighed, shaking his head. It had been foolish to leave the theatre. Viola would laugh at him—and Jack, too, no doubt, when he turned up, as he surely would. Master Edmund would be very disapproving. But it was done now, and all he could do was turn and hope he could find his way back to the Globe without losing his way again.

He'd just turned around when he felt fingers pinch tight on his shoulder.

'Jack?'

Not fear, but the memory of the cloaked figure rushing down an alleyway towards him—the last time he'd been pulled into an alley by a stranger, it hadn't been a stranger at all. All those things and so many more had scared him without need. Maybe he didn't need to be scared now either?

But as he turned his face to look, the certainty rushed in on him on a wave of blood. All those warnings. The men on horses—the toothless woman with the dead dog—even Jack in his cloak—All had been signs, telling him again and again to take care, for poison flowed through the streets and rivers of this city.

He screamed. Kicked. Twisted. Tried to bite the hands holding him. Words scraped splinters off his bones:

'I've waited a long time for you, little piglet. As soon as I saw you I knew that you were meant for me. Are you old enough to know what a rare thing it is? To see someone and know immediately that they belong to you?'

John thrashed and convulsed, kicking and scratching at the Butcher's legs and groin. He yelped and cried out.

'Help me. He's... '

A few people glanced over. The Butcher acknowledged them all with a 'good morrow'.

'Forgive the disturbance, I've caught my daughter trying to run off and see her lover.'

One man nodded, 'Aye,' and an old woman clucked disapprovingly. Most looked away and walked in different directions. John still fought, but the strength was draining from him.

Slowly, easily, the Butcher carried John out of the road and into an alleyway. He spoke so casually that John could barely comprehend the threat of his words.

'At first I was impatient. Determined to track you down. But then I told myself one night, "Richard, don't get upset, First Time John will be yours: you know it, he knows it." And here we are, bumping into each other like old friends!'

John went limp. Sometimes, that had worked with Da and the village children. Don't fight. Let it happen. People lost interest if their victim didn't seem to care. He could travel to faerie worlds while they hurt him and look at the bruises afterwards as though they belonged to someone else.

'Good. You truly are my perfect one. You know when to make noise, and when to be still and listen. You've made yourself so pretty for me in that dress, with your golden hair down. You're not like the others. Nay, don't be jealous to hear there were others, they were all rehearsals for you.'

In a movement that came from deep in his gut, John jerked his body and forced his fingers up into the softness of the Butcher's face, not thinking about the hot liquidness of what he was touching. As he felt the Butcher flinch and stumble, he screamed out.

'Jack!'

John thumped to the ground, a heap of nothing, his bones dissolving into his flesh as if he'd fallen from the roof of the sky. He looked up.

The man had both hands over one eye. The visible one was a black pit of rage, rimmed with red. Tears streamed from it. John surged, scrabbled forward, his nails catching and breaking on the dusty ground. The sharpness of the sensation—something that was part of him being ripped away and left behind—made his head hurt. How simple and unremarkable all pain was. How normal.

A hand shackled around his ankle. Flipped him over, knocking the breath from him. He was on his back, gazing up into the eternity of that black eye. The Butcher kept the injured one covered. Had John done more damage than he had realised? Was the man trying to keep his eyeball in its socket? John looked at his own fingers, slick with dirt, mucus, and blood.

He started to drift.

Please, he cried out with his mind. Where was his hobgoblin, when it had been with him for every important event of his life— Where was it now?

But then, what did the faerie folk care for the agony of tiny humans with their short lives? Like ants, they were—all the same. He knew this, had always known: in Nature there was no difference between him and the Butcher, they would both live and die and rot back into the soil. What they did when they still moved, whether they cried or screamed, hurt or helped others, was of no consequence.

Looking into the Butcher's one eye, John could see it clearly now: How this man let the shadows and darkness creep through his soul and called them his pleasure.

'Black Jack has taught you well. He's known how to survive, since he was smaller than you, so we all know that there are those who do the hurting and those who get hurt. You know which you are; I know which I am. It makes life clean when it's this way.'

John writhed and kicked out. The Butcher dragged him backwards.

'Are you going to walk, or do you want me to knock you out and carry you? I can do so without damage.' John wondered if that was the tone he used to his customers, asking them which cut of meat they preferred?

'I'll walk.' John said. He figured, then he could run. Fast. Get back to the theatre. Hide. Jack would be there waiting for him. He'd know what to do.

The man stroked his thumb over the bone of John's ankle, but his grip didn't weaken. John needed to pull away. Leap to his feet. Be gone, far gone from here. But he had to choose the moment. There would only be one chance. And if he got it wrong, he'd be unconscious until the Butcher chose to wake him again.

They stood awkwardly. The Butcher wanted to get himself upright first, without uncovering his eye, or letting the other go, and when they stood, he kept his hand pinched around John's elbow, making his arm stick out at an odd angle.

'You knew Black Jack when he was young?' Maybe this was how to play it: confuse his murderous captor with random questions. 'You said, since he was smaller than you. So I guessed you've known him for a long time. He didn't mention it.' It was a ridiculous act of rebellion that made no sense even to himself, but somehow, talking about Jack made him stand a little straighter.

'I probably know more about his origins than he remembers himself,' the Butcher said. 'If you show me that you know how to behave, I will tell you one night.'

Could John imagine a world where he and the Butcher sat

by the hearth, drinking and eating, as the man told him stories about his friend? Truer than the ones Jack told himself?

No. He didn't want to ever hear this man talk about Black Jack....

And suddenly, as swift as he could, John darted a hand up to the Butcher's one good eye. The man instinctively moved his hand to deflect the attack, which is what John had expected. Hoped for. This was his chance. He was faerie blessed.

Quick as a fish, he shifted his hand towards the bad eye, two fingers pressed together to form a knife of his own. He had to be fast: not only to catch the man by surprise, but also to beat his own revulsion. The eyeball wasn't hanging out like he'd imagined, just red and weeping with the whole of the white visible around it. All he'd done before was scratch. Now, he pressed his fingers in until the jelly sucked at them like mud on a boot, and pulled out again. The man howled. And let go.

John's stomach spewed out grey-yellow bile, over the street, over the man. The force of the acid shooting from his mouth bent him double. He'd done the hard bit. Now all he had to do was turn and run. The mists of London tightened around his body.

Not now. Yes, now.

He was inside a giant animal, clinging onto bone and tendon as red fiery fluids boiled below him.

The world turned upside down. He was on the floor, with the liquid above him, dripping down in burning dollops. He twisted around, crawling along, feeling his way through the hot slime with his hands.

I am in a street in Bankside. I am alive. I need to get up and run.

He vomited again. Not as much as before.

But it was real, it rooted him in his body.

He was close to returning.

But did he want to return?

The treasonous thought appeared bright red. Maybe he could escape from this beast and find peace on this side. But Black Jack was in the real world. He had to go back.

Oh Jack, please help me, Jack.

If he was going to call out to anyone, it should have been the faerie, wherever it was. But he was back, pinned against the wall of the alley. The air smelt of vomit, urine and dead meat. He stared downwards, avoiding the Butcher's eyes, avoiding the trails of blood on the sallow skin. And then a flash of light, and the hobgoblin was there, tugging someone with it, beckoning and pulling at his clothes...

John was drifting again, thinking about when he'd been Viola on stage, the way his body had changed to fit the clothes. The many times he had flashed into a small rabbit, or a timid deer. It was real to him, he knew that. But was it real?

He only needed it for a second. He'd never been able to control it before, but he'd never needed it like he needed it now. He tried to recapture all the fear and smallness he'd ever had; tried to remember what he'd felt like when he first saw the beast that was London. It was the briefest moment, shorter than any normal human could comprehend. But for that moment, John was a mouse, small enough to slip out of the Butcher's grasp.

Jack took advantage of the Butcher's surprise. He knelt astride the man, pummelling his face. A pause, a second's breath, a glance at John, an angry yell, 'Run, fool, Run!' Then he was back to the Butcher, smashing a fist into the man's nose. But his wrist was caught. He aimed a blow with his other hand at the Butcher's neck. The man was faster, clamping his hand around Jack's.

Jack yelled even louder, 'RUN!'

The Butcher flipped Black Jack onto his back, pinned his hands down either side of his head. 'Don't move.'

John's blood froze in his veins.

Jack cursed and grunted, but the Butcher held him as firmly as he had held the smaller boy. The faerie stood a few paces away, its head bowed, staring at something on the ground. It looked up at John suddenly, its eyes blazing, beckoning him with one crooked finger.

John crawled towards it. The ground was scarred, and then he saw what it was looking down at: two things, glinting in the light of the magic being; a ring and Jack's blade.

They must have fallen from Jack's pockets.

If he could give his friend the blade... would Jack use it?

The Butcher now had Jack's hands pinned with only one of his. He raised an enormous fist, holding a jagged stone.

John shoved himself to his feet and raced forward.

In this distorted, stretched out time, there were seconds to think. He grabbed the blade off of the ground, sprawled forward towards the Butcher, arms flailing, and crashed into the man.

Blood.

Of its own will, the blade had shredded the man's garments and found flesh. Ripped a crooked path across the Butcher's belly. That one clutched his stomach, looking down at the mess of his guts with bleeding, teary eyes. Jack pushed John away, and John pulled the blade with him. The Butcher made a rasp that was neither death nor life and Jack grabbed John's wrist.

'Drop it.'

He obeyed at once, his fingers opening up as though Jack himself was moving them.

Black Jack moved swiftly. With sweating effort, he pushed the man off him and onto his back, then he kicked him and stabbed the blade into his belly.

'You're dead, Richard! And I, Black Jack, killed you! Take that thought to hell with you. I, Black Jack, slayed you!' He shouted it out in victory.

'Jack, what are you doing? He was already dead... I...' John's voice was so quiet he barely heard himself.

Or perhaps he hadn't spoken at all, for Jack was loudly dancing around the body, spitting on it and continuing to yell out how he had killed his most hated enemy.

John sensed the stale smell of the crowd before his eyes could focus on them. So many people! Had they always been there? Hidden in shadow until they were certain which way the fight had turned? Not willing to risk helping the boys, but now swarming into the alley to bathe in all the grisly details. They pushed forward, squeezing into the space as if it they were groundlings at the Globe.

Hands grabbed Jack, and he didn't fight them, but held his arms up in surrender.

'I've no argument with any other,' he said, grinning at those who were taking him as if they were friends about to go for a drink.

Something began to return to John, his blood started to flow again. Hands gripped him, pulled him backwards through the crowd.

'Zounds, you look a mess.' Viola's voice. 'Don't meet anyone's eyes. If any stop us, let me do the talking. I'll say it is from the play, and if I flirt enough, they won't ask the wrong questions.'

John struggled, straining to look around and catch a glimpse of where Jack remained in the mass of bodies.

Master Edmund's hand, rubbing his shoulder.

'Jack has sharp wits; he'll talk his way out of this. Right now you'd only cause him trouble, he wants you safe and away from this... accident. Respect your friend's wishes.'

He didn't know if that was what he was doing, but he allowed himself to be hurried away, certain that Jack would somehow run forward and transform the whole horrific day into a bright story of merriment and adventure.

Nothing is but what is not

A laugh that failed to sound happy. Master Edmund. His Master: 'You truly are loved. You would not know this, but plague is the curse of the theatre, it closes us down. If any take ill, it is not the thing for any of the players to visit them. Not that you have anything like the plague, of course, but it is rare for so many to come and see you. I am sure if I was on my deathbed, none would risk even being on the same street.'

He recognised voices, but they were all distorted, travelling to him through thick, sludgy water. He was aware that the things that were said were not the normal things that were said. Maybe they didn't think he was listening. Maybe because they knew all he could do was listen.

'I miss the Avon. It is the river of my childhood. Where William taught me to swim. He was different then, lighter, before the writing trapped him. I know it was his choice, but it changed him. He used to pretend he was going fishing, but I trailed after him and all he did was sit and be still. I wanted to hear what he heard; I never did. But I loved the sounds of the river. The Thames will drag you under and drown you, but the Avon was my brother, looking after me and loving me. What really changed William though, wasn't the writing or London—it was when little Hamnet died. He told me one night you reminded him of Hamnet, but I have never seen the resemblance. Hamnet was only eleven, and you are older than that. At least, I think you are. It is difficult to tell with you being so slight. But Hamnet had William's looks and you are fair... though now I dwell on it, I cannot deny, even if they are different colours, you do have the same look in your eyes. You can see the things that are never more than blurred shapes to me. You can see them, can't you? Those dancing creatures... '

Master Edmund kept talking, but his voice faded away and another became louder: Viola.

'I know what you're feeling. It was a long time ago, but I was kidnapped too. I was abducted while walking to school. I can't imagine any more that person I must have been who went to school every day and studied and had a respected father who told me he loved me. I know it is fact, but it is not real or connected to who I am. I wasn't far from my home, but I was too scared to run away from my kidnappers. I don't even know why now. I was convinced my father would come and find me, but he never did. Strange, that. But it is an old story. I was sold to the Lord Chamberlain's Men and this is my life now. I think I am happy.'

As John fell, he dreamt, and his dreams took a flat but definite form. Master Edmund sat in a chair; Viola perched on his bed. They were never with him together, but he experienced their visits at the same time. He watched their faces, the movements of their lips, and realised that the words he was hearing did not match the words they were saying.

His head ached, his ears bled.

Among parchment, ink, stub-ended quills and books filled with singing words, he saw the glint of a ring. He ran from the hum of human voices towards it. But instead of being safe in the house where he belonged, he arrived outside, on a city street wearing only his smock. The clamour, the stench, the rough churned-up ground very nearly plummeted him out of his dream and back into the falling blackness.

Then he saw it: Red hair, the colour of the sun rising on a spring morning. The boy turned and gazed at him with green eyes like the first buds after a thaw. The boy grinned and winked at him.

The city was not the city. Moss grew beneath his feet and softened his every step. Apple trees sprouted where the buildings had loomed, and the scent of apples filled the air though the trees were in their summer green and not their autumn fruit. Traders and shops appeared within the orchard only as Jack moved and willed them into existence. As with Master Edmund and Viola, Jack's lips moved and he grinned and made his usual wide hand gestures, but John heard something else.

'Would he like a ribbon? Yes. He should have something pretty for all that hair. He can dress it up. When the two of us are alone. Though mayhaps I could take him out once or twice where none will ever see us again, and we can make a fine jest that he is my mort. But no. This is John's first time on stage. How can a tiny bit of ribbon be a suitable gift for such a thing?'

Jack sauntered on.

'Some clothing? That is surely more worthy. But should it be male or female? He seems to favour the female. Though he still has moments of being prickly about these things. I could get him some fabric and then it is his choice what he makes from it. It'll be bene to watch his quick fingers weave something entirely for himself, instead of mending all the theatre clothes. Yet the theatre clothes are so fine, all the discarded outfits from the gentleladies, that is what he'll be used to wearing from now on. Soon he won't even be wearing that ragged old thing he's so attached to on his sister's account. I'm sure she was relieved to give it to him. One of the many mysteries of life with John: how he's got such a sensitive nose to the flavour of the street, but his favourite clothes stink of dung and onions.'

John tried to raise a hand to his cheek. Was he blushing? Was his face hot? But he was only a dream here; he could not touch his own skin. The temperature around him was more something thought of than felt. It was the last warmth of a dying fire while you waited for winter to frost over your body.

Jack continued to stroll around looking at diverse things: books, a new writing implement called a pencil, knives, fruit and flowers. Everything was discarded as unsuitable.

Jack, what are you doing? I don't need a present. I need you.

'Od's Bod, but you are a fool, Black Jack.' The red-haired boy tilted his head back and gazed up at the tree branches. Although he probably saw something different to what John did. 'I'm supposed to be sharp-witted, always aware of my surroundings, and

I do not even recall hearing the last hour being called. I will be reaching John late with no present to explain my absence. How will he manage if I am not in the tiring room with him? Mind, he's so enamoured of the theatre folk he might not even notice I'm not there.'

No, Jack, I notice. I always notice.

Jack shook his head.

'What is wrong with me? I am not one for self-pity and I always know how others value me. You've ruined me, Fair One.' He chuckled and walked on.

Something glinted in the centre of a tree trunk: it was the ring John had seen from afar.

He touched it at the same moment that Jack did, and as their fingers met, they swirled together.

Every second they'd lived, all their dreams remembered and long-forgotten, every thought they'd ever had, entwined into a tapestry that only faerie eyes could see. John's fears disappeared under the weaving of Jack's confidence; the darkest of Jack's thoughts were decorated with sparkles from John's magic.

Jack's fist closed around the ring. John slipped backwards, he couldn't hold on, but it didn't matter: him and Jack were now the same. They didn't have to be touching. The connection was eternal.

'This is it, this is the gift,' Jack said without his lips moving. 'A charmed ring to keep him safe from all ill. The cost. I could lift it so easy. So easy. But I can't. Not for John. Not this time. It has to be honest, it has to be paid for. I've had a good run of luck, I have the coin, and what do I need it for? There'll be no starving winters to protect John from. He is safe. And... do I allow myself to imagine that I am, too? That I can live the life he wants me to? It is possible. What a strange thought. And if it is not, then I can work as I always have and ride my Fortune for as long as its lasts, just as I did before.'

Jack ran his thumb over the ring.

'Letting myself be cozened, listening to the sell, as if I believe it so I can repeat it all to John. Spending so much on a useless trinket. But it is not useless. He'll smile and he'll believe in it.'

The hobgoblin appeared beside Jack, its skin the colour of yellowing bones, its eyes like dried blood.

It gazed at John with eternal sorrow.

John grasped his hands together in pleading.

Please.

It slowly shook its head then flicked a finger against Jack's ear.

Jack looked up, a suddenly alert animal. 'What was that scream? He's calling for me. He needs me.'

No, Jack, no. Leave me. Leave me. I'll escape the Butcher on my own. Stay here. Stay safe.

He stretched out his arms, but they couldn't reach his friend.

The ring dropped out of empty air into John's hand.

The forest disappeared, and John stood in his smock as the city crashed around him.

Jack was gone.

Some rise by sin, and some by virtue fall

He was somewhere. Somewhere he wasn't supposed to be, somewhere he wasn't supposed to even think about. It might be that he wasn't here. This could be nothing, a wisp, no more than a ripple in a pond.

How could it be real?

An ordinary room with ordinary men deciding whether to kill Jack or not. Whether to hang bright vibrant Jack from his neck until he lost all colour. It was not possible that such a thing was happening. It wasn't possible that such a thing ever happened, that men gathered together and pretended to put order and rules around the chaos of choosing to kill.

Perhaps he was still in bed, coaxed and spoon fed by Master Edmund into eating cold, congealed broth.

Viola might not have twisted Andrew into lending them disguises. Viola might not have pulled him out of bed and complained constantly that he had too much hair to hide under the shoulder length dark wig. Viola might not have sneaked him out of the house past the dozing Master Edmund and led him here.

None of that had happened. He remembered now.

He heard his own voice talking to Andrew when Andrew arrived with a pile of sewing to 'distract his mind from worse things'. The hobgoblin had been there, and had touched John's tongue and given him the words he'd needed. It had been his plan. Viola's presence was down merely to the chance of her visiting John in the middle of his escape. It had been John who complained about his own hair. Viola had said that he needed to rest and how he mustn't lose his apprenticeship; how generous the Shakespeares were being. But Viola hadn't stopped him. No one could stop him.

The hobgoblin had led the way.

Eventually, Viola left, repeating that it wasn't worth the risk, and pleading with John not to mention her as being any part of this nonsense when he got caught, as he surely would.

So, he was really here. Standing at the back of a wood-panelled room with the hobgoblin touching his fingers, making him invisible so no one questioned him. Although Master William and his friend Ben Jonson were here, sitting in front of him on benches. And of course, as Master William was here, the blue faerie was too. None of them looked in his direction, though he knew they were aware of his presence.

The room had absolutely no smell, as if everything that made people human had been drained out of them before they came in. When he'd tell Jack about it later, Jack would laugh and say wasn't that just how life worked: John moaned all the time about the stink of the city, but when he got what he wanted, he still wasn't happy. Equally as mysterious as the lack of scent was the whole business of the court. There was lots of talk by people who spoke in clear voices like actors, but the words might as well have been the mumblings of mice. He and the hobgoblin stared blankly at each other. Who knew how adults decided justice.

Staying invisible at the back, he only heard Jack:

'Before you sentence me, I claim benefit of the clergy: you've heard this was not pre-planned murder out of malice, it was manslaughter by chance. You know there's no branding on my thumb, this is my first time making this claim and thus I ask for your mercy.' Jack's voice had none of its swagger, it was deferent and humble. But still Jack—still his own, brave Jack.

John smiled down at his hobgoblin. The faerie remained a creamy hue and did not smile back. But it probably didn't understand how Jack's own magic was as strong as any faerie power.

There were mutterings, something about Jack being given a Bible and being asked to read Psalm 51.

Then in the same low but strong tone, Jack's voice filled the room. 'Miserere mei, Deus, secundum misericordiam tuam... '

John could almost taste the air, giving him life. He recalled Jack's words, so soon after they'd met, that John had never given a thought to since: 'There is a certain magical Latin passage I'll have to teach you. If you recite it perfect, it stops you from being hung.'

Jack finished reading. John hadn't needed to understand the words; he felt the perfection of them in himself, and he rose up and down on his tiptoes, though it gave him no better view of what was happening.

Words were being said in stern voices, Jack's fate was being decided, and John's mind hovered, a strange morning mist above his head. The ground stretched into eternity and was fresh green grass and tiny daisies with dew on their petals. But when he looked up, all was swirling greyness. The air was scented with apples begging to be picked, but there were no trees, only flat land. He blinked, and he was outside on the street, walking between Master William and Ben Jonson.

'Where's Jack?' John jerked his head around looking for his friend's grinning face.

He wanted to run and search every shadow of every street, but his body kept walking forward with the two men as if it was controlled by a different mind. The hobgoblin was also nowhere to be seen; only the blue faerie was there, floating above Master William's head but watching John with eyes of drowning water.

'Where's Jack?' John asked it, his wariness of the faerie far outweighed by his fretting for his friend.

The blue faerie looked away.

It was only when he was back in the house and sat down at the table that he got any sort of answer to his question. Ben Jonson showed him the brand on his own thumb. And Master William said, 'Out of this nettle danger, we pluck this flower, safety.'

Much later, Master Edmund was the one who came to John and gave him a more solid explanation.

'Do not look so sad. Things could have fared so much worse. Jack has been spared hanging due to his learning. Being in our good company has elevated his mind, and he was able to recite the Latin perfectly.'

John didn't mention to Master Edmund that Jack had known the magical words long before he'd ever heard of any of them. There was only one thing he was interested in.

'Where's Jack?'

'I do not know.' The other patted John's hand. 'I believe he cares for you enough not to return for a long time, perhaps ever. The man that died was a bad man, John. He did not keep good company like you do. It may be that he has accomplices who believe that Jack should have paid for his crime with his life, and will be determined to exact justice on their own account.'

John remained quiet as his master spoke on. He'd stopped listening, but he allowed him to say all that he wanted, and even managed to give Master Edmund thanks for taking the time to come and talk to him.

'You are sensitive. The world is not kind to sensitive people, thus we must always be kind to each other,' Master Edmund said in a soft voice that sounded more like John's than his own. Then he patted John on the hand again and in his best theatre voice, boomed out:

'We will resume your training soon, you still have much to learn.'

He was genuinely grateful to Master Edmund, but also glad when he was left alone.

Until he realised how alone he was.

He lay on the floor of the room him and Jack had shared and closed his eyes. He wanted to imagine Jack was here with him as he should be, but he wasn't strong enough. And trying and failing to make his friend's body appear made his own tremble.

At some point, John started to undress for sleep.

A piece of paper folded up many times to make it into a small square fell out of the creases of his clothes. Just as quick, he felt a presence in the room. As if Jack had returned to him after all. He spun on his heel and his shoulders slumped when he saw only the hobgoblin sitting on his pillow.

'Sorry... I am happy to see you... I just... ' He walked over and gently stroked the faerie's hair.

The hobgoblin pointed him back to the note.

John gazed at it for a long time. Finally, he reached for it with only his thumb and forefinger, his muscles tensed, as if the paper had the power to burn his skin. He had no idea when or how it had come upon his person without him noticing.

John sat on the floor with the small of his back pressed into the wall. He hugged his knees to his chest, and tried not to look at the thing he continued to hold with just the tips of his fingers.

The world got dark around him.

Or maybe it had got dark a long time ago.

The hobgoblin came and floated beside him in the soft glow of faerie light.

John bit his lips and finally unfolded it:

Fair One, I have borrowed some of Master William's words which you love. They are not the right words, as there are no right words, but they are far better than any story I could tell, and use a lot less ink.

And whether we shall meet again I know not.
Therefore our everlasting farewell take:
For ever, and for ever, farewell,
If we do meet again, why, we shall smile;
If not, why then, this parting was well made.

'You do not speak untrue,' John said to the person who was not there. 'They are not the right words.'

I would not wish
Any companion in the world but you

John smiled around the bustling tiring room. It was at least half an hour before the play began, but he had already checked the apparel and makeup of the new actors hired to be in Prospero's masque. The extras had a merry energy that the company men sometimes lacked, and the air sparkled with their chatter as they danced and sang, practising and repeating their lines as if theirs was the only part that mattered. Despite his innocent pleasure in their pleasure, John kept a close eye on them all: people that would not be here working tomorrow were more likely to try and take a little extra to supplement their fee. And John was always the best at spying quick hands reaching for things that did not belong to them.

Even as he perfected his own face and hair, he watched everyone else. Their voices bubbled through his mind.

Three of the more experienced actors were in a small group, jesting about yesterday's play.

'I do not know why Romeo and Juliet remains popular with any but children and those from Bedlam.'

'I heartily agree. The killing takes far too long to begin. I've told William it should begin with a sword fight and... '

'It does. Well, after the chorus. You never pay notice to any but your own parts... '

'But do any die? If none die, my point is well made... '

'No, you both mistake me. The problem is in the whole romance. These young people who've just met each other, thinking they're in love and it's worth dying for, when it is only the excitement of the forbidden thing. If the parents had had any sense, they would've told their offspring how much they adored their choice in partner and locked them in a room together until Romeo had his fill, and grew mighty sick of his Juliet.' He made a crude gesture and the other two guffawed.

'Prithee, but you are sorely misled, my friend. Can you see any hot blooded man ever tiring of looking upon Juliet's face?'

The laughter increased, and Thomas the Older, glanced towards John with a sheepish grin.

'We speak only of the character, naturally, not thee who portrays Juliet.'

'Naturally.' John flashed a smile. 'I understand precisely. Just as any attraction I display towards others is due entirely to being on stage and playing the characters that Master William writes.'

A slim man appeared on the other side of John.

'What do you think of the new apprentice being given the part of Ariel? The role of a fairy is much more suited to you. Shall I steal this Henry's cue sheet for you and we can compare the number of lines between him and you.'

John grinned.

'That'll not be necessary, Viola, I'm quite content with playing Miranda.'

'It is sweet that after all these years, you still call me after the first role you saw me in. Despite me long playing men.' He put a light hand on John's shoulder. 'I am happy to hear you're glad to be playing the role of my love, though. Perchance, we should practice kissing so it looks more natural on stage.'

John glanced at his cue script on the dresser in front of him. There were always surprises in the first performance of a new work when you had no real knowledge of others' lines, and Viola oft liked to take advantage of that.

'No kissing,' John said firmly, and then in a softer voice: 'I do not want to ruin my make up.'

'I remember you when you were so pliable and innocent.'

'You're remembering much in the past today, coz, but forgetting the now, where I need to look after Master Edmund...'

Viola rolled his eyes.

'He's not vomiting again, is he? All his years in the company yet give him more than one line to say and he is as nervous as a boy in a brothel house.'

John giggled as he walked off, but carefully changed his expression when he came into Master Edmund's sight. The man's head drooped and there was a green hue to his complexion. John trotted forward as if he'd only just seen him.

'Master Edmund. I'm not going to ask if you ate the potage that I left for you, as I can see that you made me cook this morning for nothing.'

He said it playfully, but Master Edmund's cheeks reddened.

'I am sorry, John, it was kind of you to take note of my request. Your cooking is always preferable to the old maid's, but I...'

He touched his stomach.

'I understand you're full of excitement for the role that Master William has written for you.' John leant forward and spoke in a more confiding tone. 'In faith, I am nervous. It is so rare for Master William to take a large role, I tremble thinking of being on stage with him and playing his daughter. But then I remember all that you've taught me about speaking loud and clear and... '

'Always focus on your own lines and never add any of your own invention,' Master Edmund said.

John looked down shyly.

'If I make any misstep I know you'll be there to save the play...'

Master Edmund raised his head.

'William has always had the highest faith in my ability. And you have no need to be nervous, you've always been a good learner and a credit to me. But just to be certain, go and check on all the exits and entrances, not just your own, so you can help others if they need it. Just as I've always taught you.'

John gave a low curtsey and skipped towards the outline of the play's scenes pegged up by the side of the stage. He already knew it by heart, but he studied it as carefully as if he was looking at it for the first time.

'Have I told you how I created the character of Miranda for you at the moment of our first acquaintance?'

John had been unaware of Master William's approach, but

he turned to face the man with a warm smile. 'You know you have not; it is ever your habit to remember all things that you say to all people.'

'As do you.' Master William gazed at him for a long moment. Apart from one other person, he was the only man who could make the busy tiring room melt away.

'The first plots formed around Miranda, who was joyful to write, but it has taken me many years to discover who Prospero was.'

'I am anticipating with delight your performance of him.'

'...but you carry sadness today. You're thinking on the past more than is your wont.'

John tried to think of a frivolous reply, but Master William spoke on:

'You're young. You must believe that there is more than dead love for you in the world. Hope is a lover's staff; walk hence with that, and manage it against despairing thoughts.' Master William nodded, then turned and moved gracefully through the players, dispensing last instructions and requesting final alterations to costume and make up.

John watched him in silence, until he noticed the boy playing Ceres rubbing his eyes. He quickly hurried over and chided him. Reapplied his makeup.

John walked onto the stage with Master William by his side. He gave only the briefest glance up at the faeries dancing across the sky; today, he was more interested in the audience. A mixture of awe and excitement rippled after the opening clamour of the storm scene. They were waiting for something to continue to thrill them, some fair voice or face to lead them off to magical worlds far away from the grime of their real lives. He knew that feeling, even if he himself disappeared from this world more and more rarely as the days went by.

At the moment, all they had was John—it was his job to take them by the hand and show them the way.

He stood, listening, waiting for the character to take his body over as had happened every other time, but this time nothing came. He looked back up and let his gaze linger on the faeries. His own hobgoblin was flying amidst them, but none cast any magic his way.

Master William remained composed and stately beside him, but Viola was hissing from backstage.

'John, surely you have not forgotten your line? You never miss a word.'

He wondered, why couldn't Viola have actually given him the line?

Master William walked around the stage as if he were surveying a great world that lay before him, giving the impression that momentous silence was just what was required at this time. But the audience was becoming restless, muttering.

Why were the faeries ignoring him? In his mind, John rushed through everything that had occurred since he came off stage yesterday after successfully becoming Juliet. Did the magicfolk not like Master William's new play? But they were dancing and sparkling above as usual, and all the other actors were shining, just as they always did.

Then, something strange broke into his thoughts and the silence of the stage.

An apple was thrown. It rolled slowly to his feet.

John stared down at it. Its flesh glowed green and fresh, as though it had just fallen from the branch. As though it was still alive.

He started to speak his lines, alone. No faerie magic imbuing them with power. Only his own, quiet voice.

'If by your art, my dearest father, you have
Put the wild waters in this roar, allay them.'

He stared at the apple as Master William replied as Prospero. But instead of the lines, he heard Master William telling him how he'd inspired Miranda, back when they'd first met. Of course, Master William had written other parts since then with John in mind, but this was different. The other roles were ones that Master William had believed John could play; Miranda was the character that had sprung into life after their first meeting. Miranda would never come and take his body over, because she was already within him. The rest of the scene passed, and he felt all of Miranda's wondrous nature and all her pain as his own.

Backstage, he made jokes at his own expense and focused on preparing everyone else, though he yearned to retreat to a corner re-memorising his lines. He hadn't been prepared for this new experience of acting; this feeling of a bruised and aching soul. It was all the same entwined yearning and confusion he had experienced that very first time Jack had taken him to see Twelfth Night. He remembered how his friend had held him up on his shoulders through the whole performance so John could see Viola and the other boy-women.

It seemed too soon that he was back on stage. When he peeked at the audience, it was just like his first day in London and the terror he'd felt looking at all the strange faces, overwhelmed by their stench and noise. He clenched his fists and breathed deeply. This didn't happen to him any more; he didn't flicker out of reality into nightmares and bad memories.

He was firmly on stage, saying the words for his scene, with Viola as Ferdinand, and Master William clearly visible, but pretending to be hidden, as he played Prospero and spied on the two young people. John twisted innocence and loneliness through his words; the desire to live and love, to experience the world, but with someone he could trust always by his side.

Midway through his speech, his limbs began to tremble. Something had changed.

Now, he stood alone on the stage and the crowd had disappeared. And one person remained.

He blinked, though this wasn't like some vision trying to throw him back into the stink of London. Something in the beating of his heart and the turning of his stomach told him that this was real.

It was daytime, and the weather was fine with a clear blue sky. But when he glanced up, the faeries had disappeared as if all their magic had been consumed by that lone figure—. He lowered his eyes, stared around the whole empty Globe, before he could finally resist no longer, and he looked directly at the person standing alone in the centre.

John hadn't realised he'd stopped breathing until he started again. His eyes met dancing green ones—

Jack wasn't the same: The years had aged him, the same as they'd aged John. Black Jack had more freckles over his nose and cheeks; the lines of his jaw were more pronounced; he was taller, his shoulders broader, his whole body was thicker, in fact. The most striking change was that his hair had darkened to a rich auburn. But his mouth was the same, ever ready to jest. He smiled his widest smile, showing his crooked tooth.

'I've come a long way to see you, my Fair One. ...Will you allow me the great pleasure of seeing you shine?' It was Jack's voice, but it rang with the power of ancient magic.

And when John spoke Miranda's next lines, he said them with the meaning of his whole life.

'I would not wish
Any companion in the world, but you.'

What is love? 'Tis not hereafter;
Present mirth hath present laughter

John darted through the streets. He stared hard at everyone he passed. And he was fully aware that they were staring back at him.

Normally when he was out in the city alone, he made an effort to appear as male as possible. It was easier that way. But today his hair was loose, and he'd done nothing to cover up his face. All he'd wanted to do was get away from the theatre and the inquiring gazes of his friends as quickly as possible.

Had he been quick enough?

That was the question pounding through his mind. Though the one he should probably be asking himself was slightly different.

Had it been real?

After all this time, had it been real?

John knew he wasn't the best person at recognising the difference between his world and everyone else's. But in every part of his being, he was certain that if Viola, or Master Edmund, or any of the Thomases had looked in the right way in the right place they would have seen Jack too. True, they might not have known it was John's Jack, and wouldn't have had the experience John had of flying through the light of another, but they would have seen a flesh and blood person, not a faerie apparition.

He was sure of that.

So where was the boy with the dancing green eyes now?

John had waited so long, so patiently. Why hadn't Black Jack waited until the end of the play?

Under his breath, he muttered some of the creative curses that Jack had often used, but until this moment, John himself had never spoken. As soon as he'd seen Jack, John should have forgotten the play and jumped off the stage and into his friend's arms.

He'd been too vain, a fault none could've accused him of before, but today, when it had mattered the most, he'd been plagued with that weakness. He'd wanted his first friend to see him shining on stage in a role written especially for him. He'd fully believed that Jack had finally returned and he'd never thought that Black Jack would, after a glance, decide John wasn't worth any more of his time.

But it hadn't been a glance. Jack must have experienced the same thing that he did. That intensity could not have been his alone. And still he hadn't waited for John.

But why not?

Before he could form an answer to that question, something sharp cut through his mind.

He wasn't sure what it was at first. He studied the people around him. Then studied them again. No body and no thing of note. Yet his eyes kept wanting to look at an old hunched woman making her pained way forward on the other side of the street. He didn't know what was different about her compared to every other poor person living on the frayed edges of their luck. Then he did know. She hadn't looked at him once.

John raced over. Before thought and doubt could prevent him, he took both her hands in his and walking backwards, pulled her into the nearest alleyway.

The old woman hobbled along, unresisting, until they were in the privacy of the shadows and then, without thought, John pressed his lips against hers.

Her mouth stayed firmly closed. She yanked her hands away from his and pushed him away. Her fingers, covered in tatty mismatched gloves, remained awkwardly splayed across John's chest as she spoke.

'I shall scream,' she said in a cracked voice.

He gazed at her without blinking.

'I know it's you. I can see your eyes.' Only as he spoke the words, did he realise, he couldn't actually see her eyes. The shadows of the alleyway combined with the shadows from the layers of dull fabric concealing her face. But still, he repeated with complete confidence, 'I know it's you.'

It had to be. Who else would his body just lean in and kiss like that?

'I shall call the constables on you,' the woman rasped.

'That is something you'd never do.'

'Please, whatever madness has taken you, by troth, I am not part of it. You look like a kind one, have mercy on an aged woman with nothing that you can possibly want.'

John tried folding his arms across his chest, but couldn't keep still. His arms fidgeted, his hands clenched and unclenched, he rocked on the balls of his feet.

'I thought you'd come into the tiring room. Then when you didn't, I thought that you must desire a reunion without anyone else around, and I realised how much I desired that too. But you weren't there when I came out. You weren't anywhere. Or were you? Were you here all the time watching me desperately rush around searching for you? What game are you playing with me?'

'Please. It is surely you playing with me. This may be good sport for a young un like you, but you don't know what it does to an old body. Pray, let me be on my way now.'

'Why are you doing this now? Why come back if you didn't want to speak to me? Can't you tell me? And why did you leave me back then, Jack? Why did you leave me when we could have been together?'

'You've greatly mistaken me,' the woman said in a voice of pure pleading and anguish.

'You should be the one on stage, you've always been a better actor than me. You made me completely believe in something that was but a dream.' John bit his lips. He wouldn't cry. Not here. He turned away. 'It is as you wish it. I'll leave you. Fare thee well, Good Mistress.'

He meant to walk away with dignity, but his feet were heavy and his head drooped. And yet, he couldn't leave. John looked over his shoulder at the old woman hunched against the wall.

In his softest voice, he whispered:

'I've missed you. Every single day, I've missed you.'

The woman straightened up, her clothes rearranging themselves almost magically so that instead of fitting her, they hung oddly off a tall male body. The shawl fell off as the body stretched out and leaned its head back against the wall with a deep sigh. Then the face turned to him and smiled just as it had when he'd seen it at the Globe.

Just as it had so many times before.

'Fair One, whatever I may be, and I am a lot of things, I am certainly not a better actor than you. This is the best I can.' He held his hands out indicating his garments. 'And you saw straight through it. But when I saw you on stage, you were beyond everything. You shone so brightly. Aye, you understand now, don't you?' Black Jack said in a voice that was both warm and distant. 'I'm sure you know I had to stay away to begin with because it was the safest thing to do. And then when things appeared bene, I still couldn't come back. How is a street rat like me to keep company with the celebrated and famed beauty of John Flaxen?'

'It isn't like that.' John shook his head. 'Between us, it would never be like that.'

'Did your faerie friends tell you that?'

He looked up at the mocking tone of his friend's voice and saw eyes that weren't quite as he remembered them.

They were darker, tired.

'You see how I am?' Jack thumped the wall with the side of his fist. 'Surviving in my world hardens you. You were the one drop of light that came in my life, the one good thing I did. You cannot know how much I need that memory, it helps me sleep and even blesses me with occasional sweet dreams.'

'I am more than a memory. I am real. I am here.'

'My Fair One, for me you would kill, and for you I would die. And still would. That is wondrous and beautiful that we felt so for each other. But where are we to go from that? Only awkwardness and ugliness as you grow beyond me, as it is right you do, and I get jealous and bitter and lonely, as is wrong for me to do, trying to hold onto you long after you have flown away. We are each other's past, nothing more.'

'But you came to see me at the Globe today. And you followed me in the streets. You don't believe your own words. You don't want to keep me in the past.'

'Weakness.' Jack gazed straight ahead. 'I managed to resist for long enough. I can't answer what was different about today, so don't ask.'

John stared away from Jack, out at the busy street. Everyone bustling past, oblivious to the heartache mere steps away.

They were silent for a long time. It was John who found the strength to look back at him.

'Maybe it was faerie magic,' he said softly.

Black Jack turned his head to him and raised a questioning eyebrow.

'Maybe it was faerie magic that made you come and see me today,' John said with more confidence. He smiled a soft smile. 'Maybe from the beginning it was faerie magic that made you mistake a simple pick, and have to run into an alleyway and kiss a fool to escape capture.' He took small steps back towards Jack. 'Or our stars aligned. Or it was Fate. Or a witch cast a spell. Or we have the most powerful guardian angels in all of heaven. I don't know about those things. Or anything else. But I do know about faeries.' He reached Jack and stood in front of him. 'So I will believe that it is faerie magic.'

'You are different.' Jack smiled a half smile. 'Yet you are still the same. Which is all the more reason for me not to disturb you, no matter what magic is at play.'

John took a deep breath and licked his lips. His hands fluttered over each other. He'd said enough. He may as well say it all. This was likely his only chance.

'There always was more, wasn't there? I was just too innocent and too inexperienced to know what we were.'

Black Jack's eyes flashed; his voice was a soft contrast to the hardness in his expression. 'Am I to understand that you are no longer... innocent nor inexperienced?'

Heat rushed to John's face and the other laughed merrily:

'Od's bod, but you still blush prettier than any maiden. Whatever else has changed since last we met, you're still as sweet as ever, aren't you?'

'Perchance, if you truly want an answer and are not just teasing me, I will give you an answer. I was waiting for someone to return who I thought would return as soon as he could to me because he had the same feelings for me as I had for him. But I was a fool for not realising what a fool he was. That he'd decide all on his own that we were better off not being friends, not because we did not have a liking between us, but because we couldn't spend each and every day in excitement running around the city rescuing and dying for each other! Perchance if the fool had come back sooner and spoken to me and shown me what a fool he was with his fool ideas, I would have stopped waiting for him and could have had the fun life he foolishly thinks I could be living without him by my side.'

John's mouth was open, ready to continue; strong hands grabbed his waist and pulled him into a warm body. Lips pressed against his—. The world was apple blossoms and the greenest grass. It was crisp winter beauty and bright summer heat.

It was Jack who broke the embrace, caught the other's chin in his hand and made him look up at him.

'I was the worst kind of fool, I was so scared of losing you, that I didn't dare try to win. ...So is it too late? Has our moment passed?'

'We love each other, don't we?' John said.

'We love each other,' Jack replied.

He turned, began to reassemble his disguise. Before Jack pulled the gloves back on, John kissed the brand mark on his friend's thumb.

'Give me one promise. You won't ever make the decision I'll be better off without you again.'

Jack caressed John's lips with his branded thumb.

'Aye. That I can promise.'

The words were so simple. Compared to the magic language Master William wove, such words were mere airy nothings, of no note. Immediately lost and forgotten in the cacophony of inconsequential words spoken by the thousands of people all over the city at this exact same moment. No one but John and Jack would ever truly know their power.

They smiled at each other.

Linked arms and walked out onto the London streets looking more like a girl and her grandmother than anything else.

Author's Note

This book is a magical apparition of Shakespearean London and should in no way be mistaken for historical fact.

There was a real Edmund Shakespeare, who was the youngest sibling of William Shakespeare; he did follow William to London to become an actor. His tomb in the church now known as Southwark Cathedral remembers his death in the year 1607, at the age of 27. Although it can be difficult to date Shakespeare's plays, The Tempest is commonly believed to have been written around 1610, so it would have been unhappily impossible for the real life namesake of my character to have performed the role of jealous brother to William's Prospero.

Unfortunately, some of the more dismal elements of life in these times were much more hellish than described here. The Elizabethans and Jacobeans enjoyed pastimes that would probably scar many 21st century Britons for life; chief amongst these were regular hangings. If a prisoner was lucky, their neck would break immediately, and friends could ensure that happened, just as Black Jack helps Bess Porch; otherwise it was a slow strangulation that could take a gruesomely long time.

The one possible way for criminals to avoid the noose has a long and complicated history. It is known as benefit of the clergy and originates in the 12th century, when Henry II was forced to allow clergy to be tried separately from other people in an ecclesiastical court, which was generally much more merciful. By the time of Elizabeth I's reign, the person on trial had to prove they could read Latin to claim a leniency in their sentencing, but as the same psalm was generally always used, Miserere mei, Domine (Have mercy upon me, O Lord), it could be memorised and became known as the 'neck verse,' due to the fact that it saved you from being hung.

Convicts who benefitted from this loophole were branded on the thumb, ensuring they could only do it once. The next time they were caught, there would be no escape from the death sentence.

Outside the risks of the criminal world, many diseases, including plague, made death a regular occurrence in everyone's lives. The richer inhabitants could escape to the country in the worse years, leaving the poor to be heaped up in death carts and buried en masse. Largely due to low life expectancy, it is estimated that in the year 1600, fifty percent of London's population was under 25.

One thing that is difficult to compare between modern living and Shakespearean times is the treatment of people who did not fit normal gender stereotypes. We now have many labels and terms which have only come into everyday usage in the last few decades. But at least within the confines of the theatre, boys wearing dresses and pretending to be girls and women was a normal, accepted part of society. So we can imagine that someone like John would have found a haven here.

Shakespeare's Real Words

My William Shakespeare is entirely fictional, but scattered through this novel are the words the real, historical Shakespeare wrote hundreds of years ago. For anyone who is interested, here's a brief overview of the main quotes and where they originally come from.

The poet's eye, in fine frenzy rolling,
Doth glance from heaven to Earth, from Earth to heaven.
And as imagination bodies forth
The forms of things unknown, the poet's pen
Turns them to shapes and gives to airy nothing
A local habitation and a name.
Such tricks hath strong imagination,
That if it would but apprehend some joy,
It comprehends some bringer of that joy.
Or in the night, imagining some fear,
How easy is a bush supposed a bear!
A Midsummer Night's Dream (Act 5, Scene 1, lines 12-22)

The quote that inspired the title of this novel comes from one of Shakespeare's most magical plays; a play which contains enchanted lovers lost in a wood, plays within plays, comically bad acting, a man with a donkey's head, and of course a Faerie Queene.

In this extract Theseus (a normal human king) is telling his queen that he doesn't believe what the lovers have told of their fantastical adventures, because lovers are like madmen, who are like poets, all making up things out of nothing!

But I love this quote and instead of the disbelief that Theseus intends, I take it to display how magical the world actually is, how love and poetry, (and in John's case, some seriously mad visions), can transform the ordinary things that most people don't even notice into things of terror and beauty.

Chapter One

To unpathed waters, undreamed shores
The Winter's Tale, (Act 4, Scene 4, lines 671-675)

In this part of the play, Camillo is advising the lovers, Florizel and Perdita, to find safety in each other and not travel to some remote and dangerous part of the world. Although I am using it in the reverse way (kind of!), John is leaving the only home he's ever known to try and find the places he's only dreamed of.

Chapter Two

To-morrow, and to-morrow, and to-morrow,
Creeps in this petty pace from day to day,
To the last syllable of recorded time;
And all our yesterdays have lighted fools
The way to dusty death. Out, out, brief candle!
Life's but a walking shadow, a poor player,
That struts and frets his hour upon the stage,
And then is heard no more. It is a tale
Told by an idiot, full of sound and fury,
Signifying nothing.
Macbeth (Act 5, Scene 5, lines 19–28)

I borrowed just a couple of lines of this famous speech from Macbeth to introduce my second chapter. In the actual play, Macbeth has just heard that his wife has died and is contemplating the whole nature of human existence. I borrowed it to represent the danger John is in on his travels, how quickly it could all be over, and also how brief the moments that can change everything can seem within our little lives. This is the first time John sees a player/actor and although he is unable to follow this particular troupe, it plants an important seed in him of who he is and what he wants to be.

Over hill, over dale,
Thorough bush, thorough brier,
Over park, over pale,
Thorough flood, thorough fire.
I do wander everywhere
Swifter than the moon's sphere.
And I serve the fairy queen
To dew her orbs upon the green.
The cowslips tall her pensioners be.
In their gold coats spots you see.
Those be rubies, fairy favors.
In those freckles live their savors.
I must go seek some dewdrops here
And hang a pearl in every cowslip's ear.
Farewell, thou lob of spirits. I'll be gone.
Our queen and all our elves come here anon.
A Midsummer Night's Dream (Act 2, Scene 1, lines 369-384)

The first lines of Shakespeare that John ever hears immediately enchants him, and why wouldn't they? There are fairies, elves, and cowslips, all the sorts of things John loves to distraction.

In the play, these lines are spoken by a fairy talking to Puck, one of the most famous fairies in all of literature, so if he had seen them in the play, rather than overheard them on the road, John would have been even more besotted.

Chapter Three

I have heard, but not believed, the spirits o' the dead
May walk again: if such thing be, thy mother
Appear'd to me last night, for ne'er was dream
So like a waking.
The Winter's Tale (Act 3, Scene 3, lines 20-23)

This little bit of speech comes from a dramatic part in The Winter's Tale where Antigonus is on the verge of abandoning a baby on the orders of the King, who is mad with jealousy thinking the baby is not his (it is). This is him talking to the babe in his arms, just before he names her Perdita (as her mother instructed him to do, in a dream.)

That does not seem to have much to do with John, except he is lost and is soon to be found, but the lines 'for ne'er was dream so like a waking' capture perfectly his existence between the human and fairy worlds.

Chapter Four

What country friends is this?
Twelfth Night (Act 1, Scene 2, line 1)

Viola has just landed after being shipwrecked and is asking the sea captain what strange place she has ended up in.

Chapter Five

I can express no kinder sign of love than this kind kiss
Henry VI, Part I (Act I, Scene 1)

Taken out of the context of the complicated politics of Shakespeare's history plays, this line expresses the simple connection of a kiss, which fits perfectly John and Black Jack's first meeting.

Chapter Six

Thy friendship makes us fresh
Henry VI, Part 1 (Act 3, Scene 3, line 87)

Again, outside the bloody fight for the crown that is Shakespeare's history plays, this line captures John's feelings about having his first friend.

Chapter Seven

Fate, show thy force; Ourselves we do not owe;
What is decreed must be; and be this so!
Twelfth Night (Act 1, Scene 5, lines 317-318)

Olivia has just met Viola, disguised as the male youth Cesario. Over the course of one conversation, she moves from mourning her brother, to being interested in a romance with the stranger. She believes Fate has shown her Cesario, and now she must wait and see what happens.

Chapter Eight

For I can raise no money by vile means.
By heaven, I had rather coin my heart
And drop my blood for drachmas than to wring
From the hard hands of peasants their vile trash
By any indirection.
Julius Caesar (Act 4, Scene 3, lines 75-79)

In the original play, Brutus is explaining to Cassius that he would rather turn his own body into money than exploit the peasants, which matches how John would feel in a position of power, but not so much Black Jack.

Chapter Nine

Too much of water hast thou, poor Ophelia,
And therefore I forbid my tears. But yet
It is our trick. Nature her custom holds,
Let shame say what it will. When these are gone,
The woman will be out.
Hamlet (Act 4, Scene 7, lines 182-186)

Laertes is speaking of his sister Ophelia drowning, which I've translated to the terrifying visions John experiences crossing the River Thames for the first time.

Chapter Ten

The raven himself is hoarse
That croaks the fatal entrance of Duncan
Under my battlements. Come, you spirits
That tend on mortal thoughts, unsex me here,

And fill me from the crown to the toe topful
Of direst cruelty!
Macbeth (Act 1, Scene 5, lines 38–43)

Lady Macbeth contemplates murder to further her ambitions, but for John, 'unsex me here' has a very different meaning.

Chapter Eleven

Well, God give them wisdom that have it; and those that are fools, let them use their talents.
Twelfth Night (Act 1, Scene 5, lines 13-14)

From a scene where the fool is bantering with Maria, basically saying that everyone has their talents and should use them the best way that they can.

Chapter Twelve

Viola: I am not what I am.
Olivia: I would you were as I would have you be!
Twelfth Night (Act 3, Scene 1, lines 131-132)

Viola and Olivia are talking about identity: Viola admits that she is not what Oliva thinks she is (she is a girl, not a boy), and Olivia responds by wishing that Viola was how Olivia wants her to be (so, in love with Olivia).

This is the chapter where John sees his first play and realises he does not have to be alone in the way he experiences the world. He falls in love with the players, in particularly Viola, who can so happily and easily occupy the space between real and pretend, and boys can be girls being boys and be admired by both men and women.

Chapter Thirteen

Let me be that I am, and seek not to alter me.
Much Ado about Nothing (Act 1, Scene 3, line 29)

Don John, the baddie of Much Ado about Nothing, is telling one of his co-conspirators that he is a villain and is going to remain a villain as that is what he essentially is; he'd rather be free to act how he pleases than be false to his nature and loved by everyone.

In contrast, Black Jack wants John to like him, even as he works out how to manipulate John from pursuing his interest in the theatre and keep him under his control.

Chapter Fourteen

Foolish curs, that run winking into the mouth of a Russian bear and have their heads crushed like rotten apples. You may as well say, that's a valiant flea that dare eat his breakfast on the lip of a lion.

Henry V (Act 3, Scene 7, lines 145-149)

Orleans is talking about how stupid the English army is for coming so close to the French. Although history is going to give the English the win and the English knew what they were doing, John and Jack walk unknowingly into the human horror that is the Butcher.

Chapter Fifteen

Let every eye negotiate for itself
And trust no agent; for beauty is a witch
Against whose charms faith melteth in blood.
Much Ado about Nothing (Act 2, Scene 1, lines 178-180)

This is Claudio speaking when he is duped for the first time (yep, he gets duped again after this, some people don't learn from their mistakes) into thinking the girl he loves is unfaithful to him. I use the first line of the speech to indicate how Jack thinks him and John should both be looking out for themselves, but of course, they stay together and John looks out for Jack.

Chapter Sixteen

In nature there's no blemish but the mind;
None can be call'd deform'd but the unkind
Twelfth Night (Act 3, Scene 4, lines 332-334)

Antonio mistakes Viola for his friend, Sebastian, who happens to be her twin brother, and is confused by her reaction to him as a stranger. He says that the only real blemish in a person is not on their outside, but within their personality.

Chapter Seventeen

Here's ado to lock up honesty
And honor from th' access of gentle visitors
The Winter's Tale (Act 2, Scene 2, lines 9-11)

Hermione is locked up by her jealous husband when he wrongly thinks she has cheated on him.

Chapter Eighteen

What's to come is still unsure
In delay there lies no plenty
Twelfth Night (Act 2, Scene 3, lines 48-49)

This is a song from the Fool, who celebrates enjoying the now and does not worry about the future as it is uncertain anyway.

Chapter Nineteen

We know what we are, but know not what we may be.
Hamlet (Act 4, Scene 5, lines 43-44)

Ophelia has fallen into madness and amongst her ravings there are moments of insight, as if she understands that everyone is only capable of living in the present with no idea of who their future selves will be.

Chapter Twenty

We cannot hold mortality's strong hand
King John (Act 4, Scene 2, lines 84-85)

King John has just learnt of the death of his nephew, Arthur.

Chapter Twenty One

Neither a borrower nor a lender be; for loan oft loses both itself and friend
Hamlet (Act 1, Scene 3, line 75)

This is part of a very long list of advice Polonius gives his son Laertes, before Laertes parts on his travels.

Chapter Twenty Two

Moderate lamentation is the right of the dead,
excessive grief the enemy to the living
All's Well That Ends Well (Act 1, Scene 1, line 57-58)

Many, if not all, of Shakespeare's comedies are beset with ambiguities and problems for the audience to try and unpick if they so wish. All's Well that Ends Well begins with mourning and further separation of the living from those they love. The character Lafeu's remark consoling the Countess on the death of her husband and departure of her son, directly questions how we can and should grieve for loss.

Chapter Twenty Three

What shall you ask of me that I'll deny
Twelfth Night (Act 3, Scene 4, line 219)

Olivia is besotted by Viola disguised as a boy and will do anything for her love to be accepted and acknowledged.

When in disgrace with fortune and men's eyes,

I all alone beweep my outcast state,
And trouble deaf heav'n with my bootless cries,
And look upon myself and curse my fate,
Wishing me like to one more rich in hope,
Featured like him, like him with friends possessed,
Desiring this man's art, and that man's scope,
With what I most enjoy contented least;
Yet in these thoughts myself almost despising,
Haply I think on thee, and then my state,
Like to the lark at break of day arising
From sullen earth, sings hymns at heaven's gate;
For thy sweet love rememb'red such wealth brings,
That then I scorn to change my state with kings.

The sonnet that Black Jack gives John to read in this chapter is Sonnet 29, which is part of a long sequence of sonnets Shakespeare wrote, believed to be addressed to a young man. Instead of the frequent focus on sensuous beauty, this poem celebrates the effect a beloved has on the mind. The first eight lines display a person at odds with the society he lives in, feeling ugly and jealous in comparison with others. But the last six lines can be read as showing that the concerns of the outside world are irrelevant. His beloved can take him away from the materialistic concerns and prove that loving and being loved is true wealth.

Chapter Twenty Four

I'll fight, till from my bones my flesh be hacked
Macbeth (Act 5, Scene 3, line 34)

Whatever happens, Macbeth is declaring that he'll go down fighting, in contrast to the start of this chapter where poor Edmund runs away from John and his wooden sword.

Make me a willow cabin at your gate
And call upon my soul within the house;
Write loyal cantons of contemned love
And sing them loud even in the dead of night;
Hallo your name to the reverberate hills

And make the babbling gossip of the air
Cry out "Jack!" O, you should not rest
Between the elements of air and earth
But you should pity me

The lines that John recites as Viola to Black Jack is his version of a famous speech from Twelfth Night commonly referred to as the willow cabin speech. Viola is disguised as a boy talking to Olivia but imagining the love she feels for Orsino. Her love is based on absolute devotion and Olivia is completely enchanted by it.

Chapter Twenty Five

As flies to wanton boys are we to th' gods,
They kill us for their sport.
King Lear (Act 4, Scene 1, line 41-42)

Things go seriously wrong for the main characters in King Lear, and in these words, Gloucester contemplates the meaningless cruelty of it all.

Chapter Twenty Six

Nothing is but what is not
Macbeth (Act 1, Scene 3, line 145)

Macbeth is shaken by the prophesy that he could be king by murdering the current king. The words of the witches telling the future, take over his mind.

Chapter Twenty Seven

Some rise by sin, and some by virtue fall
Measure for Measure (Act 2, Scene 1, line 41)

After a character in this play is ordered to be executed, Escalus comments on how in this world, some people will be successful despite their wickedness, and others will fall due to their kindness. That is to say, there is no fairness in people's fates.

Brutus: Forever and forever farewell, Cassius.
If we do meet again, why, we shall smile.
If not, why then this parting was well made.
Cassius: Forever and forever farewell, Brutus.
If we do meet again, we'll smile indeed.
If not, 'tis true this parting was well made
Julius Caesar (Act 5, Scene 1, lines 118-123)

Jack borrows from Julius Caesar for his farewell note to John, although it may have been a poor choice, as both Cassius and Brutus die!

Chapter Twenty Eight

I would not wish
Any companion in the world but you.
The Tempest (Act 3, Scene 1, lines 54-55)

Miranda tells Ferdinand that although he is the first young man she's ever seen, she doesn't need to see another, because he is perfect for her.

Chapter Twenty Nine

What is love? 'Tis not hereafter;
Present mirth hath present laughter;
Twelfth Night (Act 2, Scene 3, lines 45-46)

The observant Shakespeare nerds amongst you may have noticed that I used this song also for chapter eighteen. You may wonder why over the whole Shakespearean canon of more than thirty plays and one hundred and fifty sonnets, I am quoting twice from the same song? The answer is, that this song suits Jack and John so well. In a world of uncertainty, surrounded by death, seizing the moment and enjoying being with each other in the here and now is essential. And Twelfth Night is such an important play for John, that the last quote had to come from it.

A warm thank you to the following people,
for making this book possible:

Dermitzel
Brak
Clacks
Philip O'Loughlin
Junibert
Merey Agi
Leon Soerensen
and
Gele Croom

Your support is seen, felt, and appreciated.

About the author: Clarissa Pattern studied English language and literature at the University of Oxford and has lived in the Oxfordshire area ever since. She has been writing ever since she could hold crayons and scribble across the wallpaper. Aside from writing, she spends as much time with her kids as they'll put up with, ignores almost all the housework, and has an ever increasing list of books she's frantic to read. Airy Nothing is her first novel.

About our press: Traum Books is a postqueer mini-press dedicated to telling unconventional stories, in unconventional, pretty formats. You can visit us online at our website and get updates about our other books at http://www.traumbooks.com.

Also, thank you for reading this book! If you enjoyed it, please consider leaving us a review on Amazon and/or Goodreads. Reviews really help us indie authors, and we will read and appreciate each one!

Printed in Great Britain
by Amazon

70109840R00147